# Altered
# Body Image

# Altered Body Image
## The Nurse's Role

SECOND EDITION

Edited by

## MAVE SALTER
MSc, BSc (Hons) Nurs, RGN, NDN(Cert), ENB
216, CSCT, Diploma in Counselling, Cert Ed
*Clinical Nurse Specialist, Community Liaison,*
*Royal Marsden Hospital NHS Trust, Sutton, UK*

**Baillière Tindall**
PUBLISHED IN ASSOCIATION WITH THE RCN

London Philadelphia Toronto Sydney Tokyo

Baillière Tindall   24–28 Oval Road
London NW1 7DX

The Curtis Center
Independence Square West
Philadelphia, PA 19106-3399, USA

Harcourt Brace & Company
55 Horner Avenue
Toronto, Ontario, M8Z 4X6, Canada

Harcourt Brace & Company, Australia
30–52 Smidmore Street
Marrickville
NSW 2204, Australia

Harcourt Brace & Company, Japan
Ichibancho Central Building
22-1 Ichibancho
Chiyoda-ku, Tokyo 102, Japan

First edition 1988
Second edition 1997

A catalogue record for this book is available from the British Library

ISBN 1 873853 40 8

Typeset by Phoenix Photosetting, Lordswood, Chatham, Kent
Printed and bound in Great Britain by WBC Book Manufacturers,
Bridgend, Glamorgan

# Contents

# Contributors

**Adele Atkinson**, BA (Hons), RGN, RNT
Senior Lecturer, Kingston University & St Georges Hospital
Medical School, Faculty of Healthcare Sciences, London

**Sandra Birtchnell**, MB BS, MRCPsych, MSc
Consultant Psychiatrist, Chichester Priority Care, Graylingwell
Hospital, Chichester, West Sussex

**Sue Cluroe**, BA, RGN, RSCN, RNT
Senior Lecturer/Course Leader – Children's Nursing, Centre for
Healthcare Education, Nene College of Higher Education,
Northampton General Hospital NHS Trust, Northampton

**Peter S. Davis**, MA, BEd (Hons), CertED, RN, DN, ONC
Principal Lecturer, Nurse Education Department, School of
Health and Social Care, South Bank University, Royal National
Orthopaedic Hospital, Middlesex

**Linda Davis**, RMN
Former Staff Nurse, Eating Disorders Unit, Atkinson Morley's
Hospital, London

**Tonia Dawson**, MSc, RGN, OncCert, ENB 225
Primary Care Base Macmillan Cancer Nurse, Hadleigh House,
Corfe Mullen, Dorset

**Jan Dewing**, RGN, MN, BSc, DipNurs, DipNursEd, RN
Project Worker (Community Hospitals), Oxfordshire
Community Health NHS Trust/Royal College of
Nursing/Institute, Burford, Oxfordshire

**Bridget Dolan**, BSc (Hons), PhD, CPsychol
Lecturer in Forensic Psychology, St George's Hospital Medical
School, London

**Sarah Hart**, MSc, BSc (Hons), RGN, FETC
Clinical Nurse Specialist Infection Control, The Royal Marsden
NHS Trust, Sutton, Surrey

**Margot Lindsay**, RGN, BA, ALA, MPhil
Medical Librarian, Robert Brown Postgraduate Centre, Basildon
Hospital, Basildon, Essex

**Mary Levens**, MA, DipOccTher, DipArtTher, DipPsychodramaPsychother, MA
Psychotherapist, Eating Disorders Unit, Atkinson Morley's Hospital, London

**Mave Salter**, MSc, BSc (Hons), RGN, NDN(Cert), ENB 216, CSCT, DipCounselling, Cert Ed
Clinical Nurse Specialist, Community Liaison, Royal Marsden Hospital NHS Trust, Sutton, Surrey

**James Smith**, PhD, MA, STL, SRN, RMN, OncCert
Former Chaplain to Royal Marsden Hospital, Sutton, Surrey

**Ann Tait**, PhD, MA, RGN, OncCert
Senior Nurse, Breast Care, Bloomsbury Health Authority, University College Hospital, London

**Mavis Wing**, RGN, MBE
Breast Care Specialist Nurse, Royal South Hants Hospital, Southampton

**Jacquie Woodcock**, MSc, BEd (Hons), RGN, OncCert
Lecturer in Cancer Nursing, Centre for Cancer and Palliative Care Studies, Institute of Cancer Research, Sutton, Surrey

**Louise Woodhead**, RGN, RMN
Former Sister, Eating Disorders Unit, Atkinson Morley's Hospital, London

# Foreword

Almost ten years ago I was asked to write the foreword to the first edition of this book and the invitation to prepare the foreword to the second gives me just as much pleasure. Body image is all about being comfortable with one's self, having the confidence to share life experiences with other members of our community and being accepted as an equal. Since Mave produced her first edition, society has become even more fixated with 'the body beautiful'. People who look different, have communication or physical problems or who have a health deficit can so easily feel isolated from a world where value is given to good looks or a sportman's physique.

The need to be accepted as part of our society is a fundamental human right, as is the right to live life to the full. So often it is the attitude of others who restrict this right, sadly sometimes through ignorance and lack of empathy. In the past, nurses and other healthcare workers have often found it difficult to come to terms with patients' body image problems through a lack of insight into how best to care. Mave and her colleagues have addressed that knowledge deficit, in a way which helps the reader understand the need every patient has: to be seen as an individual with their own value, beauty and uniqueness.

My first ward placement as a student nurse 35 years ago was to a female surgical ward. Amongst the many patients I met with colostomies and ileostomies was a teenager with Crohn's disease who had been having surgery for several years and who had all the physical and psychological problems such a patient would experience. The Ward Sister was at the end of a long career, and brought professional skill, compassion and understanding to her nursing. I have always remembered what she taught me about caring for that young woman as she helped her not only to heal physically but gave her the mental strength to return to school and to plan a future.

This book is written for all those who want to care with skill, compassion, empathy and a determination to improve the quality of life for their patient, their families and their friends . . . it is indeed a truly 'Nursing' text.

Dr Betty Kershaw
LLD, RGN, MSc (Nursing) RNT
President, The Royal College of Nursing

# Preface

Altered body image, once a neglected subject, is now increasingly a feature of the nursing care of many patients that is essential to consider in adopting a holistic approach to the care of patients and when drawing up their nursing care plans. This book has been written to provide the nurse and other health care professionals with a text that can be referred to when caring for patients whose body image has or may undergo alteration. It covers examples of the many different diseases and injuries, and their subsequent treatment, which may lead to a change of body image and will help professionals to become more aware of the concept of individual self-image and how this can be radically altered, often leading to profound emotional problems in patients. With this insight should come an awareness of the health care professional's own concepts of body image, and the verbal and non-verbal attitudes that may be conveyed to patients whilst caring for them.

While general nurses, both in the public and private sector, should benefit from reading this book, specialist nurses or nurses working in special units and areas should also be helped by it. Health care professionals from all disciplines also will, hopefully, find it helpful. Nurses taking post-basic courses, for example, the English National Board's Stoma Care (216 and 980), Family Planning (900), Gynaecological (225 and 228) and Burns (264) courses will find it to be a useful adjunct to their studies. It is anticipated that it will also be helpful to members of the primary health care team, and will bring to all nurses and allied professionals a greater awareness and anticipation of the problems of altered body image and how patients can be helped to resolve their loss.

The majority of chapters have been updated and mainly adopt a research-based approach. The chapter on rheumatic disease in the first edition has been replaced with one that addresses other 'medical' conditions as well. Similarly, the chapter on stoma care now addresses body image problems in patients with an internal pouch/reservoir. New chapters include measuring body image, caring for clients with HIV/AIDS and also a chapter addressing cultural issues.

In this book, an account is given of the most important and more common causes of altered body image, and appropriate nursing action has been outlined. The contributors hope that readers will acquire a greater awareness of the many facets of body image and how these can be altered by disfigurement, by injury or disease. We hope readers will extend their knowledge of caring for patients with altered body image and that this important aspect will, in future, feature as an integral part of their patient's holistic care.

Altered body image affects not only the patient but his or her partner, family and friends as well. Thus the involvement of these significant others in the reader's care is as vital to successful rehabilitation as are the specialist skills of nurses and their colleagues in the other caring professions.

In this era of the Patient's Charter, quality of care and client satisfaction, together with an economy-driven health service, it is hoped that the patient will remain the central and pivotal part of our care in body image and related issues of care.

Mave Salter

# Acknowledgements

I would like to thank the contributors for their part in this second edition and also Jacqueline Curthoys for her guidance and help. My thanks also to the many patients whose body image change has taught me so much and without whom this book would not have been possible.

This book is dedicated to my daughter, Claire, a fine example of coming to terms with an unseen altered body image and living life to the full.

## CHAPTER 1

# Introduction

*Mave Salter*

**Introduction**

Altered body image has been a neglected area but, currently, one that is increasingly a part of the nursing care of every patient. Yet, as far back as 1859, Florence Nightingale stated that volumes had been written and spoken about the effect of the mind on the body, but she wished a little more was thought of the effect of the body on the mind.

This opening chapter will explain what is meant by body image and the pressure society places on an attractive body. Some of the different types of altered body image and diseases that result in a changed body image will be mentioned as well as the way patients react and learn to cope with their body changes.

The mass media seems permanently to confront society with positive suggestions that it is essential to have a healthy, attractive body. Body image is an important part of everyday life and society places an enormous significance on having an attractive body. Smitherman (1981) states that society is very concerned with physical appearance. The ideal body image has been said to represent youth, beauty, vigour, intactness and health, and there is likely to be a resulting decreased self-esteem, insecurity and anxiety among those who deviate significantly with this ideal.

Beauty and health clinics, saunas and salons are to be found in abundance. It is evident from advertisements on both the film and television screens, and in daily papers and weekly magazines the pressure imposed to comply to the image these portray. This may be acceptable to people with an intact body but could be a real problem for those who feel that their body image is not what it should be, and the expectation of others can also have a profound psychological effect.

Body image can be simply defined as the way a person sees himself or herself and perceives how he or she is seen by others.

Various definitions of body image have been given. Smith (1984) states that we all have a body image of ourselves. This image is formed at birth and develops as we grow. In adolescence we go through a crisis as the child image is replaced with the adult one. Our image is reinforced by environmental factors and social attitudes. We all aim for perfection, but realize this is impossible.

Cohen (1991) suggests that clothes, make up and jewellery, as well as aids or accessories, such as a stick or a wheelchair, are integrated into body image. Changes in appearance and function lead to an alteration in body image that influences certain aspects of life, for example, work, social activities and sexuality. Body image is dependent to a large extent on one's upbringing. If one has lived in an environment of acceptance of both good and bad points, of spots and blemishes, and if one has had praise where praise is due, then acceptance by others leads to acceptance of oneself.

Woods (1975) comments that body image has been conceptualized as a mental picture of one's own body – the way in which the body appears to the self. Chilton (1982) suggests that body image also plays an important part in self-understanding. How individuals feel about themselves is basically related to how they feel about their bodies. The body is a most visible and material part of one's self and occupies the central part in a person's perceptions. Body image is the sum conscious and unconscious attitudes that individuals have towards their bodies. People with a high level of self-esteem will tend to have a much clearer understanding of themselves.

Gillies (1984) suggests that to utilize body image theory effectively it is necessary to differentiate the following concepts and understand their inter-relationships: self-concept, self-esteem, body concept, body scheme, body image and body image boundary. Self-concept consists of the cognitive aspects of self-perception and reflects a summary of what one thinks about oneself in an objective fashion. Self-esteem is the affective aspect of self-awareness or the evaluation of one's self-worth. Self-esteem, like self-concept, is both global and attribute specific. An individual who felt that she was a good mother, an excellent student, a valuable friend and a superior nurse would probably feel that, for those and other reasons, she was a fine person overall.

Gillies (1984) continues by stating that a major aspect of the self-concept is the body concept. Most of what we know about ourselves is knowledge of our physical being and its relationship to the social and physical environment. The self-concept is primarily a body concept because the individual can acquire self-knowledge only through the function of those body structures that specialize in perception, movement, sensation and cognition.

The body concept of many individuals is built on inadequate knowledge of normal anatomy and physiology. For instance, Pearson and Dudley (1982) observed that out of 720 subject responses relating to body organ location, 58% were wrong, 28% correct and 14% revealed only a vague awareness of normal body structures.

The body concept is composed of several subconcepts, among the most important of which are body scheme and body image. Body scheme is the concept of one's physical being as an object in space, for instance, the individual with an intact body scheme is aware of distances between various body parts, the relation of the body to the ground and to the vertical, and the effect of body movement on contiguous physical objects. The body image boundary is the individual's perception of the outermost limit of his or her physical being, or the point of interface between his or her body and the environment (Gillies, 1984).

Burnard and Morrison (1990) suggest that the terms 'self-esteem', 'self-image' and 'self-concept' are all closely related, and that if people are happy with the physical aspects of themselves (body image or physical appearance), they are more likely to experience positive feelings of self-esteem. In contrast, people who are unhappy with their physical appearance could have negative feelings regarding themselves.

Cohen (1991) suggests that body attributes affecting body image include, but are not limited to, total body size, proportion of body parts, coloration, sexuality, texture of the skin and facial features. Derbyshire (1986) suggests that factors affecting and impacting body image formation and dynamics include genetics, socialization, fashion, culture, race, education and the mass media.

Smith (1984) indicates that present and past perceptions, and feelings about size, function, potential and appearance are important. In considering size, Bradsky (cited in Burns, 1979) asked subjects which attributes characterized certain body builds. The image of the endomorph (obese) were consistently negative whilst that of the mesomorph (muscular, athletic) was regularly positive.

Appearance is a very important concept in Western society. It influences how people are perceived by others and valued by them and how they value themselves (McCall, 1990). Castledine

(1981) believes, therefore, that body image can be used as an indicator of a person's general health and that adaptation is necessary for a patient with a changed body image to be rehabilitated. Kesserling (1989) indicates that the literature pertaining to body image shows conceptualizations in which the physical presentation of the self and satisfaction with life are closely linked.

In considering gender, studies have been conducted that support gender differences in body image perception. Men are said to have a less definite body boundary sense than women. This may be a reflection of men being more likely to achieve an identity from their accomplishments rather than from their bodily attributes (Secord and Jourard, 1953). Research suggests that women are more likely than men to develop anxiety concerning their bodies. This anxiety may be due to the social importance placed on the female body (Janelli, 1993).

It is also important to consider culture. In one study, isolated black children absorbed negative views of themselves from the media and rarely encountered black role models or interacted with people of the same ethnic background. In contrast, white children avoided racial identity crisis because they regularly encountered positive images in television programmes and toys (Maxime, 1992).

Price (1990), in his model for body image care, discusses three components of body image: body reality (the way our body really is), body ideal (how we would like to look) and body presentation (which includes, for example, appearance, dress and poise). Body image is adjusted regularly in health as well as illness or injury. This adjustment is a response to puberty, maturation, ageing and other anticipated environmental events.

Price (1990) suggests that supportive care may be directed to any of the body image concepts. For instance, helping the patient to complete a clean wound dressing supports body reality. Removing a redundant nasogastric tube allows the patient to take greater charge of his or her body space (body ideal). Encouraging the patient to choose attractively designed clothing may assist the patient to improve body presentation. Thus a nurse can take steps to conceal the extensions of the patient's body image as much as possible. For example, the patient with a catheter and urinary drainage bag should have the drainage bag concealed by, for instance, the sheet draped over the side of the bed, if possible.

## Development of body image

Grunbaum (1985) states that a person's body image forms in infancy and develops throughout life. Each person derives his or her self-perceptions from the attitudes of parents, classmates and, later, adult peers.

Coopersmith (1967) states that self-esteem rests on four characteristics:

1. A child's feelings of being loved by others.
2. A sense of competency or personal efficiency.
3. A positive regard for his or her own ethics.
4. A feeling that he or she has control over their own lives or other people.

This focus suggests that children who have a sense of competency will be better able to cope with impaired appearance. They are likely to have higher self-esteem to begin with and their self-esteem does not rest on appearance. In addition, the importance of mastering one's body (an important aspect of this state of development) is being learned through sports, dance and other physical activity. Competency could, as stated above, help the child. However, bad experiences at school related to appearance could slow the acquisition of competency feelings (Hill-Beuf and Porter, 1984).

What happens when people see themselves and do not like what they see? for example, the distorted body image in a hall of mirrors at a fun fair, an unexpected glance at oneself in a shop window as one passes in the pouring rain. Seeing oneself on video or hearing one's voice on a recording for the first time often brings an embarrassed response of 'Do I really look/sound like that?' Other people's looks affect how an individual feels; how others are perceived, therefore, plays a large part in self perception.

## Adjusting to an altered body image

Donavon and Pearce (1976) discuss three components of the adaptation process. Firstly, they suggest there must be a change in the individual's value system so that physical characteristics become less important. Secondly, the effects of the disability must be confined and not allowed to affect unconnected areas of the body or unrelated behaviour (for example, stoma patients should not be handling/checking their appliances continually and it should not interfere with their daily activities).

Thirdly, the physical factor or altered function must be viewed as an asset rather than a liability. For example, patients with inflammatory bowel disease may well accept a stoma or continent pouch as an end to the misery of diarrhoea and ill-health. However, patients would need to be encouraged in these three components of adaptation – they do not just happen.

Costello (cited in Donavon and Pearce, 1976) suggests that nurses caring for clients with surgically created alterations in body image must assist patients in the following areas:

1.  Acceptance of the operation site.
2.  Touching and exploring the area.
3.  Accepting the necessity of learning to care for the defect.
4.  Developing independence and competence in daily care.
5.  Reintegrating their new body image and adjusting to a possibly altered lifestyle.

Because of the patient's need to incorporate a change in body image, some authors (Donavon and Pearce, 1976; Smitherman, 1981; Wassner, 1982) indicate that expectation is very important to the process of coping with a defect and that prepared individuals adapt more easily to body image changes than those in whom alteration occurs without warning. However, Murray (1972) suggests that adaptation is not always positive because there are individuals who will permanently avoid the reality of having undergone changes to their body. These few persons will continue to deny changes and remain regressed or develop a psychosis.

## Stigma

Stigma has to be considered too. It is important to establish whether a patient is fearful of people 'discovering' his or her secret. The person may go to great lengths to conceal their changed image. Goffman (1963) suggests that when a person's 'differentness' is not immediately apparent, he or she then has to decide whether to tell or not to tell, to let on or not to, to lie or not to lie. The same author defines stigma as the situation of an individual who is disqualified from full social acceptance; a person who has a failing or handicap and is reduced in the mind of society as a tainted person. The word 'stigma' originated from ancient Greek, and it was used to refer to bodily signs designed to expose something unusual and bad about the moral status of the signifier.

Even when individuals can keep an unapparent stigma secret, they will find that intimate relations with others, ratified in our society by mutual confession of invisible failings, cause them either to admit their situation to the intimate or to feel guilty for not doing so. Goffman suggests that, if stigmatized people are really at ease with their differentness, this acceptance will have an immediate effect upon 'normals', making it easier for them to be at ease with the stigmatized people in social situations. In brief, the stigmatized individuals are advised to accept themselves as normal people because of what others (and hence likely themselves) can gain in this way during face to face interaction. Goffman (1963) further suggests that persons who are ready to admit possession of a stigma may nonetheless make a great effort to keep the stigma from looking large. The individual's objective is to reduce tension, that is, to make it easier for himself or herself and the others to withdraw covert attention from the stigma, and to sustain spontaneous involvement in the official content of the interaction.

In all of this, special timing may be required. Thus, there is the practice of 'living on a leash' – the Cinderella syndrome – whereby the discreditable person stays close to the place where their disguise can be refurbished and where they can rest from having to wear it; they move from this repair station only that distance that they can return from without losing control over information about themselves (Goffman, 1963). This became apparent in the writer's (Salter, 1995) study when interviewing respondents with a stoma regarding body image and sexuality. Two respondents would not empty their appliance unless they were at home, and, therefore, the Cinderella syndrome applied – they could not venture far.

In his study on stigma, Goffman (1963) quotes a fictitious letter which is rich in sociological understanding and compassionate in human terms (Taylor and Bogdan, 1984).

Dear Miss Lonelyhearts
I am sixteen years old now and I don't know what to do and would appreciate it if you could tell me what to do. When I was a little girl it was not so bad because I got used to the kids on the block making fun of me, but now I would like to have boyfriends like the other girls and go out on Saturday nights, but no boy will take me because I was born without a nose – although I am a good dancer and have a nice shape and my father buys me pretty clothes.

I sit and look at myself all day and cry. I have a big hole in the middle of my face that scares people, even myself, so I can't blame the boys for not wanting to take me out. My mother loves me, but she crys terrible when she looks at me.

What did I do to deserve such a terrible bad fate? Even if I did do some bad things I didn't do any before I was a year old and I was born this way. I asked Papa and he says he doesn't know, but that maybe I did something in the other world before I was born or that maybe I was being punished for his sins. I don't believe that because he is a very nice man. Ought I to commit suicide?

Sincerely yours,
Desperate.

Taylor and Bogdan (1984) suggest that quite a few themes may be seen here. The first is despair. 'Desperate' says she looks at herself and cries and asks whether she should commit suicide; the signature itself reflects this state of mind. The next theme relates to trying to find an explanation for her situation. 'What did I do', she asks, 'to deserve such a terrible bad fate?' She goes on to speculate about, for instance, her father's sins. A third theme, which is somewhat more subtle, has to do with the meanings of physical stigma at different times in a person's life. 'It was not so bad' when she was a little girl, but now that she has reached adolescence, when other girls have boyfriends and go out on Saturday nights, it is unbearable. A final theme relates to how 'Desperate's' other qualities do not overcome the fact that she does not have a nose. That she may be a good dancer, have a nice shape and wear pretty clothes, does not get her any dates.

However, the writer would add that it would now be possible to camouflage this type of deformity by plastic surgery. It must not be forgotten also, that her parents were supportive of her, and this goes a long way in helping her. She acknowledges that her mother is upset, but that her mother loves her and her father takes time to discuss the situation with her, as well as trying to make up for the defect in a small, but necessary way, by buying her pretty clothes.

In his autobiography, *Journey into Silence* (1973), Labour MP Jack Ashley recalls several unhappy sequelae to his return to the House of Commons after becoming totally deaf. Among these is the following.

*'On one occasion in the tea-room, I took my cup of tea to a table to join four friends. When one of them asked me a question which I could not understand, the others repeated it for me but I was still unable to lip-read it. They paused while one of them wrote it down*

*and I was aware that the easy-going conversation they had been enjoying before my arrival was now disrupted. When I answered the written question it was understandable that none of them should risk a repeat performance by asking another. Within a few moments two of them had left and after a brief pause the others explained that they had to go because of pressing engagements. They were genuinely sorry and I understood, but it was small solace as I sat alone drinking my tea'.* (Ashley, 1973: 149).

Some people are born deformed, but it is only when they measure themselves against other people that they feel different. Notice a mixed group of young children playing – their difference may be, for example, physical, mental, colour or creed, but they accept each other as they are. It is adolescents and adults who have the problems about body image. Thus, if people are born with imperfections, or develop them, how they look and feel about themselves affects their health and general well-being. Few ever reach the ideal they may set for themselves, but individuals are what they are naturally, with all their faults and blemishes. A healthy, newborn baby can be said to be perfect: he or she has the correct number of 'parts' in the right proportions. If, however, over the course of life, his or her body image alters, normal then becomes abnormal as far as that individual is concerned.

A woman who has anorexia nervosa does not see her true body image. Instead, she sees in the mirror a fat, unattractive figure that must lose weight. Little does she realize that what she sees is just as awful as her present self, for, although altered body image is not just a change in appearance (take the anorexic again – her underlying problem is psychological, not just physical) or a visible disability, if one looks good, one usually feels good. Conversely, if one feels bad, one often looks bad, but it is possible to be positive. Many women, for example, recognize that, if they make a special effort to look good during the days of premenstrual tension, they will tend to feel less miserable. Such women may keep a check on when they hit this regular downward slide each month, and then perhaps treat themselves to a different hair style, buy a new shade of nail varnish or eye shadow. They will often have a list of 'support' people to contact if they should become too desperate.

McCrea (1984) suggests that probably never before has dissatisfaction with the female body (especially) been so widespread, because we are bombarded with hints as to how we should look and, inevitably, most fall short. People with body image problems should not have to go through such mental agony, so are these problems caused by society or disease? McGrouther (1996) asks if our obsession with physical beauty is creating an underclass of less than perfect people.

Take obesity, for instance. McCrea (1984) continues by stating that being fat in our society is such a stigma that obese people develop a distorted body image. The obese, therefore, may have as many problems as the anorexic. For while the person with anorexia nervosa is putting her life at risk and her body in a poor state of nutrition, with accompanying hormonal change and a cessation of ovulation, her overweight counterpart is increasing her chances of developing a cerebral vascular accident, high blood pressure, diabetes and varicose veins. However, it is necessary to say, at this point, that men can be equally apprehensive about altered body image. For example, a man with a conspicuous bald patch on his head will often alter his hair style in an attempt to cover up the baldness, or acquire a toupe.

**Body image as a continuing entity**

It would be of interest to compare the feelings of individuals with congenital disease affecting their body with those who acquire a body change in later life. It can be argued that the former have not known any difference and have, therefore, not missed what they have never had. This is a fallacy, however, for each individual has his or her particular way of accepting a change in body image and the age at the time of the body image change is also important. As one young woman with a congenital deformity put it: 'The fact that I was loved for myself, regardless of how I looked, helped me to forget my self-pity and put self-respect in its place. Being handicapped was less important than being loved and loving' (Stewart, 1975).

Olshansky (1962) introduced the term 'chronic sorrow' to explain the parental response of lifelong, episodic sadness to the parents whose children were not normal. Olshansky suggests that chronic sorrow is a pervasive psychological reaction, a natural rather than neurotic response to a tragic fact and the sadness is exacerbated at critical periods in the child's development. The parents, because of the loss of the fantasized child, experience sorrow (Teel, 1991).

Whether deformity is congenital or acquired later in life, 'normal' people will tend to stare at or reject the disfigured person. Comparison between peer groups is common, especially during adolescence, and the trauma of puberty is linked with the developing body. Body image is constantly changing, and one has also to take into account a person's cultural and religious background. Some stoics believe that they must bear bravely what God has allowed them to suffer, and feel they will be rewarded in the after life; others feel only shame with their affliction and may be treated as outcasts by their families or religious leaders.

Being unhappy with his or her body image affects the way a person behaves and functions, which in turn rebounds on others. This can show itself in something as simple and transient as a haircut that has not turned out as one imagined it would. The person may be angry and disappointed, and no amount of encouragement will improve the situation. However, if they put on a confident front they will be accepted, whereas, if they appear negative and insecure, people will react to them as such. People glow with pride when someone pays them a compliment − it seems as if they are walking on air for the rest of the day − it is a boost to their self-image and ego.

## Rating of body image

Salter (1983) suggests that different people rate body image in a variety of ways. This is apparent with the change due to natural ageing and disease, for example, the attractive wife who realizes she now has abdominal stretch marks or facial wrinkles; the balding husband; the obese father and the amputee. Creams and lotions can be bought to camouflage stretch marks and wrinkles, special preparations can stimulate regrowth of hair and one can strive to eradicate excessive weight gain. It is not the same, however, if one is fitted with an artificial leg. Although people in general are affected by the ageing process, it is a small minority who undergo limb amputation and its resulting body image consequences.

In quoting two patients it appears that surgery to take away the cancer is more important than the loss of a body part, Kelly (1995), in a letter to the Editor of BACUP states: 'I kept looking down my nightie and I do realize that my breast is gone but I feel no sense of loss, I only feel relief that the cancer is gone . . .'. Barron (1995) following a cystectomy writes 'In particular I remember a magnificent bouquet of chrysanthemums, symbolically white to say that the impurity had been taken away'.

In disease, diagnosis alone can have an adverse effect on body image with the patient or 'significant other' withdrawing from one another. This can be true if one partner of a marriage is found to have a sexually transmitted disease from an extramarital relationship. This is also true of cancer, when cancer cells are felt to be rampant in the body, destroying it. Yet, altered body image can be used to enhance one's sexuality. This is so in pregnancy – an expectant mother and father will often feel nothing but pride in such an expanding bulge and wish to show it off rather than hide it.

**Different types of body image**

Parents of physically or mentally handicapped children, or their offspring, may suffer the agony of being either avoided or offered sympathy. A mother of a Down's syndrome child remarked to the writer: 'Every time I take her out I feel people are sorry for us, despite the fact that I also have two perfectly normal children. I don't want their sympathy, I just want my daughter to be accepted for herself'. Other parents complain of the stigma they experience; the glance of self-pity or disrespect, followed by the hurried looking away and brushing past. Care for such people in the community is being hampered by the view society places on these children and adults, enhancing their (society's) unwillingness to 'spoil' the neighbourhood.

Cystic fibrosis is a common hereditary disorder; children and adults with the disease battle with daily physiotherapy, frequent hospital admissions and dietary supplements, yet they want to lead a normal life – not to be treated differently. Imagine having chronic and recurring chest infections and fighting for breath in a crowded disco or bar – people with cystic fibrosis will often prefer this to being singled out as being 'different' from their peer group because they cough continuously. In the same way, young diabetics will drink and eat things they know they should not so that they can be like their peers (Kingäs and Hentinen, 1995).

Some changes in the body's image are noticeable to everyone, such as, a young man with a full head of hair who undergoes chemotherapy treatment leading to alopecia, whilst a woman with, for example, a mastectomy is able to conceal her deficiency from the world at large. But, if people who lose a bit of hair or put on or shed a few extra pounds are concerned about their appearance (the way they see themselves), how do people feel when their body is radically altered by disease or surgery?

Those who are blind, deaf or dumb may have profound body image problems because their vital communication pathways are affected. Skin disorders such as acne, psoriasis and eczema can

**Table 1.1** Examples of types/categories of altered body image.

| Congenital | Hereditary | Reproductive | Medical | Trauma | Surgery |
|---|---|---|---|---|---|
| Muscular dystrophy<br>Spina bifida | Huntingdon's chorea | Pregnancy<br>Sterility<br>Miscarriage<br>Premature ejaculation | Arthritis<br>Anorexia nervosa<br>Bulimia<br>Obesity<br>Skin diseases<br>Multiple sclerosis<br>Sensory impairment | Burns | (Encompasses oncology) |

| Ageing | Revealed | Concealed | Permanent | Temporary |
|---|---|---|---|---|
| Balding<br>Obesity | Head/neck<br>Amputation | Stoma<br>Breast<br>Gynae<br>Impotence<br>Teratoma<br>Sterility<br>Incontinence | Stoma<br>Head/neck<br>Breast<br>Brain tumour | Alopecia<br>Stoma<br>Incontinence<br>Fistula |

NB Some of these examples are not necessarily specific to their categories; for example, a stoma, a fistula and alopecia may be temporary or permanent.

cause much misery, coupled with feelings of uncleanliness. Such people feel untouchable and can convey their negative feelings to others. Women with gynaecological conditions, which although unseen, may result in an abortion, sterilization or hysterectomy and male patients undergoing prostatectomy will often comment on their feelings of 'loss of woman/manhood'. This is particularly so in infertility where the infertile woman can long for the altered body image of pregnancy.

Burns can be another cause of altered body image, especially if they are facial or on other parts of the body that are normally uncovered, or uncovered especially during the summer. Other types of facial repair can make the person depressed, despite good camouflage techniques. Rheumatoid arthritis, Parkinson's disease and multiple sclerosis are all disabling and disfiguring illnesses. The patient with a slowly progressive change in body image, such as the often gradual weakening experienced in multiple sclerosis, may be able to cope more effectively with that change than some-one involved in traumatic paraplegia. The person with multiple sclerosis may progress from walking stick to frame, then to wheel-chair, and may well feel frustrated and angry as each step on the downward slope means more loss of independence; but to have been a healthy, sports-orientated individual one minute and be transformed to a paraplegic the next, must be a heavy cross to bear. However, it is not only the permanent conditions that alter the body's image.

In considering chronic illness versus the critically injured per-son, Morse and O'Brien (1995) suggest that, although the former has been addressed (Charmaz, 1983; Morse and Johnson, 1991; Thorne, 1993), the experience of the critically injured patient has not been described in its entirety.

**Temporary conditions**

In considering the temporary conditions within oncology, a large field of altered body image is encompassed where people have to come to terms not only with a change to their normal body, but with the fact that they may not have the permanent cure that they hoped their treatment would bring. Chemotherapy regimens with cytotoxic drugs are common in the treatment of cancer, but often it is apparent that patients may cope with the reality of having cancer. They may cope with coming for treatment month in month out, but their response to losing their hair is 'No, please, not that'. Young children with leukaemia are not so concerned with altered body image and peer group acceptance as other family members (especially parents) may be. To them it may be a game to have a moustache 'like Daddy's' (brought about by the side effects of treatment, with growth of hair in unusual places). Similarly, little girls may not mind having to wear a scarf to cover their bald heads, but teenagers can be devastated. Imagine the feelings of a girl in a sleek, fashion-conscious family having to 'shave' various parts of her body as a result of her treatment.

Patients can be rendered virtually incontinent by radiotherapy to the pelvis, firstly with more frequent trips to the toilet and then perhaps uncontrollable diarrhoea or frequency of micturition. They, too, feel that their body image and the healthy regard they once had for themselves has been altered by sheaths, catheters, leg bags, or pads and pants – a regression to childhood. They are embarrassed by the alteration they have to make to their style of dress to accommodate bulky pads. If nurses are the patient's advocate, then it is only right to discuss ways of making their incontinence garments less noticeable and to supply slim pads for special occasions or outings. Assisting in practical ways helps patients to adjust emotionally.

Consideration must also be given to brain tumour patients. They walk into objects, they are forgetful, they make odd comments at times and they know it. How do they rate their self-esteem and how does their partner or family accept or not accept their personality change? The astute businessman may find all this very undignified, as indeed does the blue-collar worker. He objects to having his wife waiting on him when he feels he should be the bread winner and head of the family. He may be fighting for his last bit of independence and, therefore, his carers must seek ways of enabling him to do this. Diplomacy is needed in the nurse's interactions with such people. Many patients would prefer to press on without nursing intervention, especially in the community. Families may, therefore, decline the services offered because they prefer to keep 'a stiff upper lip' and pretend to the neighbours that all is well.

Men with testicular tumours may not look any different, but again, this is a very personal area of life and of their anatomy that is affected. They may find it hard to give the proper name to their genital organs and thus the carer's language is important. A nurse can be guided by the terms the patient uses and, if a patient is more at ease using them, the nurse should not insist on correct anatomical labelling.

A woman with cervical cancer, whose vagina is a mass of adhesions or has the problems of fistulae that impede sexual intercourse, may feel guilty and see that, being unable to satisfy her partner as she once could, he will have no positive regard for her and seek pleasure elsewhere. It may be right to suggest to such a couple an alternative way of satisfying each other which does not involve intercourse and it may be appropriate to advise them on the type of sex aids which could help in their situation.

Referral to a sexual counsellor can assist people to seek more specific help to enable them to come to terms with their problem. Although patients may attach stigma to such a referral, it can be explained to them that, if they are depressed or suicidal, the psychiatrist may well be the most appropriate person to help. Stewart (1975) comments: 'If a marriage is solidly based – one in which the partners are mature and understanding of each other, frank and without reservations in their satisfaction – then they can withstand crisis'.

## Permanent changes

One must also consider those who undergo a permanent change of body image – that young man with a sarcoma, once so athletic, but now reduced to one leg – a prosthesis, crutches, wheelchair. And, if that is not enough, his healthy self-regard is further assaulted as metastases develop and his aggressive treatment results in the loss of his hair.

Head and neck surgery requires careful preoperative counselling together with help and patience during the various stages of treatment, healing of wounds and skin grafts. For patients undergoing changes in body image, support is paramount and the carer's positive attitudes can enhance those of the family. If nurses are seen to be willing to sit close to a patient and approve of him or her, then family and friends will feel more confident in doing so. Patients cope with their illnesses and come to believe in themselves again in different ways. Some patients can cope with mammoth disfiguring operations, whilst others go to pieces over something which may seem trivial to us but obviously is important to them. Although, medically, all tumours may be classed alike and all surgery is similar, it is a unique crisis for them. Kissing is part of loving for most people, but for someone with a facial impairment it is not easy to kiss a loved one, and harder still to be that person.

Yet there is another category of patients – those who some may say are fortunate inasmuch as they are able to hide their problems, but hidden or not, they are still there. Such people often feel that they are rotting away inside. Within this category is the woman with a mastectomy or lumpectomy. She is concerned as to what she is going to tell her husband and their children, and about the further assault on her body of radiotherapy, chemotherapy or hormonal treatment. She is troubled by how thin she is going to become as her disease progresses, or how fat and bloated she will feel when treated with steroids. Complimenting her on the natural traits which she can be positive about is a boost to her self-confidence, for instance, a new hair style or dress. Giving support and providing a listening ear when it is needed will help her overcome her fears. A patient with a changed body image can be asked if they would like a member of the nursing staff to discuss his or her surgery with their children, adapting the conversation to the age and gender of the children. The patient can be supported through the traumatic treatment by the nurse emphasizing that, if help is only a telephone call or visit away, the client can make that contact and a nurse will be there to offer advice and give support.

Others falling into the category of hidden disability are patients with a stoma. However, they do not get off all that lightly: 'their anal equivalent is placed on their abdomen in a prominent position, often demanding continual attention. It can be subject to various complications and thus become a dominant part of the person's daily life' (Salter, 1983). How the nurse seeks to enable stoma patients to come to terms with their altered body image is dealt with in a later chapter, but it is of benefit here to compare how patients with hidden altered body image differ from those whose change in body image is noticeable to everyone.

Wassner (1982) suggests that adults' reactions to mutilating surgery are bound to the degree of development of body image, but certain factors cause variation of the reaction. Some of these variables are age, sex, personality, beliefs, values, expectations and sociocultural background. Also, the degree of preparation for the change, the cause of the change and the relationship with the health team all have their effect.

**The effects of altered body image in illness**

For people who are ill, undergoing investigations and treatment often involves admission to hospital at least once and perhaps several times for varying periods. Such patients will miss home, family and social contact, and may feel confused about life, unsure of themselves and inadequate. Pritchard (1981) supports this statement by suggesting that hospital means that the individual is suddenly translated from a family to a strange environment, which functions according to rules and regulations that have no meaning or relevance outside the hospital setting. The individual has to enter new relationships with authorities upon whose skills his or her very existence may depend. Their pattern of life is changed completely.

Kubler-Ross (1969) suggests 'There are five stages of dying (or loss). On first learning of the loss, the person denies the seriousness of the condition. This is followed by anger at the situation and this anger is likely to be expressed towards nurses and medical staff, as well as towards family and friends, or God and fate. In the third stage the patient bargains with life, or fate in an attempt to escape from the situation. This is followed by a stage of depression as the inevitability of the condition is realized, and the loss and separation it involves is acknowledged. Finally, there is acceptance and the opportunity to respond realistically to the situation.'

The following describe in more detail some of the stages of loss:

*Denial:*   1.   'The doctor has just told me that I have cancer and need major surgery, but I feel so well. How can he possibly be right?' (Discussion with this patient would focus on disbelief/denial.)

*Anger:*   2.   A patient is fitted with an appliance preoperatively to get used to the 'feel' of wearing a bag. The nurse asks him how he is feeling about his impending surgery, to which he responds by tearing off the bag, throwing it across the room and saying 'This is my doctor's fault – if he'd listened to me, I wouldn't need this terrible operation'. (Discussion with this patient would centre around displaced anger.)

*Bargaining:*   3.   The 'bargaining' period of grief often displays itself in bargaining with God. If . . . then . . ., for example, 'If you make me well, I promise I'll make up for my bad deeds and live a better life'.

Patients progress through the stages of grief on different time scales. They often remain depressed and can go backwards and forwards through the various stages, progressing and regressing until they accept the situation. It may be helpful for nurses to ask themselves how they would feel in the following situations:

'You are on the bus going home after being told in outpatients that you will be admitted to hospital for a colostomy in one week's time'. Or

'Your wife has been home for three months after her breast surgery. Despite encouragement she has made no move to re-establishing the sexual side of your marriage'.

Emerson (1983) recognized that a crisis occurs when the previous equilibrium is upset. All the usual responses are completely out of tune and inadequate to meet it. One's own behaviour becomes unpredictable as a loss of self occurs. It is best to try to ensure that conditions make it possible for the person facing a loss to grieve, to reassure him or her of the normality of strange and often frightening feelings and thoughts which may be experienced, and, when the peak of grief is past, to point the way towards a more realistic and satisfying adjustment of life.

Wilson-Barnett (1980) suggests that giving the right information reduces anxiety and also aids a rapid adjustment to stressful events because patients can prepare before they occur, when they are more able to concentrate, rather than when they are in pain. Preparation is really a process of sharing nursing and medical knowledge with patients so that their coping strategies are more effective. Forewarned is forearmed; if patients trust nurses to anticipate their need for information, other events which require more adjustment may seem less harmful.

Illness inevitably blocks off some of life's goals, and it becomes a vicious circle of mood change, depression and unfulfilled hopes. Patients may pretend that they are managing when they are not; they may try to protect and to prevent their relatives from knowing what they know or suspect, and in turn relatives will put on a facade of cheerfulness for the patient's sake. False laughter and outward show, the conspiracy of pretence, can be detected in both. If these intense feelings are not acknowledged or expressed, they are turned inwards, leading to deeper depression.

Smith (1984) stresses that each patient has individual needs and worries which only a careful history and awareness of the family and social background will reveal. 'The carer's reactions and acceptance of this new change will in turn affect the attitude of the patient towards himself.' Sometimes too much information is given to patients without allowing them sufficient time to grasp it all. To be told their diagnosis, treatment and prognosis all in one go is a bitter pill to swallow, and resolution of crisis is often unreached. All patients are individuals and information must be carefully spaced; some will stoically face 'the truth, the whole truth and nothing but the truth', but they are a small minority. Others will deny even the slightest mention of complications or problems. It may be kinder to deal one cruel blow at a time, giving opportunity for recovery, and in stages that lead to acceptance.

It is important for the nurse to be a communicator, a counsellor and a patient advocate. She or he must take a careful history and assessment, organize, where applicable, patient conferences, encourage patient/family-centred care, and arrange discharge planning and rehabilitation within her role in the multidisciplinary team.

Regression feels safe when the outside world is intolerable. Regression is begging, pleading: 'Won't you cure my disease, give me my independence back, help me fulfil my ambitions, take away this mental agony?'. The emotional pain patients experience here and now is related to their past experiences of such grief. The kind of illness they have and the kind of loss they have to face, is an attack on their identity, yet their progress through the various stages of mourning towards acceptance shows that reality is being faced. There are so many losses – loss of hair, loss of mobility, loss of weight, loss of continence, loss of role, loss of control, loss of dexterity, loss of sight, loss of sensible thoughts . . . the list could go on.

## Body image in end-stage disease

Cancer is among those diseases that particularly evoke a feeling of fear, dread and revulsion. It is not only frightening and stigmatizing for the cancer patients, their families and the public in general, but also for medical and nursing professionals (Macdonald and Anderson, 1984).

Gillies (1984) suggests that severe pain in any body part can create body image distortions. Because the painful part receives a disproportionate amount of the patient's attention, the part is perceived as being increased in size so that it occupies a prominent position in the body image. If severe pain persists, however, the painful part becomes progressively isolated from the rest of the body to the point that it is eventually pushed out of the body image entirely (Fisher and Cleveland, 1968). Grunbaum (1985) suggests that pain can interfere with adaptation to change. For example, a patient was in severe pain for several days following major surgery. Only after the pain subsided was she ready to start adapting to her change in body image.

An important account of palliative care is the randomized survey conducted in England and Wales by Cartwright *et al.* (1973) as noted by Fitzpatrick *et al.* (1984). The data were based on retrospective accounts, mainly from the nearest surviving relative. They could hardly have been disinterested observers, but their reports largely have the ring of truth. One of the many tables records the symptoms occurring to a 'very distressing degree' during the last year of life in the following percentage of patients: pain (42%), breathing troubles (28%), vomiting (17%), sleeplessness (17%), loss of both bladder and bowel control (12%), loss of appetite (11%) and mental confusion (10%) (Cartwright *et al.*, 1973: 18–24).

In terminal illness the slow destruction of the body seems to cast a great shadow over the last few weeks and months of life, but when the individual is loved and cared for, the emotional pain can often be relieved. Even here the nurse can encourage the patient gradually to let go of life but still continue on, hopefully, to acceptance. As one patient's wife put it: 'He has all kinds of tubes and plumbing fastened to him but I should have known that just as long as he had a heart and a brain he wouldn't change. That body is just a house for the man I love. They can add to, or take away from it, remodel the whole structure, but he will still be in there' (Randall, 1972).

**Case study**

*Tom Harris was a middle-aged hairdresser who was to have major life-saving surgery. The nurse met him for the first time in outpatients, after the surgeon had explained the nature of his impending surgery. He was about to undergo four weeks of radiotherapy prior to surgery and, because it could be seen from the outset that he would need much support, it was of benefit to have a long period of time to work with him. He cried helplessly 'Why me?'. The nurse explained that, although she did not know 'why him' they could all – family and professionals alike – work together, and he would come through. He asked if she would be there to see him through, and she promised that she would. The nurse explained that there was no quick, easy or painless way out, but eventually he would 'make it'. During his treatment she listened to his denial, his anger, his bargaining and slowly his acceptance. As he was prepared for theatre, he said 'I am resigned to this now; I don't want it; if there was another way out I'd take it, but I know I must make the best of my future'. And he did.*

The care plan that follows details the patient's main areas of need and the following brief notes are provided to accompany the plan.

*Problems 1 and 2*
On two occasions Mrs Harris accompanied her husband to the radiotherapy department, where it was possible to explain to her, in her husband's presence and with his agreement, the extent of his surgery. She was seen once on the ward with Tom (preoperatively) when the patient, his wife and the nurse discussed the patient education booklet in detail. (Many appliance companies produce information booklets on stoma care, for example, *How to Live with your Urostomy* by Coloplast Ltd). Part of the conversation is repeated here:

*Nurse*:   Mrs Harris, as you know, your husband did discuss with the surgeon and me the problem of impotence that arises after cystectomy and I wonder if you would like to discuss this?

*Patient's wife*:   Well, I, I know Tom's told you that that side of our marriage is still important to us – I think it's more important to him than me. I . . . I've, um, tried to reassure him that it won't matter, but I think he's still quite upset about it all.

*Nurse*:   So you feel that, although the sexual side of your marriage is still important to you both, your husband will feel it more of a problem than you?

*Patient*:   I suppose it's because I still feel fairly young and fit. This tumour has come like a bolt out of the blue. (laughs) I'm at the age when I need to prove myself. I mean, I like to feel I'm still a man!

*Patient's wife*:   But I've told you, Tom, you'll still be attractive. After all, I'm the only one that'll see you undressed. I'd rather have you any way than not have you at all. . . .

*Problem 3*

*Patient*:   This operation, Doctor, it has taken all the growth away, hasn't it?

*Doctor*:   As far as we can tell, Mr Harris, your previous radiotherapy treatment and now the operation gives us confidence that the cancer has been removed. We'll keep a careful check on you in the future and . . .

*Patient*:   But you can't tell me for sure that it's all gone? After all this treatment? I've been up and down to this hospital every day and now a big operation. *Still* you can't tell me if everything is all right?

*Doctor:*   Mr Harris, we have many patients doing exceptionally well after 5 years, even 10 years after surgery. You've just met . . . I believe I saw one of my patients with you the other day – eight years since his treatment – still working and enjoying life, and his out-look is good. (Silence. Doctor moves away and nurse takes up conversation.)

*Nurse:*   It seems you're worried, Tom, in case the disease hasn't all been removed?

*Patient:*   I suppose I want an answer no one can give me – that I'm cured completely.

*Nurse:*   I suppose that we all want assurances that we'll stay healthy indefi-nitely – I must accompany Mr Cox on his ward round – I'll come back afterwards and have a few words with you, or shall I ask staff nurse to come now?

*Patient:*   No, I'm sorry. I suppose I just feel I've been at or in hospital so much, and I just want to get better and get out fighting fit.

*Footnote*   Mr Harris continued to have difficulty in accepting his angry feel-ings that cancer had caused such a radical change in his life, but before leaving hospital, he had worked through most of his anger.

*Problem 4*

*Nurse:*   Tom, we want to take your appliance off today and have a look at the stoma. I'll give you a mirror when I've cleaned around your urostomy and you can have a look yourself if you feel you are ready to. . . . Do you remember that we discussed how your stoma would look – swollen, red and unhealed – almost like a raw piece of meat? (Nurse removes appliance and cleans around stoma) I won-der if you feel you are ready to have a look?

*Patient:*   It's not as bad as I thought it was – not very nice, mind you! (laughs) I wonder what Pat will think of it?

*Nurse:*   You'd like your wife to see it soon, or wait until you can show her how to change the bag?

*Patient:*   I think I'd like to get it over as soon as possible – can I show her tonight when she comes in?

*Nurse:*   That's fine; just call one of us when you are ready and we can come along and give a bit of moral support, or would you rather be alone?

*Patient:*   I don't know . . . maybe I'll opt for some moral support the first time around!

## Problem 5

*Nurse*:  I understand your wife was quite reassured by the operation site yesterday – I'm wondering if you feel more relaxed now she has seen it?

*Patient*:  Yes, but we did wonder what the children would think – whether we should show it to them once I get home, or just not let them see it at all?

*Nurse*:  How do you feel about that?

*Patient*:  I'm not exactly proud of it, but then, on the other hand, it's a bit of a novelty isn't it? Pat thinks Jenny might be a bit put off – you know what these teenagers are like. . . . I think I'll see what happens when I get home. I mean, if they ask to see it, I'll show them, but if they don't, we'll forget about it.

*Nurse*:  That sounds wise, and don't forget, it's not goodbye when you walk out of here – your own doctor, the district nurse and the hospital staff are available to help. You'll be coming back here for outpatient appointments. If anything worries you in the meantime, just get in touch with your doctor, or with us here.

## Problem 6

*Nurse*:  Tom, would you like to come down the corridor to a spare room we have. I thought it might be nice to discuss your discharge plans in a little privacy?

*Patient*:  Thanks, nurse, it's amazing how everyone's conversation stops as soon as the curtains go round the bed!

*Nurse*:  As you know, Tom, Mr Cox has suggested that you can go home tomorrow. Your stitches are out, you're managing your own stoma care, but we did wonder if you were still a little unsure of going so soon?

*Patient*:  I want to get home – I've had enough of this place! I suppose I'm still a little bit uncertain, sort of down; um, depressed. (silence) I mean what's going to happen when I get home? I'm really nervous about that because I'm going back a different person.

*Nurse*:  You'd like to go home but you feel depressed and nervous because you don't think it'll be the same Tom Harris? To your family, to your friends who've been to see you, and to us, you are still you.

*Patient*:  What shall I do when Pat and I go to bed tomorrow night? I shall feel really uncomfortable – I suppose I'm scared really – chickening out.

*Nurse*:  It's natural for you to have such concerns and we are here to discuss them with you if that's what you would like. Mr Cox has

**Table 1.2** Nursing care plan.

| | Patient's problems/needs | Aim | Implementation | Evaluation |
|---|---|---|---|---|
| 1 | Need for preoperative counselling incorporating partner/relative if possible, stressing return to normal lifestyle, continuance of social life, adaptation to change in body image | To ensure patient is physically and emotionally able to cope with surgery. 1 How does he feel about his surgery that will cause a change of body image? 2 Does he foresee any specific problems? | Discussion with staff – invited to ask questions. Referral to patient booklet to show altered anatomy | Understands all that is being said. Feeling able to cope |
| 2 | Thinks wife won't find him sexually attractive | To promote the idea that he will be sexually attractive still | Suggest patient and partner talk to someone of their own age and background who has undergone similar treatment | Feels more relaxed following visit |
| 3 | (Second postoperative day). Frightened that all the cancer hasn't been removed and that he will have altered body image and the disease | To reduce anxiety about possible residual cancer | Encourage patient to talk about how he feels | Remains angry and resentful and does not believe surgery has cured him |
| 4 | Need for patient to look at operation site when he feels ready | To be willing to view wound | Encourage patient to look at wound and remind him what we said operation site would look like | Is happy to view scar |
| 5 | Worried about what he will tell rest of family and friends about operation | To help patient decide what he will tell others | Will talk to his children when they next visit. Feels he will only tell his two best friends | Feels relaxed and thankful that 'relevant others' have taken it so well |
| 6 | Physically ready for discharge but is depressed | Elevation of mood and creation of environment where patient is able to talk about future | See patient in privacy of a side room. Ask open-ended, leading questions regarding his feelings over the future | Reluctant to talk at first but says he is feeling better having discussed his problems and knowing he will receive follow-up care |
| 7 | Home visit – apprehensive about going out | Encourage to get out and about more, e.g. shopping, restaurants, visiting friends | Discuss how he feels about his lifestyle (self-assessement) | Filling time more profitably and gradually coming to terms with change in self-image, identified by more frequent social activities |

suggested to you that you give yourself plenty of time to consider if you would like a penile implant. Your wife knows this too, so it will be a matter of acting naturally, of finding alternatives in love making. . . . You could always go home for the afternoon tomorrow and if you feel OK, go home permanently the next day – a gradual getting used to it. . . .

*Problem 7*

District Nurse: I wonder how you feel about discussing how you're managing now, Tom? Your first follow-up outpatient appointment is next week and the staff there will be interested in how you are adjusting.

Patient: I'm definitely feeling stronger physically – eating well as you know, and pottering in the house and garden. But I'm still not happy about going out – the bag is fine, but I don't trust it in a restaurant or shop, so how will I trust it back at work, in close contact with my customers?

District Nurse: I'm sure your confidence in the appliance will increase as time goes by. Have you been out shopping with your wife yet? You could always try a short trip and lengthen your outings as time goes by . . . (Conversation goes on to self-assessment of adjustment to changed body image). Your wife seems very supportive – I had a chat with her yesterday, if you remember, and she said you seemed to be coping emotionally all right?

Patient: Yes, I feel less depressed, may be still uncertain about the future, but I really don't mind the bag and all the connotations that go with it. . . .

*Summary*

Thus it can be seen that, as Wood (1975) suggested, body image is a dynamic concept, subject to change in responses to influences on the body itself. Altered body image may be the result of the ageing process, illness (disease) accident or injury and each individual will react differently to his or her changed body image.

**References**

Ashley, J. (1973) *Journey into Silence*. London, Bodley Head.

Barron, C. (1995) Chronicle of a recovery. *Urostomy Association Journal* no. 45, Spring, 34–41.

Burnard, J. and Morrison, L. (1990) Body image and physical appearance. *Surgical Nurse* **3**, 4–8.

Burns, R. (1979) *The Self-concept*. London, Longman.

Cartwright, A., Hockey, L. and Anderson, T. (1973) *Life Before Death*. London, Routledge & Kegan Paul.

Castledine, G. (1981). In the mind's eye. *Nursing Mirror* **153**, 16.

Charmaz, K. (1983) Loss of self: a fundamental form of suffering in the chronically ill. *Sociology of Health and Illness* **5**, 168–195.

Chilton, S. (1982) Identity crisis. *Nursing Mirror* **158** (June 13), ii–iv.

Cohen, A. (1991) Body image in the person with a stoma. *Journal of Enterostomal Therapy* **18**, Mar/Apr.

Coopersmith, S. (1967). *The Antecedents of Self Esteem*. San Francisco, Freemond.

Derbyshire, P. (1986). Body image – when the face doesn't fit. *Nursing Times* September 24, 28–30.

Donavon, M. and Pearce, S. (1976) *Cancer Care Nursing*. New York, Appleton-Century-Crofts.

Emerson, J. (1983) Living through grief. *Nursing Mirror* **157** (November 9th), ii–x.

Fisher, S. and Cleveland, B. (1968) *Body Image and Personality*. New York, Dover Publications.

Fitzpatrick, R., Hinton, J., Newman, S., Scambler, G. and Thompson, J. (1984) *The Experience of Illness*. London, Tavistock.

Gillies, D.A. (1984) Body image changes following illness and surgery. *Journal of Enterostomal Therapy* **11**, 186–189.

Goffman, E. (1963). *Stigma: Notes on the Management of Spoiled Identity*. Eaglewood Cliffs, NJ, Prentice Hall.

Grunbaum, J. (1985) Helping your patient build a sturdier body image. *Registered Nurse* **48**, 51–55.

Hill-Beuf, A. and Porter, J. (1984) Children coping with impaired appearance; social and psychologic influences. *General Hospital Psychiatry* **6**, 294–301.

Janelli, L. (1993) Are there body image differences between older men and women? *Western Journal of Nursing Research* **15**, 327–339.

Kelly, A. (1995) Deciding is the hardest part. *BACUP News* Spring, 7.

Kesserling, A. (1989) Knowledge about the body in nursing. (Unpublished paper).

Kingäs, H. and Hentinen, M. (1995) Meaning attached to compliance with self care, and conditions for compliance among young diabetics. *Journal of Advanced Nursing* **21**, 729–736.

Kubler-Ross, E. (1969) *On Death and Dying*. London, Tavistock Publications.

Macdonald, L. and Anderson, H. (1984) Stigma in patients with rectal cancer – a community study. *Journal of Epidemiology and Community Health* **20**, 284–290.

Maxime, O. (1992) Image crisis for black children. *Nursing Times* **88** (January 8), no. 2, 88.

McCall, J. (1990) Fostering self-esteem. *Surgical Nurse* **3**, 5–9.

McCrea, C. (1984) First get rid of the stigma. *Sunday Times* (Supplement), 10 June.

McGrouther, G. (1996) The perfect body. *Nursing Times* **92** (14 February), no. 7, 23.

Morse, J. and Johnson, J. (1991) Toward a theory of illness: the illness constellation model. In: *The Illness Experience: Dimensions of Suffering*. Newbury Park, CA, Sage, pp. 315–342.

Morse, J. and O'Brien, B. (1995) Preserving self: from victim, to patient, to disabled person. *Journal of Advanced Nursing* **21**, 886–896.

Murry, R. (1972) Principles of nursing intervention for the adult patient with body image changes. *Nursing Clinics of North America* **7**, 697.

Nightingale, F. (1959) *Notes on Nursing: What It Is and What It Is Not*. London, Duckworth. Reprinted 1970.

Olshansky, S. (1962) Chronic sorrow – a response to having a mentally defective child. *Social Casework* **43**, 190–193.

Pearson, J. and Dudley, H. (1982) Bodily perceptions in surgical patients. *British Medical Journal* **284**, 1545–1546.

Price, R. (1990) *Body Image – Nursing Concepts and Care*. London, Prentice Hall.

Pritchard, P. (1981) Stress and anxiety in physical illness. *Nursing Times* **77** (22 January), 162–164.

Randall, N. (1972) *This Road Can Be Travelled*. London, Readers Digest Association.

Salter, M. (1983) Towards a healthy body image. *Nursing Mirror* **157** (14 September), ii–vi.

Salter, M. (1995). Body image study shows most patients need support. *Eurostoma* Autumn, 10–11.

Secord, P. and Jourard, S. (1953) The appraisal of body-cathexis: body cathexis and the self. *Journal of Consulting Psychology* **17**, 343–347.

Smith, R. (1984) Identity crisis. *Nursing Mirror* **158**, ii–vi.

Smitherman, C. (1981) *Nursing Action for Health Promotion.* London, F.A. Davis.

Stewart, W.F.R. (1975) *Sex and the Physically Handicapped.* London, Masham National Fund for Research into Crippling Diseases.

Taylor, S. and Bogdan, A. (1984) *Introduction to Qualitative Research Methods: The Search for Meanings*, 2nd edn. New York, Wiley.

Teel, C. (1991) Chronic sorrow. *Journal of Advanced Nursing* **16**, 1311–1319.

Thorne, S. (1993) *Negotiating Health Care: The Social Context of Chronic Illness.* Newbury Park, CA, Sage.

Wassner, A. (1982) The impact of mutilating surgery or trauma on body image. *International Nursing Review* 29 March, 86–90.

Wilson-Barnett, J. (1980) Prevention and alleviation of stress in patients. *Nursing* 2 (February), 432–436.

Woods, N. (1975) *Human Sexuality in Health and Illness.* St Louis, MO; C.V. Mosby and Co.

CHAPTER 2

# The nurse's further contribution

*Mave Salter*

For all the disfigurements mentioned thus far, and for those to be discussed in the following pages, nurses should be provided with the resources to help patients cope with their altered body image and to enable them, as far as possible, to come to terms with their changed circumstances. Members of the multidisciplinary team play their part, yet it is the nurse, as the prime caregiver, whose role is one of the most important in helping patients to come to terms with their altered body image. Integral to body image is sexuality, and this chapter will examine the way nurses can function in enhancing patient care and the resources they will require to do so.

Firstly, nurses must consider how they feel about their own body image. They must have a healthy acceptance of themselves before they can be part of the enabling process in helping patients with body image problems to come to terms with theirs. They may find this heart-searching: what values were they influenced with at home, at school, during adolescence and since commencing nursing? Have they learned to accept themselves, or do they have difficulty in confronting a mirror? How does the individual nurse feel about caring for patients with a changed body image, or people who have a different outlook on life than the nurse's own? It is courage, not failure, if nurses recognize they themselves may have problems for which they need help, or refer a patient to another health care professional when they feel out of their depth.

Rogers (1961) calls acceptance 'unconditional positive regard'. Nurses should be non-judgemental in their approach. They can begin the helping process by explaining to a patient that what seems unbearable now will recede with time. Technological advance has meant that surgical and medical methods are improving all the time. However, unless people accept their appearance and are motivated to go forward, modern technology might just as well have been used elsewhere. A patient may well make some progress and then regress; it is normal in the stages of loss to go backwards and forwards until acceptance is reached. It is the nurse's role to support patients when they need him or her most. An alteration in body image, visible or not, by itself changes the body; however, its effect upon the personality can be great unless caring professionals seek to prevent it.

## Sexuality

Few (1993) states that sex is complex. The accumulated impact of parents, family, friends, religion, media, sex-role conditioning, sexism, heterosexism and sexual experience will have shaped, in part, our attitudes towards sex and influenced who we are sexually. Social and cultural codes about sexuality and sexual activity may be less rigid now than they were 50 years ago, but they still have an impact on sexual freedom (Metcalf and Humphries, 1985).

Ellis (1981) suggests that sexuality is an integral aspect of every person, its components are awareness of one's body as a source of pleasure, perception of oneself as feminine or masculine, and a sense of oneself as an inherently sexual being. According to Maslow (1970), the fulfilment of man's need for love, intimacy and sexual gratification is a critical link in the mature, healthy personality. Weston (1993) states that everyone has a right to enjoy a state of sexual health and this right is unaffected by age, illness and disability. It must be seen as an integral part of delivering holistic care, Van Ooijen (1995) postulates that whether or not we are sexually active and whatever our sexual orientation, our sexuality cannot be divorced from who we are as people, even when we are ill.

Andrew and Andrew (1991) suggest that sexuality includes both physical and psychological factors, physical appearance as well as sexual activity. Psychological aspects of sexuality include our body image or the mental picture we carry around of ourselves. Frequently, it is hardly possible to distinguish between the physiological/anatomical and psychosocial sources of sexual dysfunction. Therefore, there is a need to be cautious in attributing a psychogenic cause to a disorder, when organicity is possible and vice versa (Schultz *et al.*, 1992).

Beacham (1995) suggests that communicating about sex is often an area left out of health professional's training or is only covered by biological facts. Similarly, Savage (1990) suggests that if sexuality is to be more centrally incorporated into nursing care, the training and support available for nurses must be improved. Briggs (1994) states that an in-depth study of sexuality must be included in the Registered General Nurse syllabus, and individual students should be encouraged to look at their own attitudes and prejudices to sexuality and increase their own awareness. Excuses can no longer be made for ignoring the concept of sexual health in nurse education or in frameworks for care. It is time nurses brought this concept into the assessment and daily care of all their clients (Weston, 1993).

Savage (1990) states that nurses are not helped by an over-simplification of the meaning of sexuality. One study, cited in Savage, suggested that nurses are interested in sexuality, but are unsure as to what the term covers. Not surprisingly, they feel inadequately prepared to make any assessment of patients' needs concerning sexuality. Nurse tutors have offered little help in this matter as their own training has generally glossed over this issue. Van Ooijen (1995) realizes that some nurses will operate from a different knowledge and experience base from that of the patient. The subject of sexuality is a difficult one to broach with patients; care and attention need to be paid to the manner, skills, knowledge and attitude of the nurse. However, the nurse who feels embarrassed about discussing sexual activity with a patient may not be able to look towards colleagues for guidance, as they may also feel inadequate.

Similarly, the practical constraints that nurses face are often underestimated. There is often little acknowledgement that a significant number of the nurses expected to carry out sexual assessments are young and still unconfident about their own sexuality. This may lead to the nurse becoming embarrassed if the subject is broached by the patient (Savage, 1990). Van Ooijen (1995) also suggests that the understanding of our own beliefs about sexuality have to be handled with care.

Weston (1993) feels that nurses clearly have an important role to play in promoting the sexual health of clients, but how should we proceed in this area, and, indeed, should nurses be expected to discuss clients' concerns about sexual health? Some nurses would claim it is none of their business. However, in a survey of 73 health workers, the overwhelming majority (92%) said that nurses should discuss sexual matters with their clients (Waterhouse and Metcalfe, 1991). The authors referred to a survey of 108 women who had undergone a hysterectomy; the survey found that only a small proportion felt that nurses were the most valuable source of information on sexual matters. Almost half those surveyed said they would have liked nurses to have initiated a discussion on sexual concerns (Weston, 1993).

Information given to the patient while in hospital may not be recalled (Briggs, 1994). Elliot and Smith (1985) found that stress factors reduced the individual's ability to retain and comprehend much-needed information and Braulin et al. (1982) found that frequent repetition of details given was necessary to ensure that the information was understood.

Briggs (1994) suggests the nurse may be guilty of sexual prejudice. It is well documented that single patients, the elderly and homosexuals do not receive as much information as married heterosexual patients. Booth (1990) found that many nurses presumed that elderly patients did not have sexual needs, did not think that it really mattered at that age, and concluded that it was highly unlikely that they would be having sexual relations. However, many couples enjoy a warm, loving and active sexual relationship until late in life.

Knowledge about actual and potential problems associated with sexuality and an alteration in body image enables the nurse to assess the meaning of this for the individual patient and family, provide counselling before and after the surgery, and intervene so that the individual will be able to adapt to an alteration in body image and return to his or her previous activities of daily living and lifestyle (Cohen, 1991).

Andrew and Andrew (1991) state that many people with a life-threatening illness will have worries about how the illness will affect their sexuality and the impact this will have on a sexual partner. It must not be assumed that, because patients do not express an interest in sexual problems, they do not exist. Lamont et al. (1978) and Dempsey et al. (1975) mention partner education, and their acceptance and interest as the most important factors in the process of achieving total sexual rehabilitation. Referral to one of the voluntary organizations, for example, Relate or the Sexual and Personal Problems of the Disabled may be appropriate. If a crisis is unresolved, further professional help may be required.

Webb (1985) states that anyone recovering from a life-threatening illness needs to feel loved and cared for; the partner may want to show his or her love but be afraid of any intimacy. Patients should not be deprived of this relationship through lack of counselling. The more knowledge nurses have, the more favourable their attitudes will be and they will feel more able to give advice that is needed. Briggs (1994) suggests that it is important that advice and counselling take place in a comfortable, private environment and include, if possible, the patient and his/her partner. However, single patients must not be denied this information. The main aim of offering sexual guidance is to facilitate communication between the couple.

It is necessary to point out that sexual intercourse is not the only way of expressing love and it is acceptable to use other means if both partners agree. A patient can be complimented on their genuine sexuality, such as their clothes, make up and jewellery. Loss can be discussed and explained as part of the grieving process, and touch is important to enable the patient to still feel 'touchable'. Giving permission after the convalescent period to try lovemaking and advice (and referral if necessary) on what to do if things do not go as planned form part of the counselling process (Salter, 1996).

Hine and Daines (1987) suggest that, within the nursing process, a suitable goal for nursing care in the area of sexuality could be defined as to assist people in their understanding of sexuality so that patient and partner will be able to assume responsibility for their own sexuality under the most helpful circumstances. Some patients will need sexual advice on a mainly practical level. These authors also agree that it is important that nurses are both educationally and emotionally prepared to give such advice when asked. Equally, what seems like a request for practical advice may be the tentative presentation of a more complex problem. The nurse needs to be receptive to the less obvious, and alert to the fact that a sexual problem is often a symptom of general disharmony in the relationship.

Often people have difficulty in thinking about making love except in the man-on-top 'missionary' position. They may feel offended at other positions and may need some help in talking through their feelings and deciding what to do. In this instance, as in most others, it is important that the patient should be able to talk to his or her partner about this and the nurse could have a role in helping them to talk to each other (Hine and Daines, 1987).

## Homosexuality

Homosexuality must also be considered as a concept that alters one's body image, Stewart (1981) states that, like so many other areas rarely discussed openly in the past, homosexuality has now become an acknowledged option. It has been established that 1 in 20 of the adult population are so inclined and this must obviously involve many people with disabilities.

The following suggestion is offered to ease the discussion of sexual orientation: 'Every patient is concerned about how their current partner, or if single, a future partner might react. Is there some special person, a woman, or man, in your life?' (Etnyre, 1990).

Wells (1990) states that 'if we really believe that the sexual health of our patients is as important as their physical well-being, then we will demand that health professionals are educationally prepared for and professionally supported in this vital aspect of care. How well the patient functions sexually after we have finished with him or her will depend largely on how effective we have been. If sexuality is part of the quality of life, then we as professionals can no longer ignore these components of individual care'.

## Counselling

Whether nurses work on a particular ward or unit, in the outpatient department, or as community or specialist nurses, one of their primary functions is to help patients as they try to come to terms with their lot in life. If that includes a change in the way that they see themselves, it is inevitable nurses will want to help. But how can they assist? Most people help others every day without being aware of the helping process; what then is this helping, this counselling? It is not always necessary to have attended special courses in counselling to be able to assist patients, although such courses do have their place, not least in helping nurses as individuals to face their own stress or tension.

The Standing Conference for the Advancement of Counselling (1975) (cited in Hollister, 1982) states that counselling is a process through which one person helps another by purposeful conversation in an understanding atmosphere. It seeks to establish a helping relationship in which the one counselled can express their thoughts and feelings in such a way as to clarify their own situation, come to terms with some new experience, see the difficulty more objectively, and so face their problems with less anxiety and tension. Its basic purpose is to assist the individual to make his or her own decision from among the choices available. Rogers (1961) suggests that it is not upon the physical sciences that the future will depend. It is upon us who are trying to understand and deal with interactions between human beings – who are trying to create relationships.

What is this purposeful conversation? It is an unhurried sharing and understanding; it is both verbal and non-verbal communication. Types of non-verbal communication include position/closeness of patient and nurse, gestures made that may help nurses understand how a patient is feeling, eye contact and facial expression, touch, tone of voice and feelings.

**Communication**

Anderson's (1959) definition of communication states that communication is the process by which we understand others and in turn endeavour to be understood by them. . . . 'Emotional pain . . . is often expressed in body language . . . because it is too agonising and too difficult to express in words' (Earnshaw-Smith, 1982).

What is an understanding atmosphere? It is certainly not that created by a screen pulled round a bed with everyone listening in from the outside! An important aspect of counselling is to choose a room that is comfortable and free from any likely disturbance. The two chairs in the room should be comfortable and identical. If an interview room as such is not possible, then as quiet, relaxed and informal a setting as is possible should be used.

Nurses involved in caring for people must instil confidence in an unhurried manner; draw up a chair, sit on the bed, give verbal and non-verbal cues that they are interested, have time and want to become involved. It is the nurse who performs the caring duties and, therefore, has the greatest patient contact time. If a nurse allows a patient to express thoughts and feelings, and then acts as a sounding board in assisting the patient to come to terms with some new experience, then hopefully the nurse will enable the patient to face the problems with less anxiety and tension. Counselling is not advice-giving – it is exploring with the patients/clients the various options open and assisting them to make their own decisions.

Nurses need to spend time talking to patients about how they feel and not just pass the time of day, hoping that they will not be asked awkward questions that they want to avoid. Nurses should indicate that they care about the individual's emotional as well as physical well-being, and not give the impression that they are too busy to listen.

So often in a busy ward or department, patients ask questions just at an inconvenient time. The nurse can explain the dilemma, make a note of the problem and agree to come back and discuss it as soon as possible. It may be that a carer is so emotionally exhausted, that the last thing they want at that moment is to give to others when what they do need is to reaffirm their own resources. If another professional person is available to help, this help can be offered, but again an agreement can be made with the patient to return when the nurse is able. If time is spent in caring and listening to patients' emotional needs, it will pay dividends in their recovery or peace of mind.

Branden (1982) states that people sometimes find it hard to give of themselves. This may be because we feel we are inadequate; we are afraid to risk using just our warmth and caring. To be committed to change within yourself is the single, most important function in helping others. Only then can you communicate a message of unrealistic hope borne out of your own survival. For it is those difficulties that provide a concrete base for communication with people in distress. Thus it can be seen that, first, members of the caring professions must be aware of themselves, and their problems, stresses, and tensions, and they must seek to resolve them in order to help others. So the question needs to be asked by the carer: 'Can I deal with the salt as well as the sugar in life?'. To be able to do this means that caregivers will also need support and so nurse to nurse communications are vital. A life apart from work is necessary where one can relax and switch off from time to time.

**Stress in nursing**     Much has been written recently about the stressful nature of nursing. 'Nurses and, in particular, nursing students undergo a great deal of stress. Often they have no way of coping with it but by distancing themselves from their patients, hiding behind task-orientated care or by leaving the service. There is an appalling lack of support reinforced by the notion that nurses must not get emotionally involved with their patients. They must not cry and they must not show that they are upset. As professionals, we fail to care for the carers. We fail to facilitate their grief and fail to encourage a frank and open exchange of feelings about the job we do. We should allow our nurses to have a human relationship with their patients and the patient's relatives. This is part of good total patient care' (MacDonald, 1983).

Firth (1984) says 'What can happen when personal support in a stressful job is not sufficient? If other supports – good staffing levels, training opportunities, support outside of work – are not available, then the nurse may suffer professional depression or burn out. The following tips may be useful for senior staff to improve support among their colleagues:

- Make clear to staff that you have time available to give attention to their concerns.
- Seek staff's own opinion as well as giving advice or instructions.
- Practise listening skills when with other staff at any time.
- Check your understanding "So are you saying . . .?"
- Endeavour to provide plenty of feedback to staff, and make it positive and constructive.
- Criticism should always be accompanied by some positive feedback.
- Pay attention to non-verbal aspects of speech (tone, speed, eye contact, gesture and so on) which are vital in conveying attention, positive or negative feedback.
- Emphasize to others the importance of the skills of listening and seeking views, opinions and feelings of others.
- Emphasize training in communication skills. These will need to be taught using role play and other practical exercises'.

'A severe result of stress and fatigue is burn out. Surely burn out would be less frequent if nurses supported each other and were able to admit their problems to each other without being labelled failures? A profession whose members are concerned for the welfare of each other is much stronger than one divided by uncaring attitudes. Nurses spend every working day caring for others, so why can't they care for each other? Perhaps they are too tired at the end of the day to listen to others' problems; perhaps they have too many worries of their own. If nurses knew they could turn to colleagues without fear of being castigated for the occasional inability to cope, these occasions would become fewer. No-one is infallible, and it is time nurses recognized this. Occasionally being unable to cope does not mean that you are a failure, it means that you are human' (Laurent, 1984).

'Burn out' is a recognized problem in nursing at the present time. Economic stringencies, shortage of staff, young nurses dealing with life-and-death emergencies with little support lead to stress with sickness levels and occasional days off work rising. Thus it is important that a support system is built up to keep one's own head above water. The inner resources of the nurse, therefore, will help in coping with the denial, anger, bargaining, depression and acceptance of the patients. Such reactions/responses all require listening, reflecting and questioning on the part of the nurse.

Nurses should be encouraged to learn and use effective skills that will allow them to recognize these stages and respond appropriately, thus helping patients as they pass through them. Patients fear the unknown, but they can be helped by talking about it. Salter (1983) recognized that: 'Discussing the subject freely creates an understanding and understanding hopefully leads to acceptance. Discussion and education commence by explaining why the disease has progressed in this way, or why treatment or surgery is necessary. Patients must be given confidence in the caring profession, which wants to do the best for them. Nurses need not fear treading on the toes of other colleagues involved in the patients' care. Provided there is liaison with other members of the health care team to ensure that conflicting information is not being given, the more discussion that can take place with clients, even covering the same ground – the better it is for them. The advice given and the listening undertaken all need to be reiterated before, during and after the disease process or treatment. It is an on-going education for patients and their families and we can help them see themselves as healthy, acceptable people'.

For example, if someone has always dealt badly with a crisis, it is no use expecting them to change this time around. If a person has found solace in the attention that illness brings, they will need a lot of encouragement to get better and our care should extend to the wider family unit. A partner may need encouragement to take time off and get away without feeling guilty. This may be necessary on a regular basis, despite the protestations of the sick person.

**Social support networks**

The concept of social support first rose to prominence in the 1970s: however, scattered observations for hundreds of years have drawn attention to the importance in the genesis of illness of how people feel about their social environments (Oakley, 1992). While gender is the most significant social factor affecting friendship patterns (Bell, 1981), the historical importance of friendships, particularly among women, has been veiled by a deep-seated cultural anxiety about the 'sexual' meaning of these friendships (Raymond, 1986). Conceptually, social support overlaps with friendship, and both with family, kin and neighbourhood relations. While interest in social support and sociable relations is now increasing in different fields, this is nowhere more so than in the study of health. An important reason for the current 'fashion' in social support research is the increasing realization that conventional risk factors are able to explain only a small part of the picture of individual and group differences in health, death and disease (Oakley, 1992). It is a common finding that women report more supportive relationships than men at all stages of the life cycle (Leavy, 1983). As Madge and Marmot (1987) have observed, there seems to be little controversy that something about social relationships can be good for health, although quite what is important remains unclear.

Price (1989) suggests that social support networks provide the milieu in which a normal body image is first formed and an altered body image is reintegrated into society. Patients with an active social support network are likely to make better progress.

The distinction between emotional, informational and instrumental aspects of social bonds is commonly made: 'Emotional support includes intimacy and attachment, reassurance and being able to confide in and rely on another – all of which contribute to the feeling that one is loved or cared about, or even that one is a member of the group, not a stranger. Tangible support involves direct aid or services and can include loans, gifts of money or goods and provision of services such as taking care of needy persons or doing a chore for them. Informational support includes giving information and advice which could help a person solve a problem and providing feedback about how a person is doing' (Schaefer et al., 1981: 385–386).

These distinctions are summed up in what Kahn and Antonucci (1980) phrase as the 'three As' – affect, affirmation and aid. Oakley (1992) suggests that the term 'social support network' implies that social ties do not form isolated units but are interconnected, so that one person's friends and relatives are likely to know each other and the extent of interconnectedness between network members then becomes potentially a feature of the social support available to any individual. Oakley (1992) further states that social support extends to a wide range of physical and psychological health outcomes.

Price (1993) postulates that individuals who enjoy a rich source of contact (both quantity and quality of relationships) are better able to adapt to the threat of mutilating surgery and altered patterns of elimination thereafter. Families assist the patient to rejoin social activity, to return to work and to form positive appraisal of their progress under challenging circumstances. Supportive social networks, Price further suggests, values the individual, reminding them of their personal worth and developing ways of talking comfortably about the changed circumstances. Therefore, one should be aware of the patient who has few friends, a limited family or unconstructive relationships in the first place.

**Nursing support**     Salter (1992) suggests that incorporating body image into patient care can be developed by using a model of care. Peplau (1969) suggests a relationship of closeness between the nurse and patient which can be a springboard for enabling healthy adaptation to body image changes. Where possible, patients should be able to choose the person in the caring team to whom they best relate for their continuing support, and, with the patient's agreement, relatives and friends with whom they share their social life, and colleagues at work who are best suited to play a part in their recovery. Thus care does not stop at family; it goes as far as friends, social and work colleagues. To incorporate them (with the patient's permission) into the programme of care means the caring profession is extending rather than limiting the resources of the patient, and preparing him or her for going home. Surely this is what rehabilitation is all about – encouraging the patient's return to their previous or an acceptable lifestyle.

Titmus (1976) in his *Essays on the Welfare State* says 'How often one comes across people who have been discharged from hospital, bewildered, still anxious and afraid, disillusioned because the medical magic has not apparently or not yet yielded results, ignorant of what investigations have shown, what the doctors think, what the treatment has been or is to be, and what the outlook is, in terms of life and health. Why should all this be so? Why is it not understood that courtesy and sociability have a therapeutic value? Most of us in our homes know this instinctively, but somehow or other it gets lost in hospital. Partly, I suppose, it is the effect on people of working and living in a closed institution with rigid social hierarchies and codes of behaviour. The barrier of silence is one element in a general failure to treat the patient.'

It is hoped that with the Patient's Charter (1991) the above is changing and the hospital is becoming less of an alien environment for the family, but the nurse needs to be there both for the sake of the anxious relative as well as the patient. Sitting rooms for relatives with refreshment facilities are becoming essential in hospital settings. Just as a nurse needs a break from the ward situation to relax over a coffee, so do caring relatives.

It is essential that patients receive help as soon as they undergo, or it is known that they will be undergoing, a change in body image. Often someone of the same age and sex who has experienced a similar disease process and who has readjusted well can be incorporated into rehabilitation. To begin counselling as soon as possible facilitates a quicker recovery. Preoperative counselling and the postoperative contact are of great value in assisting each patient to adapt more easily to a new and unwelcome body image. By trusting our patients, we show we have faith in their ability to cope, for part of the nurse's job is to give patients permission to take responsibility for themselves. Tschudin (1981) states that empathy has been described as the ability to see the world through another's eyes and by allowing the patient to talk of their illness, it becomes more of a reality to them and their family.

Unfortunately, nurses are still guilty of reassuring the patient before they find out exactly what it is the patient is worrying about. Most patients strive to maintain the appearance that they are coping well, but it is like wearing a mask to hide their true self. Accompanying them into the consulting room may help them voice their feelings to the doctor. What the doctor or nurse thinks he or she has told the patient, and what the patient actually understands about their illness or proposed operation are often at great variance.

It is important, therefore, for nurses to be communicators, counsellors and patient advocates. They must take careful histories and assessments, organize, where applicable, patient conferences, encourage patient/family-centred care discharge planning and rehabilitation within their roles in the multi-disciplinary team.

The support of the nursing team is necessary throughout every stage of the patient's illness. Patients should be encouraged to express their feelings about their altered body image. When a patient sees her deformity for the first time, she should be encouraged to express her feelings about it. The nurse can reassure her that it is natural to feel apprehensive about going out in public and facing the world again. The nurse needs to support her when her hair starts to fall out (and provide a wig in plenty of time), and when she wakes up and takes a look at her mutilated breast, or sees her stoma for the first time. If the carer's face shows acceptance, then the patient will learn to accept herself. But patients must be active participants in their care.

The loss of identity and independence patients feel when ill and especially when in hospital has been mentioned previously. One way of counteracting this dependence is to suggest that they should be responsible for what they are capable of doing for themselves, e.g. taking care of their own medication, if well enough. Teaching self-care is an important step back to a normal life. With compassionate guidance, patients can regain their self-esteem and be restored to normal social activity. If nurses reinforce the fact that they expect their patients to be self-caring, that they expect them to be able to wear the same clothes, for example, and go on holiday, etc., then patients will have enough trust and hope in their own ability to move forward.

Smith (1984) states that each patient has individual needs and worries that only a careful history and access to the family will reveal. The carer's reaction and acceptance of a changed body image will in turn affect the attitude of patients towards themselves. How people have reacted in the past will affect their present coping mechanisms.

## Rehabilitation

Broadwell (1987) states that rehabilitation is the dynamic process directed toward assisting the individual to function at an optimal level within the limitation of the disease or treatment. The physical, mental, emotional, social and sexual components are domains of the rehabilitation process. Pre- and postoperative counselling is aimed towards returning the patient to the lifestyle enjoyed prior to illness, enabling the patient to pick up the threads of life again. Rehabilitation must include the patients, their partners (or other significant people) and should be an enabling process on the part of the nurse.

As patients progress through the rehabilitation period, non-invasive questioning in follow-up, either when attending the hospital, or at home in the community, can establish how a person is fitting back into their previous lifestyle once again. Questions like: 'Do you mind if I ask if . . . you go out shopping . . . see your friends . . . eat out at a restaurant . . . go on holiday . . . go to work . . . how does your partner feel about how you are progressing?' and observations of a person's looks, voice, clothes and mood can help, the nurse assess how the patient is managing. If patients are neglectful in their appearance when previously they were not, they may well be in need of further support and help.

Whilst in hospital patients are sheltered from their normal environment, but on their return home may wait to see how those around them react – family, friends and the primary health care team. The trend today is for a shorter stay in hospital with patients returning home as soon as possible, thus community staff are having to deal increasingly with the physical and psychological effects of body image change. Caring and involved partners play an important role in their spouse's rehabilitation and the nurse can explain from the outset that there is no need for their sleeping arrangements to change because of the altered body image implications.

Nurses must seek to give quality to life, instilling confidence in an unhurried atmosphere and encouraging the patient to return to self-respect and independence. Goal-setting, both short and long term, is a good tool to use, although it must be remembered that physical well-being alone is not a sufficient reason on which to base the discharge of patients. Often they will need support when a relative or friend first sees their changed image. Their first outing from hospital is important and an afternoon away from the ward, extending to a day, then a weekend, is necessary for some people in their gradual letting go of the security of the inpatient world. The ability to obtain an acceptable prosthesis and to be able to use it properly is essential. Planning for discharge should never be an afterthought the day before the patient is due to go home. It must start right from admission and case conferences that include the patient have their place in discharge planning and rehabilitation. Patients will be ready for discharge at different times and, again, the nurse must be the patient's advocate in this respect. Careful liaison with, for example, the primary health care team, the social worker and the occupational health nurse is important for a patient prior to discharge. If these colleagues can visit the patient whilst in hospital, or a member of the hospital staff can meet the district nursing sister at home, continuity of care is established.

Nurses working with clients and patients may be able to soften the knocks but they are nevertheless hard; they may be able to help them but they cannot go through their circumstances instead of them. But with the right help, the pain and outrage of a changed body image can bring such insight and growth to each individual, for as one patient put it: 'Do you understand this grief of mine, my despair, and my fear? I cannot stop what is happening to me. I'm not who I was a few weeks ago and I don't know who I am anymore'. How reassuring if we can say in reply: 'Yes, to me you are still you' (Tschudin, 1981), and to see patients gradually accept themselves once again.

Most nurses know patients who have never come to terms with their altered body image – the recluse, the bitter, angry people. Hopefully, they know many more who have sobbed it out and come through smiling. What makes people do this? Is it the nurse's contribution? Is it the nurse's role as a member of the wider caring team? Is it the inner resources of the patient and their family support, and/or their belief in God to turn the disasters of life into something good? It would be of benefit if this could be measured but, more than that, it is important to know that nurses are playing their part, a cog in a wheel towards a patient's healthy body image.

What is normal? What is an intact body image? Society appears to dictate the normal and the eccentric. A television programme showed an audience of handicapped people. The programme host referred to them as such and asked them how they had come to terms with the fact that they were different. It was heartening to hear one such person say: 'I am not handicapped; I am normal. How about you?' He had developed a healthy body image despite his incapacity. This is what nurses should be striving for in all their patients. Thus a patient's rehabilitation is not complete until he or she can look in the mirror and accept the person they see there.

Communication videos are a useful educational tool and Hollister's (1982) 'Communication in Patient Care' series video includes the following points which can provide a helpful checklist whether applied to viewing communication videos or to one's own communication with patients. It is envisaged that this be used as an exercise.

| | |
|---|---|
| *Position*: | What do you notice about the way you and the patient are sitting in relation to each other? What do you notice about your position and that of the patient? When do either of you change position? What effect does this have? |
| *Gesture*: | What do you notice about the gestures made by you and the patient? What do the gestures made by (a) the nurse, and (b) the patient tell you about how each is feeling? |
| *Eye contact and facial expression*: | How much eye contact is there between the patient and the nurse? Discuss the use made by the nurse of eye contact to check the patient has understood what the nurse is saying. Discuss the use the patient makes of eye contact to check if the nurse has understood what they are saying. How does the patient assess whether |

it is acceptable to raise certain topics with the nurse? Study the nurse's and patient's facial expressions. What do these tell you about how they are feeling?

*Touch*:    When does the nurse touch the patient and vice versa? Do you think this touching is useful and if so, why?

*Listening*:    How does the nurse show that he or she is paying attention? How relaxed as well as attentive should one be?

*Tone of voice*:    What do you notice about the tone of voice used by the nurse and the patient? What does it tell you about how both patient and nurse are feeling? Discuss the use of silence (a) by the nurse and (b) by the patient.

*Passage of information*:    What do you notice about the way the nurse gives information and seeks it from the patient?

What do you notice about the way the patient gives information to the nurse?

How many changes of subject occur in the conversation?

Who changes the subject?

Why do you think the subject is changed?

How do you encourage the patient to express feelings?

How do you discourage the expression of feelings?

How do you ensure that the patient understands what you are saying?

How well do you think that the nurse understands what the patient is saying?

*Feelings*:    What feelings or worries do you think the patient was trying to express in this conversation?

*Understanding*:    What does the nurse say or do to show she understands the patient's concerns and intends to help? How much do you think the nurse has understood of what the patient has said?

*Glossary of terms used in video*

*Open question*

An open question is one which is worded in such a way that the respondent is free to answer as he or she wishes, e.g. 'How are you feeling today?'

*Closed question*

A closed question is one which is worded in such a way that the respondent's possible range of answers is limited, e.g. 'Are you feeling better?' The answer to this question will be 'Yes' or 'No'.

### Leading question

A leading question is one in which the question leads the respondent towards a desired or preferred answer, e.g. 'You are feeling better, aren't you?'. Here a patient will know that the expected answer is 'Yes'.

### Conversation cue

A conversation cue can be either a direct or indirect question, or any statement made in the expectation (or hope) of a certain response from the listener.

### Conversation lead

A conversation lead is where one or other of the participants takes the initiative in the course the conversation takes.

### Reflection

Reflection is a technique which involves picking up signals in words or feelings expressed by a patient and repeating them in such a way that they encourage the patient to enlarge on the topic or thought, e.g. a patient may say 'I feel so worried', in which case the nurse could reply 'You feel worried?', which could effectively encourage the patient to extend his or her thoughts and feelings.

**References**

Anderson, A. (1959) Cited in Hollister (1982) *Communication in Patient Care.* Video teaching package.

Andrew, C. and Andrew, H. (1991) Sexuality and the dying patient. *Journal of District Nursing*, November, 8–11.

Beacham, S. (1995) Talking sex. *Nursing Standard* **10** (November 29), no. 10, 56.

Bell, R. (1981) *Worlds of Friendship.* Newbury Park, CA, Sage.

Booth, B. (1990) Does it really matter at that age? *Nursing Times* **86**(3), 50–52.

Brandon, D. (1982) *The Trick of Being Ordinary.* London, Mind.

Braulin, J., Rook, J. and Silts, G. (1982) Families in crisis: the impact of trauma. *Critical Care Quarterly* **5**(3), 38–46.

Briggs, L. (1994) Caring for patients recovering from M.I. *British Journal of Nursing* **3**(16), 837–842.

Broadwell, D.C. (1987) Rehabilitation needs of the patient with cancer. *Cancer* **60**, 563–568.

Cohen, A. (1991) Body image in the person with a stoma. *Journal of Enterostomal Therapy* **18** (March/April), no. 2, 68–71.

Dempsey, G.M., Buchsbaum, H.J. and Morrison, A. (1975) Psychosocial adjustment to pelvic exenteration. *Gynaecologic Oncology* **3**, 325–334.

Earnshaw-Smith, E. (1982). Emotional pain in dying patients and their families. *Nursing Times* **78** (November 3), 1865–1867.

Elliot, J. and Smith, D.R. (1985) Meeting family needs following severe head injury. *Journal of Neurosurgical Nursing* **17**, 111–113.

Ellis, J. (1981) *Nursing: A Human Needs Approach*. Boston, Houghton Mifflin, Ch. 17.

Etnyre, W. (1990) Meeting the needs of gay and lesbian ostomates. *Proceedings of 8th Biennial Congress, World Council of Enterostomal Nurses*, Hollister, Canada.

Few, C. (1993) Safer sex. *Community Outlook*, September 7, 13–18.

Firth, H. (1984) Sources of good staff support. *Nursing Times* **78** (October 12), 60–62.

Hine J. and Daines, B. (1987) Sexuality and the renal patient. *Nursing Times* **83** (May 20), 35–36.

Hollister (1982) *Communication in Patient Care*. Video teaching package. Hollister Ltd, Rectory Court, 42 Broad St, Wokingham RG11 1AB.

Kahn, R. and Antonucci, T. (1980) Convoys over the life course: attachment, roles and social support. In: Boltes, P. and Brim, O. (eds) *Lifespan Development and Behaviour*. Boston, Lexington Press.

Lamont, H.A., De Petrillo, A.D. and Sargeant, E.J. (1978) Psycho-sexual rehabilitation and exenterative surgery. *Gynaecologic Oncology* **6**, 236–242.

Laurent, C. (1984) Help to prevent burnout. *Nursing Mirror* **159** (November 21), 37.

Leavy, R. (1983) Social support and psychological disorder: a review. *Journal of Community Psychology* **11**, 3–21.

Macdonald, D. (1983) More help for nurses in distress. *Nursing Times* (October 12), 60–62.

Madge, N. and Marmot, M. (1987) Psychosocial factors and health. *Quarterly Journal of Social Affairs* **3**(2), 81–134.

Maslow, A. (1970) *Hierarchy of Human Needs in Motivation and Personality*. New York, Harper.

Metcalf, A. and Humphries, M. (eds) (1985) *The Sexuality of Men*. London, Pluto Press.

Oakley, A. (1992) *Social Support and Motherhood*. Oxford, Blackwell.

Ooijen, van E. and Charnock, A. (1995) What is sexuality? *Nursing Times* **91** (April 26), no. 17, 26–27.

*Patient's Charter* (1991) London, HMSO.

Peplau, H. (1969) Professional closeness. *Nursing Forum* **8**(4), 343–360.

Price, R. (1989) *Body Image – Nursing Concepts and Care*. London, Prentice Hall.

Price, R. (1993) How to make an assessment of altered body image in stoma patients. *Eurostoma* no. 4 (Autumn).

Raymond, J. (1986). *A Passion for Friends: Towards a Philosophy of Female Affection*. Boston, Beacon Press.

Rogers, C. (1961) *On Becoming a Person*. London, Constable and Co.

Salter, M. (1983) Towards a healthy body image. *Nursing Mirror* **157** (September 14), ii–vi.

Salter, M. (1992) What are the differences in body image between patients with a conventional stoma compared with those who have had a conventional stoma followed by a continent pouch? *Journal of Advanced Nursing* **17**, 841–848.

Salter, M. (1996) In: Myers, C. (ed.) *St. Mark's Manual of Stoma Care Nursing and Surgical Techniques*. Kent, Edward Arnold.

Savage, J. (1990) Sexuality and nursing care: setting the scene. *Nursing Standard* **42**(37), 24–25.

Schaefer, C., Coynes, J. and Lazaraus, R. (1981). The health-related functions of social support. *Journal of Behavioural Medicine* **4**(4), 381–405.

Schultz, W., van de Weil, H., Hahn, D. and Bouma, J. (1992) Psychosexual functioning after treatment of cancer of the vulva: a longitudinal study. *Cancer* **66**, 402–407.

Smith, R. (1984) Identity crisis. *Nursing Mirror* **158**, ii–vi.

Stewart, B. (1981) Finding feelings behind the words. *Nursing Mirror* **153** (September 16), 43–51.

Titmus, R. (1976) *Essays on the Welfare State*. London, Allen and Unwin.

Tschudin, V. (1981) A question of mind over matter. *Nursing Times* **77** (March 12), 455–459.

Waterhouse, J. and Metcalfe, V. (1991) Attitudes towards nurses discussing sexual concerns with patients. *Journal of Advanced Nursing* **16**, 1048–1054.

Webb, C. (1985) *Sexuality, Nursing and Health*. Chichester, John Wiley.

Wells, R. (1990) Sexuality: an unknown word for patients with a stoma. In: Senn, H. and Glaus, J. (eds) *Results in Cancer Research*. Berlin, Springer-Verlag, pp. 115–121.

Weston, A. (1993) Challenging assumptions. *Nursing Times* **89** (May 5), no. 18, 26–31.

**Further reading**

Burt, K. (1995) Effect of cancer on body image and sexuality. *Nursing Times* **91**, 36–37.

Steinke, E. (1994) Knowledge and attitudes of older adults about sexuality in ageing: a comparison of two studies. *Journal of Advanced Nursing* **19**, 477–485.

CHAPTER 3

# Measuring body image

*Bridget Dolan and Sandra Birtchnell*

**What is body image?**

Body image is a complex theoretical concept and, although the term is widely used, its specific meaning remains unclear (Lacey and Birtchnell, 1986). The difficulties in deriving relevant measures of body image are apparent in the diversity of techniques which have been used and which are differentially sensitive to different aspects of what may be understood as body image (Feldman, 1973).

The concept of body image was originally developed by neurologists such as Head (1920). The neurological aspect of body image – the accumulated sensory experience of the body organized into the preconscious body schema and postural model – has been termed the *body percept*. This is the neural representation determining bodily experience from which body phantoms may emerge after the loss of parts (Kolb, 1975). A broader view of body image involving psychological functioning, the sociological significance of appearance, and including a person's attitudes and feelings towards their own body, was largely developed by Schilder (1935). This aspect of body image has come to be termed the *body concept*.

Schilder (1935) defined body image as 'The picture of our own body which we form in our mind, that is to say, the way in which our body appears to ourselves'. However, it is not strictly speaking a visual image, but organized out of the individual's attitudes and feelings, both to the body as a whole, and its constituent parts. These in turn are influenced by a number of factors, which are summarized in Figure 3.1. Actual body appearance plays an obvious and significant role, influencing both the individual and others in social interaction with them. The social advantages of attractiveness are well documented (Dion *et al.*, 1972; Berscheid and Walster, 1974; Adams and Crossman, 1978; Adams, 1981) as are

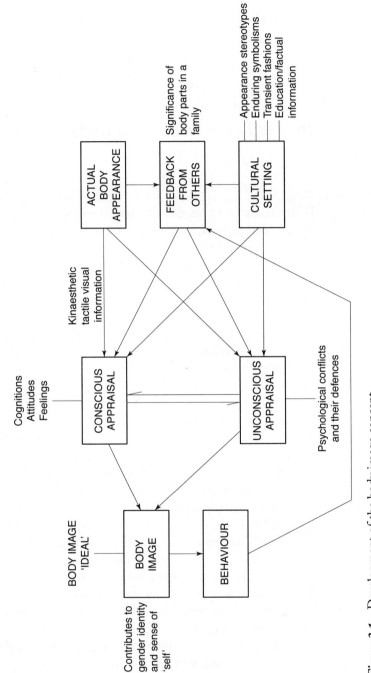

*Figure 3.1* Development of the body image concept.

the negative consequences of deformity (Clifford and Bull, 1978). Within a family, as well as within a culture, certain body parts and appearances will be valued or despised, and carry stereotypic assumptions and symbolic meanings. A store of experiences and memories for the individual will shape their attitudes and feelings towards their body in their conscious appraisal, and contribute to the psychodynamics of their unconscious appreciation of it. That a complaint about appearance may reflect and defend against an underlying psychological conflict is well recognized (Meerloo, 1956; Meyer *et al.*, 1960; Jacobsen *et al.*, 1960; Beale *et al.*, 1980).

Psychoanalytically body image is conceptualized as the internalized representation of the body and its component parts in the individual's 'inner world' (Sandler and Rosenblatt, 1962). The relationship between the psychoanalytic concept of ego and body image is unclear. Federn (1953) writes of the mental ego experienced as inside the bodily ego when awake, and Szasz (1957) proposed that the ego related to the body as an object, with a process of progressive ego–body integration. The ego may maintain an 'ideal' body image and conflicts may arise out of discrepancies between body image and this 'ideal'. Schilder (1935) wrote of body image as a personality construct with an expressive as well as perceptive component and the concept of 'body boundary' as related to different modes of personality function has been examined (Fisher and Cleveland, 1968).

Disorders of body image arise in a wide variety of circumstances. These include primary and secondary neurological disorder with or without clouding of consciousness and phantom phenomena. Psychiatric disorders including schizophrenia, manic depressive psychosis, non-psychotic depression, anxiety, hysteria, obsessive compulsive disorder and personality disorder may all give rise to secondary disturbance of body image including dysmorphophobia (as a symptom), hypochondriacal preoccupations, depersonalization and bizarre beliefs concerning the body. The body-image distortions that accompany the eating disorders have been of particular interest. Disturbances of body image may also be present in the absence of other diagnosable psychiatric disorder, and the isolated psychotic beliefs of deformity (dysmorphophobia), skin infestation (Ekbom's syndrome), internal parasitosis, emitting a foul stench and 'phantom bite' have been gathered together under the term monosymptomatic hypochondriacal psychosis (Munro, 1980). Thomas (1984) has argued that dysmorphophobia should exist as a diagnostic entity where the belief is held in isolation, but not to psychotic intensity. It is important to distinguish the dysmorphophobic patient from those whose complaint about their appearance is based upon the reality of a noticeable or minimal but culturally significant defect (Birtchnell, 1987).

## Measuring body image

Given the complexity of what may be understood by body image and the protean manifestations of its disturbance, either in primary isolated form or secondary to a wide range of neurological and psychiatric disorders, it is not surprising that difficulties have been encountered in attempting its systematic study. This is apparent in both the variety and range of the literature, and the numerous techniques that have been developed as attempts to measure it. These techniques can be classified into four main categories – projective techniques, questionnaire studies, objective measurement and silhouette techniques – although in many cases these categories are not mutually exclusive (see Table 3.1).

### Projective techniques

#### The 'Draw-A-Person' test

One of the earliest methods used to evaluate body image was the 'Draw-a-Person' test devised by Machover (1949). Machover suggested that, when directed to 'draw-a-person', a subject calls upon various sensations, perceptions and emotions which have become associated with their body. Thus a body image developed from personal experience guides the structure and content of the picture drawn. She postulated that 'the drawing of a person, in involving the projection of the body image provides a natural vehicle for the expression of one's body needs and conflicts'.

The 'Draw-a-Person' test has been used extensively with children and adolescents, indeed a survey in the United States found that it was amongst the ten most frequently used psychological tests between 1935 and 1982 (Lubin *et al.*, 1984). The test commonly consists of asking subjects to draw one person, and may also be followed with the instruction to draw another of the opposite sex. The drawings can be rated on a variety of aspects such as anatomical and proportional accuracy, size of the drawing, positioning on the page and the sex of the first person drawn. The assumption is that any distortions in the child's body image will be reflected in the picture drawn. The 'Draw-a-Person' test and its derivatives have been used to examine the body image of a range

*Table 3.1*  A summary of techniques used in body image measurement.

Projective techniques
  'Draw-a-Person' test
  Repertory grids
  Homonym test of body concern
  Body image projective test
  Thematic apperception test
  Body prominence test

Questionnaire studies
  Body cathexis scale
  Body parts satisfaction scale
  Body experience questionnaire
  Body esteem scale
  Body–self relations questionnaire
  Body shape questionnaire
  Body attitudes questionnaire

Body silhouettes
  Body shape ratings
  Silhouettes as repertory grid elements
  'Color-a-Person' test

Objective measurement
  Distorting mirror technique
  Distorting photography/video image
  Body image testing system
  Image marking method
  Visual size estimation

of groups of children, including those with severe burns (Stoddard, 1982), congenital heart disease (Green and Levitt, 1962), cancer (Paine *et al.*, 1985) and with orthopaedic disability (Silverstein and Robinson, 1956). However, although some studies find significant differences between clinical groups and 'normal' children's drawings, others have not found any distinction. Because of these equivocal findings there remains doubt as to the utility of the 'Draw-a-Person' test in assessing specific body image disturbances. Yama (1990) has suggested that despite its non-specificity the 'Draw-a-Person' test is useful as an index of overall adjustment and that it has advantages over other tests of adjustment in having cross-cultural applicability.

One interesting example of the use of the 'Draw-a-Person' test with adolescents was in an investigation of the importance of menarche in pubertal body image assimilation (Koff *et al.*, 1978). Menarche was considered to be an important event in the organization of an adolescent girl's image of her body and herself as a woman, premenarcheal confusion of sexual identity giving way to postmenarcheal acceptance of womanhood and an associated reorganization of body image. Although many people have suggested the importance of puberty in body image, Koff *et al.* felt that the 'proof' of the menarcheal event allowed assimilation of these pubertal changes. To demonstrate this they asked 12-year-old girls to complete the Machover test twice at 6 month intervals. Initially, compared with premenarcheal girls, post-menarcheal girls drew more sexually differentiated figures and all drew a female figure first. In the second testing they found that 30 girls who had changed from pre- to postmenarcheal status drew significantly more sexually differentiated pictures and they more often drew females first. There was no change in the girls who were still premenarcheal at the second testing. They also found a greater acceptance and satisfaction with bust, waist and hip shape after menarche. However, another study of adult women's reproductive status found no differences in drawings made by pregnant women in the first, second and third trimesters of their pregnancy nor were there major differences between pregnant women and those who had delivered recently (Tolor and Digrazia, 1977).

Several variations on the 'draw-a-person' method have been devised. Tait *et al.* (1955) investigated the body image represen-tation of internal organs by asking subjects to draw the inside of their body and label relevant organs. Lerner and Brackney (1978) used this 'Inside-of-the-Body' test with late adolescents and found that females demonstrated greater knowledge of their inner body and attached greater importance to their inner (and outer) body parts than males. Another derivation is the 'Color-a-Person' test (Wooley and Roll, 1991), which is described on page 65.

However, Offman and Bradley (1992) have reviewed the use of human figure drawing to measure children's body image and they have highlighted the difficulties in assuming reliability of the measure. Despite, or perhaps because of, extensive use of the tech-nique a fundamental problem of finding a reliable scoring method, which can account for differences in individual drawing skills, has not been overcome. In addition, there is a dearth of studies in nor-mative populations and very few studies have controlled for those factors which may confound the drawing produced, such as, intel-ligence, cognitive dysfunction, attentional deficits and perceptual disturbances. Thus the validity of data produced by this method remains equivocal.

*Repertory grids*

Repertory grid techniques have proved to be a useful tool in the projective evaluation of body image. The grid approach involves subjects scoring a set of items (elements) such as 'myself', 'my mother' or 'my nose', on a set of bipolar adjectives (constructs), e.g. happy–sad, ugly–beautiful. The statistical analysis of these scores provides data from which a two-dimensional graph can be plotted, visually demonstrating the relationship between different elements and the importance assigned to various constructs by the individual. Based upon Schilder's (1935) assumption that 'experience of our body image and experience of the bodies of others are closely interwoven with each other. Just as our emotions and actions are inseparable from our body image', Feldman (1973) used this technique with two anorexic and two non-eating-disordered females. He found that anorexics viewed their body parts as cold and unattractive in comparison to the normal girls. Notably the non-eating-disordered girls saw their belly, breasts and sexual organs as positive features in direct contrast to the anorexics. Grid results may give some indication of the object relations of the subjects. The extent of identification with parents and the ideal self can be examined, whilst circumventing many defensive processes. The controls rated themself and their ideal self as quite close together whilst for the anorexics their ideals were closer to their mothers'.

Patients requesting cosmetic rhinoplasty were studied using the repertory grid technique (Birtchnell, 1985). An example of the grids generated in this study is shown in Figure 3.2. The subject was a single 41-year-old woman, seeking rhinoplasty to correct what was a noticeably large, broad nose. Her father, but not her mother, was Jewish and her nose was very like his. From school days she had suffered from stigmatic comment, often with racial content. Her only sister (aged 45) had benefited greatly from a rhinoplasty 3 years earlier. This history is confirmed by the grid showing her own nose in proximity to her father's nose, and the striking shift of her sister pre- and post-rhinoplasty. The sister now occupying the same space as the nose of the patients' mother and her own ideal nose.

Grid studies have an advantage over objective methods of body image assessment in that they are a sensitive instrument which can reflect aspects of the subject's 'inner world', the qualities they attribute to different objects (or people) and the relationship

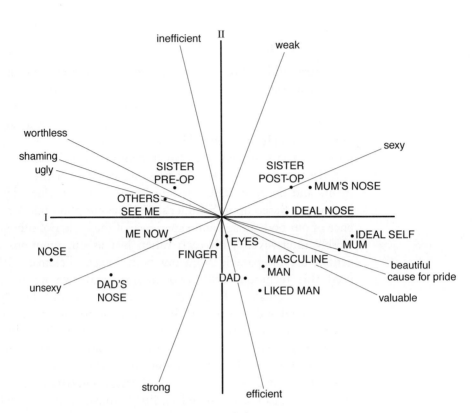

***Figure 3.2*** Repertory grid; female, noticeable deformity.

between these objects. However, administration of grids is extremely time consuming and interpreting the data requires complicated mathematical analysis. Grids are essentially an idio-graphic tool and thus are best suited for assessing individual subjects. They have particular application in clinical situations for exploratory and therapeutic work. However, statistical problems arise when using grids in nomothetic analysis of results from groups of subjects.

### Homonym test of body concern

Secord (1953) designed the 'homonym test of body concern' based on word association principles. The test involves the subjects writing their first response to an aurally presented list of words some of which have both body and non-body homonyms, e.g. 'colon' – gastrointestinal or grammatical. The number of responses to the body-type homonym showed the degree of importance of body parts for each person. Results for a female sample correlated with the score on the 'Body Cathexis Scale' in which subjects indicated the level of satisfaction with various body parts and features (see page 60). However, no correlation was found in male subjects. Wheeler (1971) also found that the test differentiated subjects in a bodily oriented encounter group from those in a verbally oriented group, but others have found poor discriminant validity of the test (Jasker and Reed, 1963). There is, however, some evidence of the homonym test having reasonable inter-rater, test–retest and split-half reliability (Jupp and Collins, 1983).

*Other projective tests*

The difficulty of deriving an accurate measure of body image is highlighted by the number of complex tests, carefully designed but subsequently found to be of limited value. Often their application is reported only once or twice in the literature. In the *Body Image Projective Test* (Hunt and Weber, 1968) subjects stated which of the four figure silhouettes was most like themselves, and which they would most and least prefer to look like. It was hoped to identify the most dominant aspects of body image, but no conclusive results were found. Fisher and Schneider (1963) used a version of the *Thematic Apperception Test* in an attempt to distinguish the body concerns of schizophrenic, neurotic and control populations. The stories produced were rated for 'body concern', i.e. reference to body parts or sensations. However, they found that 'body concern' on this measure was highly correlated with the length of the story told and the schizophrenic group told longer stories. Another test devised by Fisher (1964), the *Body Prominence Test*, involved subjects being asked to write down 20 things they were aware of at that moment. If the subject produced any phrases or words related to the body these were scored to give a total 'Body Prominence Score'. The test shows sex differences with women having higher body prominence scores than men, and scores have also been shown to increase after exposure to body-related experiences, such as a gynaecological examination (Fisher and Osofsky, 1967).

*Questionnaire studies*

There has been a plethora of questionnaires developed to measure aspects of body image. Some of the earlier instruments are concerned only with dissatisfaction with aspects of the body and appear as a list of body parts to simply be rated for satisfaction. Other scales take more account of body-image affect and its influence on feelings, behaviours and self-image.

### The Body Cathexis Scale

One of the earliest attempts at measuring body image through the use of self-report questionnaires was the Body Cathexis Scale developed by Secord and Jourard (1953). By 'body cathexis' they referred to 'the degree of feeling of satisfaction or dissatisfaction with the various parts or processes of the body'. Secord and Jourard saw body cathexis as being integrally related to self-concept and postulated that feelings about the body would be commensurate with feelings about the self. They found a significant correlation between body cathexis and self-cathexis, with women showing a larger correlation between the scales than did men.

This link between body satisfaction and self-satisfaction has now been shown repeatedly in a variety of studies using different measures of body image and self-esteem (Champion *et al.*, 1982; Mable *et al.*, 1986) in adolescents (Lerner and Brackney, 1978) and also in cross-cultural studies (Lerner *et al.*, 1980).

### The Body Parts Satisfaction Scale

The Body Parts Satisfaction Scale (Berscheid *et al.*, 1973) takes a very similar approach to the Body Cathexis Scale, listing 24 body parts which are rated for satisfaction on a six-point scale. Scores are given for satisfaction with particular body aspects such as weight, mid-torso, upper torso and face. In a survey of 2000 people the authors found that body satisfaction was related to personal happiness; teenagers who reported being unattractive being the most unhappy group of respondents.

### The Body Experience Questionnaire

Fisher and Schneider (1963) developed the Body Experience Questionnaire. They were particularly concerned with collecting empirical data to investigate the clinical findings of strange body-image distortion and bodily sensation in schizophrenics. However, comparing schizophrenic, neurotic and control populations, the only significant score difference was between the psychiatric patients as a whole and controls on the total test score.

Another questionnaire study of body-image distortions in schizo-phrenia was conducted by Chapman *et al.* (1978). Using a true/false questionnaire design asking about deviant perceptual body experiences (e.g. 'sometimes feel parts of my body no longer belong to me'), they found a significant difference between schizophrenics and controls.

### The Body Esteem Scale

Franzoi and Shields (1984) developed the 35-item Body Esteem Scale (BES) to measure body concerns and attitudes. The BES contains three subscales which assess feelings of sexual attractive-ness, weight concern and physical condition. The scale has been psychometrically tested and shows reasonable internal consistency and convergent, discriminant and construct validity (Thomas and Freeman, 1990). Although the scale was developed using male and female college populations, it has been shown to discriminate between anorexic women and non-anorexic controls (Franzoi and Shields, 1984).

### The Body–Self Relations Questionnaire

The Body–Self Relations Questionnaire (BSRQ) (Noles *et al.*, 1985) is a lengthy scale consisting of 140 items, which the subject rates on a five-point scale from agree to disagree. Items relate to the person's attitudes and actions in three somatic domains (phys-ical appearance, physical fitness and physical health). The scale has now been validated in several psychometric studies. Using this scale and the Body Parts Satisfaction Scale, Noles *et al.* (1985) have shown significant differences in body-image ratings between depressed and non-depressed individuals. Scores on the BSRQ have been shown to improve following cognitive–behavioural body image therapy (Butters and Cash, 1987).

### The Body Shape Questionnaire

Since Bruch's assertion (1962) that body-image disturbance was an essential characteristic of anorexia nervosa, the study of body image in the eating disorders has dominated the body-image literature. Many questionnaires which measure general aspects of eating disturbance include scales related to body disparagement, e.g. the Body Dissatisfaction Scale of the Eating Disorders Inventory (Garner *et al.*, 1983). However, one questionnaire which concentrates on the typical body image issues in women with eating disorders is the Body Shape Questionnaire (BSQ; Cooper *et al.*, 1987).

The BSQ is a 34-item self-report measure of concerns about body shape, especially the experience of 'feeling fat', including its antecedents and consequences. In an initial validation study, concurrent validity was assessed by correlating the BSQ with other measures of eating-disordered attitudes. For bulimic women, a moderate but significant correlation between the BSQ and the Eating Attitudes Test (EAT) (Garner and Garfinkel, 1979) total scores, and a high correlation with body dissatisfaction was found. For control subjects a positive significant correlation between BSQ and EAT was also reported. Initial results indicate that 84% of bulimic women and 17% of asymptomatic controls have an elevated BSQ score, although no reliability assessments are reported.

In a more recent study of 559 British White and Asian schoolgirls, Mumford *et al.* (1991, and personal communication) carried out a principal components analysis of the BSQ and found a first factor accounting for nearly 50% of the variance in each ethnic group. Twenty-five of the BSQ items loaded on this first factor (the same ones for each group) and it was concluded that most items were measuring the same underlying construct – concern with shape. No other meaningful factors emerged. Mumford *et al.* found a significantly positive correlation between this factor and EAT score.

The unidimensional nature of the 34 items suggests that the BSQ may be unnecessarily long for use in studies when body disparagement is not the main or sole focus of investigation. Evans and Dolan (1993), in a study of 342 adult women, have derived shorter 'alternate forms' of the BSQ (two 16-item and four 8-item versions) which showed equivalent means and excellent internal consistency in both derivation and replication samples. These shorter versions may be more efficient than the original BSQ, where body disparagement is not the sole focus of a study, where speed of completion and economy are of the essence, or where a repeated measures research design is employed.

### The Body Attitudes Questionnaire

Ben-Tovim and Walker (1991a) have reviewed techniques for measuring women's body attitudes, and concluded that many instruments and procedures were restricted in the range of attitudes measured and were poorly developed technically. In particular they felt that the central importance of 'satisfaction' was a construct imposed on women by research rather than one which had emerged from empirical study of a wide-ranging examination of body attitudes.

With this in mind, Ben-Tovim and Walker (1991b) have developed the Body Attitudes Questionnaire (BAQ), which measures the broad range of attitudes which women hold towards their bodies. Using unstructured interviews with women with eating problems, psychiatric patients and women without pathology, they derived 215 statements encapsulating attitudes towards the body. With further testing and psychometric evaluation, a 44-item scale was finally derived with six subscales labelled: 'feeling fat', 'disparagement', 'strength', 'salience', 'attractiveness' and 'lower body fat'. The BAQ shows good split-half and retest reliability, and discriminant validity between 'normal' and anorexic women. The BAQ has also been used to show cross-cultural differences in women's body attitudes in Samoa and Australia (Wilkinson *et al.*, 1994).

*Body silhouette studies*

Several body-image researchers have resorted to the use of body silhouettes or line drawings in an attempt to evaluate visual representations of the body (Figure 3.3). This technique is most often used to evaluate attitudes to weight and shape, and thus the stimuli used are drawings ranging from very emaciated to extremely overweight representations.

Fallon and Rozin (1985) used line drawings to survey what women and men felt to be their current and ideal body shape, and the shape they felt was most attractive to the opposite sex. Each subject is given a sheet of paper which contains two rows of nine human figure drawings, one row of female and the other of male figures arranged from very thin to obese. Four questions about the figures are asked and subjects must mark the appropriate figure. The questions are: 'Which figure best approximates your current figure?', 'Which figure best approximates your ideal figure?', 'Which figure do you think the opposite sex finds most attractive?' and 'Which figure of the opposite sex do you find most attractive?'. Their results indicated that women perceive their current body shape to be larger than their ideal and larger than that which they believe men prefer. Fallon and Rozin found that men also prefer women to be thinner than women actually

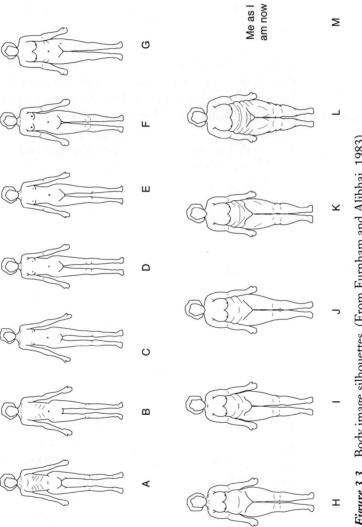

*Figure 3.3* Body image silhouettes. (From Furnham and Alibhai, 1983).

felt themselves to be, indicating that both men and women prefer a woman's body shape to be thinner than women feel they
are. These results have been shown to be consistent for two different generations of American men and women (Rozin and
Fallon, 1988).

Ford *et al.* (1990) have replicated Fallon and Rozin's method in
Egypt. A total of 230 university students in Cairo were shown figures of male and female body shape ranging from very thin to
obese. Results showed that, even within a culture which places less
emphasis on weight and shape, women selected an ideal shape
which was significantly thinner than their current shape, while
men did not. Hence the appraisal of body shape showed gender
differences in Egypt. Nevertheless, there were also other differences between the findings of the two studies in that Egyptian
women showed less discrepancy between ratings of their ideal and
current body shape than did the American sample.

*Silhouettes as repertory grid elements*

Furnham and Alibhai (1983) conducted a cross-cultural study
using an ingenious combination of the silhouettes with a repertory
grid methodology (using the body silhouettes as elements for the
grid) (see Figure 3.3). They compared how Kenyan Asian, British
and immigrant Kenyan British women evaluated female body
shapes. The Kenyans in Kenya gave a positive rating to the larger
figures than both the other two groups, yet surprisingly the
Kenyan British group was even more extreme than the British
group in their positive evaluation of slimness. These latter two
studies have both suggested that exposure to Westernized society
possibly can lead to internalization of Western attitudes, and
alteration of traditional cultural views about weight and body
shape.

*The 'Color-a-Person' test*

One recent test which combines the use of silhouettes with aspects
of the 'Draw-a-Person' test and the principles of dissatisfaction
questionnaires is the 'Color-a-Person' test (Wooley and Roll,
1991). The subject is presented with two outline drawings of the
human body (front and side views) and is given five different
coloured pens with which to colour in the areas within the lines
like a colouring book to indicate levels of satisfaction or dissatisfaction with their bodies. The test has been shown to have good

internal consistency and retest reliability. Wooley and Roll found that the test could discriminate between eating-disordered and non-eating-disordered women, and the scores of eating-disordered women decreased after treatment.

*Objective measurement*

The experimental techniques used for the objective measurement of body image are of two main types – 'distortion studies' and 'size-estimation studies'. Both approaches have been used widely to assess eating-disordered subjects.

### The distorting mirror technique

This technique, which was first used by Traub and Orbach (1964) with obese women, produces an image which can be manipulated in horizontal and vertical planes. Subjects must set the mirror to give a true image of themselves. A development of this method is the *distorting photograph technique*, which has been used extensively with anorexic patients (Glucksman and Hirsch, 1969; Garner and Garfinkel, 1977). A series of slide photographs is taken of the subject with a lens distorted up to 20% wider or narrower. The subjects' task is then to select the most accurate image of themselves. A further adaption of this method uses an on-line video image with the subjects altering their image on a television monitor to fit their current view of their body (Freeman, 1984). Using these techniques, approximately one half of subjects with anorexia nervosa have been shown to overestimate their total body size. This seems related to clinical pathology and is a poor prognostic sign (Garfinkel *et al.*, 1978). However, many studies have also found overestimation of body size in control women with no eating disorder.

### Body Image Testing System

One criticism of the image distortion technique has been that instruments introduce an equal amount of distortion at all body parts. However, as technology has developed, so has the intricacy of distorting image techniques. Schlundt and Bell (1993) have now devised an interactive computer program named the Body Image Testing System (BITS), which allows for assessment of distortions of separate components of the body by allowing subjects to change the size of nine body parts independently on a front and profile image. Cognitive representations of the body can be assessed by either considering the absolute size of the images created or by comparing images generated under different instructions (e.g. current and ideal bodies). Subjects can also be asked to provide satisfaction ratings for the body parts.

The BITS was tested in 500 subjects and shown to have strong associations with other body-image measures. In addition, BITS scores explained as much as 60% of the variance in measures of eating disturbance.

### Visual size estimation

Size estimation studies are of two types – image-marking technique and visual size-estimation studies. Image-marking technique involves the subject standing in front of a sheet of paper and marking the widths of specific body regions as if it were a mirror (Askevold, 1975). Visual size-estimation studies used calipers or more recently movable lights on a horizontal bar. Standing away from the apparatus the subjects moves the lights until they represent the width of specific body regions, usually chest, waist and hips. Using this method, Slade and Russell (1973) first demonstrated that anorexics overestimated body widths as compared with controls and that overperception decreased as weight was restored. However, other studies have found no difference between anorexics and controls. Crisp and Kalucy (1974) showed that the degree of overperception of body width increased after a high carbohydrate meal in anorexics but not in control subjects.

Research has indicated that a similar overperception of body widths occurs in bulimic women and is corrected after therapy (Birtchnell et al., 1985; Willmuth et al., 1985). However, other work has indicated that the overperception of body width is not limited to an eating-disordered population, but is also a feature of women who are free from any eating-disorder pathology (Birtchnell et al., 1987) and also asymptomatic men (Dolan et al., 1987). These findings highlight one of the problems with any measurement of body image. Although one cannot deny the obvious clinical difference between eating-disordered and asymptomatic subjects in the attitudes towards weight and shape, objective measurement does not always demonstrate these differences as it is perhaps the meaning of that weight and shape to the individual rather than their objectification of it which is of paramount importance.

Slade and Brodie (1994) reviewed all controlled studies to 1992 which applied these objective techniques in eating-disordered subjects. Although all types of experimental techniques produced inconsistent results, they found that, overall, in 60% of size-estimation studies and 58% of distortion studies, eating-disordered subjects overestimated their body size to a greater extent than controls. There was a tendency for anorexics to over-estimate their size more than bulimics on 'size-estimation' procedures, although the opposite tendency was found for 'image-distorting' procedures. They concluded that the tendency to overestimate physical size is neither unique to individuals suffering from eating disorder, nor is it diagnostic.

**Summary**

Most workers would now agree that body image includes more than the mere perceptual appraisal of the body, and that cognitive aspects play an essential and important part in the formation of an individual's body image concept. It is perhaps because of this complex interaction of perceptual, attitudinal and emotional factors in the development of body image that the specific meaning of the concept is often unclear. In addition, in investigating body image, individual researchers have chosen to focus upon different aspects of this enigmatic concept, directed by the concerns of the societal or clinical group with whom they work.

Workers derive measures of body image which are relevant to their particular position and thus are differentially sensitive to different aspects of what may be understood as body image. Given the resulting diversity of techniques which have been generated, it is not surprising that difficulties have been encountered in attempting systematic study.

Although a large variety of measurement techniques have been reviewed here, no one measure can claim to measure 'body image' successfully in its entirety. Problems particularly arise when trying to devise measures which can combine the perceptual, attitudinal and emotional components of the body image concept, and the search for a reliable and meaningful method of measuring body image is not yet complete. It may, of course, be unrealistic to expect one single universally reliable, valid and meaningful measure of body image ever to be found, and workers will probably continue to use and devise measures which are most relevant to their own view of this complex phenomenon.

**References**

Adams, G. (1981) The effects of physical attractiveness on the socialisation process. In: Lucker, Ribbens and McNamara (eds) *Psychological Aspects of Facial Form*. Ann Arbor, Center for Human Growth and Development.

Adams, G. and Crossman, S. (1978) *Physical Attractiveness: A Cultural Imperative*. Roslyn Heights, NY, Libra.

Askevold, F. (1975) Measuring body image. *Psychotherapy and Psychosomatics* **26**, 71–77.

Beale, S., Lisper, M. and Palm, B. (1980) A psychological study of patients seeking augmentation mammoplasty. *British Journal of Psychiatry* **136**, 153–158.

Berscheid, E. and Walster, E. (1974) Physical attractiveness. In: Berkowitz (ed.) *Advances in Experimental Social Psychology*. New York, Academic Press.

Berscheid, E., Walster, E. and Bohrnstedt, G. (1973) The happy American body: a survey report. *Psychology Today* July, 119–131.

Ben-Tovim, D.I. and Walker, M.K. (1991a) Women's body attitudes: a review of measurement techniques. *International Journal of Eating Disorders* **10**(2), 155–167.

Ben-Tovim, D.I. and Walker, M.K. (1991b) The development of the Ben-Tovim Walker Body Attitudes Questionnaire (BAQ): a new measure of women's attitudes towards their own bodies. *Psychological Medicine* **21**, 775–784.

Birtchnell, S.A. (1985) *Social and Psychological Factors Motivating the Request for Cosmetic Rhinoplasty*. M.Sc. thesis, University of London.

Birtchnell, S.A. (1987) Dysmorphophobia: a centenary discussion. Presented at *2nd Leeds Symposium on the Psychopathology of Body Image*.

Birtchnell, S.A., Harte, A. and Lacey, J.H. (1985) Body image distortion in bullimia nervosa. *British Journal of Psychiatry* **147**, 408–412.

Birtchnell, S.A., Dolan, B.M. and Lacey, J.H. (1987) Body image distortion in non-eating disordered women. *International Journal of Eating Disorders* **6**(3), 385–391.

Bruch, H. (1962) Perceptual and conceptual disturbances in anorexia nervosa. *Psychological Medicine* **24**, 187–194.

Butters, J.W. and Cash, T. (1987) Cognitive-behavioural treatment of women's body image dissatisfaction. *Journal of Consulting and Clinical Psychology* **55**, 889–897.

Champion, V.L., Austin, J.K. and Tzeng, O. (1982) Assessment of relationship between self-concept and body image using multivariate techniques. *Issues in Mental Health Nursing* **4**, 299–315.

Chapman, L.J., Chapman, J.P. and Raulin, M.L. (1978) Body-image aberration in schizophrenia. *Journal of Abnormal Psychology* **87**(4), 399–407.

Clifford, B. and Bull, R. (1978) *The psychology of person identification*. London, Routledge and Kegan Paul.

Cooper, P.J., Taylor, M.J., Cooper, Z. and Fairburn, C.G. (1987) The development and validation of the Body Shape Questionnaire. *International Journal of Eating Disorders* **6**(5), 485–494.

Crisp, A.H. and Kalucy, R.S. (1974) Aspects of the perceptual disorder in anorexia nervosa. *British Journal of Medical Psychology* **47**, 349–361.

Dion, K., Berscheid, E. and Walster, E. (1972) What is beautiful is good. *Journal of Personality and Social Psychology* **24**, 285.

Dolan, B.M., Birtchnell, S.A. and Lacey, J.H. (1987) Body image distortion in non-eating disordered men and women. *Journal of Psychosomatic Research* **31**(4), 513–520.

Evans, C.D.H. and Dolan, B.M. (1993) The body shape questionnaire: shortened alternate forms. *International Journal of Eating Disorders* **13**(3), 315–321.

Fallon, A. and Rozin, P. (1985) Sex differences in the perceptions of desirable body shape. *Journal of Abnormal Psychology* **94**(1), 102–105.

Federn, P. (1953) *Ego Psychology and the Psychoses*. New York, Basic Books.

Feldman, M.M. (1973) The body image and object relations: exploration of a method utilizing repertory grid techniques. *British Journal of Medical Psychology* **48**, 317–332.

Fisher, S. (1964) Body awareness and selective memory for body versus non-body references. *Journal of Personality* **32**, 138–144.

Fisher, S. and Cleveland, S.E. (1968) *Body Image and Personality*, 2nd edn. New York. Dover Publications.

Fisher, S. and Osofsky, (1967) Sexual responsiveness in women: psychological correlates. *Archives of General Psychiatry* **17**, 214–226.

Fisher, S. and Schneider, R. (1963) Body experiences of schizophrenic, neurotic and normal women. *Journal of Nervous and Mental Disorders* **137**, 252–257.

Ford, K.A., Dolan, B.M. and Evans, C.D.H. (1990) Cultural factors in the aetiology of eating disorders: evidence from body shape preferences of Arab students. *Journal of Psychosomatic Research* **34**(5), 501–507.

Franzoi, S. and Shields, S. (1984) The body esteem scale: multi-dimensional structure and sex differences in a college population. *Journal of Personality Assessment* **48**, 173–178.

Freeman, R. (1984) A modified video camera for measuring body image distortion: technical description and reliability. *Psychological Medicine* **14**, 411–416.

Furnham, A. and Alibhai, N. (1983) Cross-cultural differences in the perception of female body shapes. *Psychological Medicine* **13**, 829–837.

Garfinkel, P.E., Moldofsky, H., Garner, D.M., Stancer, H.C. and Coscina, D.V. (1978) Prognosis in anorexia nervosa as influenced by clinical features: treatment and self-perception. *Canadian Medical Association Journal* **117**, 1041–1045.

Garner, D.M. and Garfinkel, P.E. (1979) The eating attitudes test: an index of the symptoms of anorexia nervosa. *Psychological Medicine* **9**, 273–279.

Garner, D.M. and Garfinkel, P.E. (1977) Measurement of body image in anorexia nervosa. In: Vigersky, R.A. (ed.) *Anorexia Nervosa*. New York, Raven Press.

Garner, D.M., Olmstead, M.P. and Polivy, J. (1983) Development and validation of a multi-dimensional eating disorder inventory for anorexia nervosa and bulimia. *International Journal of Eating Disorders* **2**(2), 15–33.

Glucksman, M.L. and Hirsch, J. (1969) The response of obese patients to weight reduction. 3. The perception of a body size. *Psychosomatic Medicine* **31**, 1–7.

Green, M. and Levitt, E.E. (1962) Constriction of body image in children with congenital heart disease. *Pediatrics* **29**, 438–441.

Head, H. (1920) *Studies in Neurology*. London, Oxford.

Hunt, V. and Weber, M. (1968) Body image projective test. *Journal of Projective Techniques* **24**, 3–10.

Jacobsen, W., Edgerton, M., Meyer, E., Canter, A. and Slaughter, R. (1960) Psychiatric evaluation of male patients seeking plastic surgery. *Plastic Reconstructive Surgery* **26**, 356–372.

Jasker, R. and Reed, M.R. (1963) Assessment of body image organisation of hospitalised and non-hospitalised subjects. *Journal of Projective Techniques and Personality Assessment* **27**, 185–190.

Jupp, J.J. and Collins, J.K. (1983) Instruments for the measurement of conscious and unconscious aspects of body image.

*Australian Journal of Clinical and Experimental Hypnosis* **11**(2), 89–110.

Koff, E., Rierdan, J. and Silverstone, E. (1978) Changes in representation of body image as a function of menarcheal status. *Developmental Psychology* **14**(6), 635–642.

Kolb, C. (1975) Disturbances of body image. In: Areti, S. (ed.) *American Handbook of Psychiatry*, Vol. 4, pp 749–769. New York, Basic Books.

Lacey, J.H. and Birtchnell, S.A. (1986) Body image and its disturbances. *Journal of Psychosomatic Research* **30**(6), 623–631.

Lerner, R.M. and Brackney, B.E. (1978) The importance of inner and outer body parts: Attitudes and self-concept of late adolescents. *Sex Roles* **4**(2), 225–238.

Lerner, R.M., Iwawaki, S., Chihara, T. and Sorell, G.T. (1980) Self-concept, self-esteem and body attitudes amongst Japanese men and female students. *Child Development* **51**, 847–855.

Lubin, B., Larsen, R.M. and Matarazzo, J.D. (1984) Patterns of psychological test usage in the United States: 1935–1982. *American Psychologist* **39**, 451–454.

Mable, H.M., Balance, W.D. and Galagan, R.J. (1986) Body image distortion and dissatisfaction in university students. *Perceptual and Motor Skills* **63**, 907–911.

Machover, K. (1949) *Personality Projection in the Drawing of the Human Figure*. Springfield, IL, Charles C. Thomas.

Meerloo, J. (1956) The fate of one's face. *Psychiatric Quarterly* **30**, 31.

Meyer, E., Jacobsen, W., Edgerton, M. and Canter, A. (1960). Motivational patterns in patients seeking elective plastic surgery. *Psychosomatic Medicine* **22**, 193.

Mumford, D.B., Whitehouse, A.M. and Platts, M. (1991) Sociocultural correlates of eating disorders among Asian schoolgirls in Bradford. *British Journal of Psychiatry* **158**, 222–228.

Munro, A. (1980) Monosymptomatic hypochondriacal psychosis. *British Journal of Hospital Medicine* **24**, 34–38.

Noles, S., Cash, T. and Winstead, B.A. (1985) Body image, physical attractiveness and depression. *Journal of Consulting and Clinical Psychology* **53**, 88–94.

Offman, H.J. and Bradley, S.J. (1992) Body image of children and adolescents and its measurement: an overview. *Canadian Journal of Psychiatry* **37**, 417–422.

Paine, P., Alves, E. and Tubino, P. (1985) The size of human figure drawing and the Goodenough–Harris scores of pediatric oncology patients: a pilot study. *Perceptual and Motor Skills* **60**, 911–914.

Rozin, P. and Fallon, A. (1988) Body image, attitudes to weight and misperceptions of figure preferences of the opposite sex: a comparison of men and women in two generations. *Journal of Abnormal Psychology* **97**(3), 342–345.

Sandler, J. and Rosenblatt, B. (1962) The concept of the representational world. *Psychoanalytical Study of Children* **17**, 128–145.

Schilder, P. (1935) *The Image and Appearance of the Human Body*. London, Kegan Paul.

Schlundt, D.G. and Bell, C. (1993) Body Image Testing System: a microcomputer programme for assessing body image. *Journal of Psychopathology and Behavioural Assessment* **15**(3), 267–285.

Secord, P.F. (1953) Objectification of word-association procedures by the use of homonyms: a measure of body cathexis. *Journal of Personality* **21**, 479–495.

Secord, P.F. and Jourard, S. (1953) The appraisal of body cathexis: body cathexis and the self. *Journal of Consulting and Clinical Psychology* **17**, 343–347.

Silverstein, A.B. and Robinson, H.A. (1956) The representation of orthopaedic disability in children's figure drawings. *Journal of Consulting and Clinical Psychology* **20**(5), 333–341.

Slade, P. and Brodie, D. (1994) Body-image distortion and eating disorder: a reconceptualisation based on recent literature. *Eating Disorders Review* **2**(1), 33–46.

Slade, P.D. and Russell, G.F.M. (1973) Awareness of body dimensions in anorexia nervosa: cross-sectional and longitudinal studies. *Psychological Medicine* **8**, 317–324.

Stoddard, F.J. (1982) Body image development in the burned child. *Journal of American Academy of Child Psychiatry* **21**(5), 502–507.

Szasz, T. (1957) *Pain and Pleasure*. New York, Basic Books.

Tait, Fr., Ascher, C.D. and Ascher, R.C. (1955) The inside-of-the-body test. *Psychosomatic Medicine* **17**, 139–148.

Thomas, C. (1984) Dysmorphophobia: a question of definition. *British Journal of Psychiatry* **144**, 513–516.

Thomas, C. and Freeman, R.J. (1990) The Body Esteem Scale: construct validity of the female subscales. *Journal of Personality Assessment* **54**(1 and 2), 204–212.

Tolor, A. and Digrazia, P.V. (1977) The body image of pregnant women as reflected in their human figure drawings. *Journal of Clinical Psychology* **33**(2), 566–571.

Traub, A.C. and Orbach, J. (1964) Psychophysical studies of body image: 1. The adjustable body distorting mirror. *Archives of General Psychiatry* **11**, 53–66.

Wheeler (1971) *Effects of Encounter Group Methods upon Selected Measures of Body Image* Unpublished Ph.D. thesis. Cited in Ben-Tovim, D.I. and Walker, M.K. (1991a).

Willmuth, M.E., Leitenberg, H., Rosen, J.C., Fandacaro, B.A. and Gross, J. (1985) Body size distortion in bulimia nervosa. *International Journal of Eating Disorders* **4**, 71–78.

Wilkinson, J.Y., Ben-Tovim, D. and Walker, K. (1994) An insight into the personal and cultural significance of weight and shape in large Samoan women. *International Journal of Obesity* **18**, 602–606.

Wooley, O.W. and Roll, S. (1991) The Color-a-Person body dissatisfaction test: stability, internal consistency, validity and factor structure. *Journal of Personality Assessment* **56**(3), 395–413.

Yama, M.F. (1990) The usefulness of human figure drawings as an index of overall adjustment. *Journal of Personality Assessment* **54**(1 and 2), 78–86.

CHAPTER 4

# Cultural issues associated with altered body image

*James Smith*

*'The ethics of caring is the ethics of a caress. The caressing hand remains open, never tightening its grip, never "getting hold of", it touches without pressing, it moves obeying the shape of the caressed body'.* (Marc Alain Ouaknin, 1992).

**Introduction**

Throughout history, diverse cultures have deliberately changed their physical demeanour in a variety of ways and for a variety of purposes. Some of the rites were and are extremely simple to initiate and transient in their effect, for example, the cutting of a lock of a male child's hair on the eighth day of life as was the case in early Semitic cultures (Morgenstern, 1966), others such as body piercing or tattooing at birth or puberty initiation rites are long, complex and extremely painful.

**Circumcision**

Of all the birth initiation cultural procedures, the circumcision of the male child is the most universally practised, and still remains the normal practice within the Semitic and Arab worlds (Morgenstern, 1966). Alex Haley in his book *Roots* refers to the practice of circumcision at puberty for boys within 'Twi' culture. Although early circumcision is now the norm, circumcision at puberty is still widely used within Central Africa and among tribal groups of the Australian Aborigines, and among some American Indian groups from both North and South of the continent (Soyinka, 1992). Invariably the event of the circumcision of a male child is one of great celebration among all cultures who practise it as a religious or cultural norm.

Whilst male circumcision is almost universally accepted within a Western cultural tradition, its female counterpart is almost universally condemned within that same western tradition. Yet, according to the World Health Organisation (1986), over 84 000 000 women are estimated to have undergone some degree of genital surgery, with an estimated 3000 operations continuing worldwide each day.

El Dareer (1983) offers evidence that over 90% of the female population of the Sudan have undergone some form of circumcision. Although mainly confined to the societies of the Middle East, there is evidence to suggest that the practice continues in the remoter parts of Siberian Russia, and among some small North American Indian groups (El Dareer, 1983). Female circumcision varies in its severity as does the age of operation. The operation is usually performed by an older woman or women within a community group, often the girl or woman's grandmother. The commonest and simplest procedure involving the excision of the clitoral hood, which is the most usual in Egypt, takes place between the sixth and eighth year of life, whereas the more radical wide excision may take place just before the commencement of the menses or after first menses (El Dareer, 1983), or, in the case of some Swahili and some Nigerian Igbo-speaking groups, wide excision may take place after the birth of a first child (Egwuato *et al.*, 1981).

It is a matter of both historical fact and interest that clitoridectomy and even some wider excisions of the labia, were commonplace within the Europe of the nineteenth and early twentieth century. Such procedures were employed for a variety of reasons including epilepsy, hysteria and other psychiatric disorders. The procedure, deemed to lower the libido, was also seen as promoting emotional stability (Barker Benfield, 1975).

**Cultural aspects of disease**

To understand and define the issues which may present problems to people within certain cultural and ethnic groups, which relate to medically influenced altered body image, the nurse should acquire background knowledge about how disease is viewed within specific communities, and what determines a person's individuality and status within their cultural hierarchy. As health carers now tend to work in an increasingly complex multicultural environment, there is an increased need for a deeper understanding of its constituent groups. In displaying a willingness to learn and understand traditions and customs other than our own, we have the opportunity to enrich our own lives and we will find that such knowledge may dispel latent prejudices.

Comeroff (1982) suggests that, in all people, illness of any kind constitutes a threat to the body of the patient and their understanding of themselves. If the illness is severe in nature, the change in the person's status may be threefold, that of a movement of understanding from well person to patient, to one who is less able than before. Further, Comaroff implies that, irrespective of cultural tradition or background, dysfunction of the body disturbs the harmony which exists between the physical, social and moral aspects of being. Change of body image or functional change may well become to its subject a constant reminder of their altered or dysfunctioned state.

Suffering illness when a permanent change in body image is involved, especially where surgery has been involved, may well have permanent consequences about an individual's notion of themselves as a being. Illness which results in either a temporary or a permanent visible functional change (i.e. loss of a limb) may not only cause the patient to reassess their social roles and activities, but may also have a bearing upon how they as individuals are viewed and accepted by their social communities. Further, within some cultural groups, change of image and function may affect the person's social standing both in their family, and also their community as a whole. The psychological manifestations of such changes in status may also threaten the individual's capacity for some kinds of employment, and in some cases it will result in the exclusion from community activities such as worshipping in a holy place.

In addition to the effect which the treatment of disease has in terms of the patient's self-esteem, and their understanding of their role within particular cultural and social groups, the requirements of such groups in terms of physical completeness may serve either to boost or undermine the patients' sense of self-worth. The needs of patients with obvious changes such as those occasioned by such radical measures as amputation, breast loss or the formation of a stoma are frequently understood and well supported. However, there needs to be a greater awareness of the effects of hidden body image change, such as change of fertility status in most patients who undergo total body irradiation, or particular types of high-dose chemotherapy.

Much of what patients 'feel' concerning the perceived change in their body image, can be described as pain in its broadest sense. Not all cultural groups will respond to a particular form of altered body image in the same way. How this is perceived by the self and others can be largely influenced by their social and cultural background. The way in which patients communicate or fail to communicate with those who care for them, according to Volosinov (1976), is a reflection of the way in which their cultural background influences their understanding of the disease process and the professional language used to describe the disease.

**Cultural factors influencing body image**

What are these cultural factors which may influence the patients' view of themselves? The most important determinants in relation to this chapter must include a patient's ethnic background, skin colour, gender identity, religious background, the role of the family within the individual's community, and the place of the individual within the community, to name but a few. To analyse the effect of the infinite number of variations which may occur with such a group of determinants, and to consider the role of each determinant in depth is beyond the scope of this chapter. It is hoped though that this general introduction will stimulate and be a catalyst for further research.

Helman (1992) states that concepts surrounding the idea of body image may be divided into three categories:

1.  Beliefs about the optimal shape and size of the body, including clothing and surface decoration.
2.  Beliefs about the inner structure of the body.
3.  Beliefs about how the body functions.

All three of these factors can work singly or in combination to influence the way that both the patient, the patient's family and the carer perceive the patient's new place within society.

**Hair loss**

One of the more obvious and very rapid changes which can affect a patient's self-image is that of hair loss induced by chemotherapy. Visually, hair loss for women is perceived as more serious than it is for men, as many men lose hair in the ageing process. This may certainly be a typically white, Western view of the loss of hair. For many cultural groups, however, hair loss in such a way would be devastating and have effects at a much deeper level of the person's identity. Hair loss may well be symbolic of a future which is bleak, and a visible manifestation of a progressive and unrelenting disease process within.

Although hair usually regrows after chemotherapy, the temporary loss of hair may well have a permanent effect in the way that patients understand themselves. Watson in his work on death and pollution in Cantonese society (cited in Bloch and Parry, 1994) ascribes a wide range of significances to hair. It is believed that hair has both the power to absorb life forces, and also that it is a medium for losing toxins and impurities, which arise from both disease and the death of a family member. If then a person from such a community suffers acute hair loss, there may be fears within as to his or her ability to recover, when one major medium for eliminating toxins or impurities is taken away.

In many cultures, hair is seen in the male as a sign of strength and in the female as a sign of her fertility and desirability as a partner. This is certainly true within most cultures and religions of the Indian subcontinent. For people of the Sikh faith, the intactness of the body is of paramount importance. According to Guru Gobind Singh: 'Sikhs shall be in their natural form, that is without loss of hair, and in the case of men without loss of foreskin, in opposition to the ordinances of the Hindus and the Mohammedans' (Macauliffe, 1909). The significance of hirsutism within the Sikh tradition are manifold, suffice it to say that the abundance of hair is an outward visible sign of the gift of life which they are given. To lose hair is to be diminished both as an individual and, in the case of orthodox Sikhs, to have diminished status within a community (Uberoi, 1992). For the Sikh woman, her hair is a visible barometer of her health and status. It is also a visible and public statement of her beliefs, and her role as a child bearer within the Sikh community. Loss of hair induced by such procedures as chemotherapy may not only be assumed to be a sign of her inability to bear children, but may in reality be the case.

Grief at the loss of hair is not, however, contained within Asian and Chinese communities. Freedman (1994) in her study of women with hair loss subsequent to breast cancer, suggests that in white American society 'hairstyle reflects a personal message about self concept and self identity' and further she writes that 'the loss of hair is an extremely traumatic experience precisely because it is the precursor to loss of self'.

Leach (1968) and Strathern (1994) in their separate works describe many significances which hair carries within a variety of African cultures. In many of these cultures, loss of hair, especially for the woman, is an outward sign of her loss of fertility, but may also be seen in some groups as someone who has a hidden and sinister disease. Within some African cultural groups, many old folk myths still exist and, within these, one of the roles of hair was to provide a barrier against the spirits of the air. Although a superstition, this may also be an underlying factor in the fear of hair loss shown by some patients from a sub-Saharan African culture (Soyinka, 1992).

Within the majority of African communities within the British Isles, the maintenance of hair is a matter of importance. This includes patients who have settled from both the continent of Africa and those of African descent from the Caribbean. Although hair loss is a matter of concern to both sexes, more so to women usually, there is one group within the Afro-Caribbean community for whom hair loss is an issue of major importance.

Rastafarianism is a relatively recent religious development in terms of religious history (Smart, 1994) but at its heart it has a very African orientation. The movement was inspired by Marcus Garvey in Jamaica in the 1930s. Garvey advocated pride in black consciousness as a result of unjust white domination of a black society. He is reported to have exorted his followers to look to Africa for the crowning of a black king as a sign for a redeemer of the black community. This sign was accomplished in 1930 with the crowning of King Haile Sellasse, the first king of Ethiopia, also known as Ras Tafari. Thereafter, the movement grew rapidly in Jamaica and spread to other parts of the Caribbean, the United Kingdom and other mainly white parts of the 'Old Commonwealth' as well as to the mainland of the United States in the 1950s. One of the main features of the Rastafarian was the hair, which was worn long in what came to be known as 'dreadlocks'. These dreadlocks were an outward sign of the commitment of the person to Ras Tafari, whose other title among many was 'Lion of Judah'. The dreadlocks were symbolic of the lion's mane, black dignity and the right of the black person to self-determination (Smart, 1994). Thus, this distinctive hairstyle became an outward sign of the inward power and dignity of the black person. The induced loss of hair to people of the Rastafarian religion may also be symbolic of the loss of power and dignity in their community.

Within the British Isles there are still some folk myths in existence which cause anxiety about hair loss, or at least may command a passing comment. Of the superstitions which do still exist, most are from the Celtic fringes. Sudden hair loss according to Wilkie (1866) is a foretelling of the loss of children, and Opie and Tatum (1989) write that in some communities, hair should not be discarded but either carefully kept or buried. This would accord with the writing of Frazer (1911), who in his study of rural communities in County Tyrone found that hair was carefully saved so that at the general resurrection in the last days, those who were called by God would not have a hair of their head missing.

In other communities, hair loss may be seen as a sign of disfavour or punishment; indeed, the shaving of the hair is still an outward sign of criminality in some penal systems. The bald head can also be seen as either a voluntary surrender of the self (as in some religious communities) or as a mark of disfavour in others.

As previously mentioned, religion is one of the major determinants in cultural identity. According to Spector (1991) it is often difficult to distinguish between those aspects of a person's belief system arising from a religious background and those that stem from an ethnic and cultural heritage. This would certainly be the case in terms of assessing the trauma of hair loss within some Jewish, Christian and Muslim communities (in chronological order). The importance of the hair, especially in the women of these 'people of the book', may be attributed by some to the Old Testament reference to the fact that hair is the crowning glory of a woman. Although the custom for women within Orthodox Jewry is to have short hair or even completely shorn (often covered by a wig), the majority of Jewish women value their hair very highly. Within the enormous breadth of observance within the Christian faith, it is the more insular of Christian communities who value hair the most, especially such groups as the Amish, Exclusive Brethren and the Taylorites. Long hair in groups such as these is perceived to be an outward sign of God's favour, and loss of hair may well be viewed by the individual and by their community as a form of punishment.

## Breast loss

Helman (1992) writes that 'in every society, the human body has a social as well as a physical reality. That is, the shape, size and adornment of the body are a way of communicating information about its owner's status within society'. In Western society this is certainly true about that part of the anatomy which is called the breast. The loss of a breast, or a major change in its shape as a result of surgery and/or disease, invariably alters a woman's view of herself and her role within society. In the first instance, many women who suffer with breast cancer are more aware of chemotherapy-induced hair loss, but when the hair regrows, it is the lingering image of her changed body shape which disturbs her concept of self-worth and also challenges that part of her being which encompasses her sexuality.

Scheper Hughes and Lock (1987) suggest that, in Western society, the social body is an important part of the body image, as it provides the framework within which an individual interprets his or her own physical and psychological experiences. It is also the means whereby the physiology of the individual is influenced and controlled by the rules of the society within which he or she lives. This larger society exerts powerful messages and control about the ideal body within it, and, consequently, within Western society, there is little compassion for those who are unable to conform to the norms of the 'body politic'.

Whereas much of the anxiety surrounding breast deficit in Western society can be associated with an idealized anatomical form, the loss of a breast or change in breast shape within Chinese and Vietnamese cultural groups has different significances, especially if the sufferer is of child-bearing age. James Watson, in company with other anthropologists, stresses the importance of breast feeding within traditional Chinese medicine and suggest that it is seen as an essential part of the preparation of the growing infant to face a world of disease. In Chinese folk medicine it has long been held that breast milk provided the newborn with immunity against a wide range of infant diseases (Watson, 1994) and that it was also important for the nursing mother to eat certain foods whilst avoiding others to maintain the quality of her milk. For a woman from these communities, disease of the breast may then be perceived in terms of her whole being. Her diseased or damaged breast is an outward sign of her inner turmoil. The integrity of her breast is an outward sign to her and her partner that all is well within.

Beliefs about breast milk as a conveyor of life forces or as an antipollutant are by no means confined to the traditional beliefs of Chinese and Vietnamese families. Within many African cultures a variety of beliefs about the magical healing properties of milk are held, and also that the mother's milk conveys a type of regenerative power. This is also true of many of the tribal groups of Papua New Guinea. Strathern (1994) writes of the parallel symbolism of the power of the semen of the man, which creates the new being, being restored in the young infant through the breast milk of the mother. The spirit of life force is cyclical and conveyed from father to mother, and from mother to child. This life force is engendered and is seen as the passage of the male life force through their community.

Frequently there is an associated notion of shame for the woman who has either had her breast removed or a change in shape as a result in surgery. This often results either in the drawing away of the woman from an intimate relationship with her partner or, within some cultures, an enforced separateness on the part of the husband or male partner.

Within the group of women who have cultural roots within the Indian subcontinent, there is often a much greater anxiety expressed about hair loss, which may result from adjuvant chemotherapy, than the loss of a breast. Particularly for women from an orthodox Sikh tradition, the loss of hair may become a symbol of loss of status, personality and sexuality. Although there is frequently a compliance to the needs of Western medical technology, one of the continuing problems for many women, especially those from communities where modesty is widely practised and highly valued, is the assumption within many hospitals that people are quite willing to expose themselves as a part of medical treatment. This assumption that immodesty is both reasonable and necessary, merely serves to continue prejudices on the part of health care staff, and a perception that patients from other cultural and ethnic groups are invariably potentially 'difficult patients'. The maxim 'when in Rome . . .' will certainly not do in a modern multicultural health practice.

The idealized and commodified shape and size of the perfect breast in Western society has brought with it many problems for women from that very Western culture. Because of the huge symbolism of the breast as representative of the perfect woman, many women have immense psychological traumas when their breast shape and size is changed as a result of surgery or disease. (Much surgery is sought for enhancement or size change to attain the 'perfect breast'.) The feminist movement within medicine and nursing is working to redress this imbalanced and ill-informed view of the perfect woman. Although writing in particular about the role of the ovaries, Lacquer (1987) writes in general about the view of a woman's body thus: 'Whatever one thought about women and their rightful place in the world could, it seemed, be mapped onto their bodies'. Issues related to breast alteration or augmentation, and the psychological effects and benefits of such procedures, are dealt with in Chapter 8 and are outside the remit of this chapter.

**Stomas**

Of all the visible physical alterations to body integrity, the formation of stomas (colostomy, ileostomy and urostomy) present the
most complex problems in terms of the patients' cultural and religious integrity and observance. In some patient groups, they may
threaten not only the individual's self-esteem, but in reality change
their position within a social or cultural group. In some cultural
groups, where religious observance, cultural secrecy and superstition combine, the formation of a stoma may be the beginning of a
life of isolation and ostracism, for it may mean separation from
their family in terms of cooking, eating and caring, and within
terms of a worshipping community, preclusion from a place of
worship. In the extreme, the presence of a stoma may be seen as
evidence of permanent ritual uncleanness and in terms of a sexual
relationship with a partner becoming untouchable.

The lack of definitive research into this area of problems associated with altered body image means that much information presented here is from an oral tradition through interviews with a third
party as translator and, therefore, highly subjective and open to
challenge. Ongoing research into the area will hopefully give a
clearer picture in future writings on the subject. The lack of documented research, however, must not detract from the potentially
serious consequences of this type of surgery for some patients.
Within the Bengali community, there is a reticence to speak about
those who have had stomas formed, especially in the case of women.
There is anecdotal evidence to suggest that those, especially women
who have had a stoma raised in an emergency for intestinal obstruction from a variety of causes, subsequently live lives in self-imposed
isolation, and have not availed themselves of surgery to resect the
offending gut and thus have normal function restored.

The acceptance of a degree of difficulty for patients of the
Islamic faith is problematic. Followers of the Islamic faith are not
permitted to perform ablutions during prayer times. Obviously,
because stomas are not under voluntary control, this prohibition
may cause difficulties. To seek an opinion on this issue, the man-
ager of Convatec Middle East, wrote to the Islamic Commission
for guidance. This is the verbatim reply:

> '... whoever is in such a situation is considered to have a
> legitimate excuse. Since the stoma patient cannot replace the pouch
> for each prayer, he may perform ablutions at the onset of each
> prayer interval. He may then pray as many times as he may wish
> within this prayer interval. At the onset of a new prayer interval,

*the ablutions performed in the last interval are no longer valid and he performs a new ablution for the new prayer interval and so on for each of the five prayer intervals. "Allah Glory be to Him who is more knowledgeable than all"'.* (Chairman of the Fatura Commission of Al-Azhar).

The problem at issue with such a ruling is that it does not appear to take account of the involuntary nature of the stoma and, therefore, does not make provision for the person, who having performed the ritual ablutions in accordance with the law, then has stomal activity within the holy confines of the Mosque. Is the person required to leave and start again each time there is excretory activity?

The Muslim community are by no means alone in coping with difficulties in terms of social and religious observance when a member of that community has a stoma. Within the Chinese community, such a change in body image and function may well be a cause for withdrawal from public life, especially if the recipient is a woman. As we have seen with the loss of breast integrity, any alteration in function may well be seen as a reflection of the inner turmoil and unhealthiness of the individual. Although the acceptance of a stoma may be problematic to the male in terms of his own self-esteem, his position within a cultural hierarchy will probably not be affected. Although an extreme response, this author was told by one Chinese woman who was very immersed in her culture, should such a disaster fall upon a wife, she would have to be sufficiently gracious to allow her husband another sexual partner, but the reverse would not be the case.

Within the Orthodox Jewish community, there is no stigma attached to the person with a stoma, although there are ordinances for those with stomas who intend to worship at a synagogue. The following is a verbatim quotation offered to the author by the principal of Jews' College London.

*'Colostomy: A patient who passes faeces through an artificial opening (colostomy or ileostomy) may engage in prayer and other religious duties if the external opening is clean and covered'.*
(Responsa Ziz Eliezer 9;6; Responsa Minhat Yitzhak 6:11–12.) *'It is also pertinent to include at this point the ordinance for patients with permanent catheters'.*

*'Catheter: A patient who has a catheter in the bladder through which urine passes into a bag, is permitted to perform religious*

*duties, provided that both catheter and bag are kept covered'.*
(Responsa Ziz Eliezer 8 : 1.)

**Language**

Within this short chapter it is only possible to introduce the idea of the complexities of cultural, social and religious issues associated with altered body image. The carer will by experience be able to build up his or her own understanding of such issues through experience, and by dealing sensitively with the needs of the individual patient. In order to achieve these skills, carers should ensure that the dialogue between them and the patient is clear, unambiguous and easily understood. As health care workers, we need to be aware that medicine uses unique language and common language uniquely.

Mischler (1986) highlights the need for health care workers to have an understanding of their patient's distress, and the patient's resultant incapacity to assimilate and convey information. Szasz (1982) contends that the patient's understanding of the language used in the description of the treatment of their disease has particular implications for the way that they, as a unique individual, interpret their disease and its treatment. The phenomenon of 'the undermined concept of self' in sick people is viewed by Needham (1981) as both a social fact and as an issue which cannot be separated from the person's illness.

Misunderstanding of information by patients and/or their relatives is by no means uncommon. Ardener (1982) states that '. . . cross cultural or subcultural misunderstanding is a very real problem at the level of close interaction between individuals' and, whether we like it or not, the way that we convey information and the language we use to convey it looms very large in such situations. There is no doubt that many workers in health care interpret and categorize the signs, symptoms, treatments and outcomes of an illness in a totally different way from the patient. Whorf (1956) suggests wryly that health care workers 'cut nature up, organise it into concepts, and ascribe significances'.

Whilst not meaning to suggest that all health care workers are so arbitrary and insensitive in their dealings with patients of other cultures, there can be little doubt that health care workers are tempted to and sometimes succumb to establishing their own classification of what the patient needs most. If we are aware that the area in which we work is a subcultural entity in itself, with a practice and language of its own, then this may be a beginning in developing a more sensitive cultural practice. To provide an environment where a patient does not feel threatened when asking questions or explaining their beliefs and needs will certainly open the door to better all round understanding and care.

Sadly, if the carer and the cared for are not in harmony with their aims, then the words of Solzhenitsyn's dialogue between doctor and patient are altogether too true: 'No sooner does a patient come to you than you begin to do all his thinking for him. After that, the thinking done by your standing orders, your five minute conferences, your programmes, your plans, and the honour of your medical department; and once again I become as a grain of sand, just as I was in the camp. Once again, nothing depends on me' (Solzhenitsyn, 1988).

## References

Ardener, S. (1982) *Perceiving Women*. London, Dent.

Barker Benfield, B. (1975) Sexual surgery in late nineteenth century America. *International Journal of Health Services* **5**, 279–298.

Bloch, M. and Parry, J. (1994) *Death and the Regeneration of Life*. Cambridge, Cambridge University Press.

Comaroff, J. (1982) Medicine, symbol and ideology. In: Wright, P. and Treacher, A. (eds) *The Problem of Medical Knowledge*. Edinburgh, Edinburgh University Press.

Egwuatu, V. (1981) Complications of female circumcision in Nigerian Igbos. *British Journal of Obstetrics and Gynaecology* **88**, 1090–1093.

El Dareer, A. (1983) Complications of female circumcision in the Sudan. *Tropical Doctor* **13**, 131–133.

Frazer, J.C. (1911) *The Golden Bough*. Tyrone, Coal Island.

Freedman, T. (1994) Social and cultural dimensions of hair loss in women treated for breast cancer. *Cancer Nursing* **17**(4), 334–341.

Hayley, A. (1992) *Roots*. London, Hutchinson.

Helman, C. (1992) *Culture, Health and Illness*. London, Wright.

Lacquer, T. (1987) Orgasm, generation and the politics of reproductive biology. In: Gallagher, C. and Lacquer, T. (eds) *The Making of the Modern Body: Sexuality and Society in the Nineteenth Century*. Chicago, University of Chicago Press.

Leach, E.R. (1968) 'Magical hair'. *Journal of the Royal Anthropological Institute* **77**, 164–167.

Macauliffe, A. (1909) *The Sikh Religion*. Oxford, Clarendon Press.

Mischler, E. (1986) *The Discourse of Medicine*. Cambridge, MA, Harvard University Press.

Morgenstern, J. (1966) *Rites of Birth, Marriage, Death and Kindred Occasions among Semites*. Chicago, Quadrangle.

Needham, R. (1981) *Belief, Language and Experience*. Chicago, University of Chicago Press.

Opie, I. and Tatum, M. (eds) (1989) *A Dictionary of Superstitions*. New York, Oxford University Press.

Ouaknin, M.A. (1992) *Meditations Erotiques*. Paris, Ballard.

Scheper Hughes, N. and Lock, M.M. (1987) The mindful body: a prolegomenon to future work in medical anthropology. *Medical Anthropology Quarterly* **1**, 6–41.

Smart, N. (1994) *The World's Religions*. Cambridge, Cambridge University Press.

Solzhenitsyn, A. (1988) *Cancer Ward*. London, Bodley Head.

Soyinka, W. (1992) *Myth, Literature and the African World*. Cambridge, Cambridge University Press.

Spector, R. (1991) *Cultural Diversity in Health and Illness*. New York, Appleton and Lange.

Strathern, A. (1994) Witchcraft, greed, cannibalism and death. In: Bloch, M. and Perry, J. (eds) *Deaths and the Regeneration of Life*. Cambridge, Cambridge University Press.

Szasz, T. (1989) Psychiatric justice. *British Journal of Psychiatry* **154**, 864–869.

Uberoi, J.P. (1992) Five symbols of Sikh identity. In: Madan, T.N. (ed.) *Religion in India*. New Delhi, Oxford India Paperback.

Volosinov, V.N. (1976) *Freudianism, A Critical Sketch* (translated by Titunik, I. and Bruss, N.). Bloomington, Indiana University Press.

Watson, J.L. (1994) Of flesh and bones. In: Bloch, M. and Parry, J. (eds) *Death and the Regeneration of Life*. Cambridge, Cambridge University Press.

Whorf, B.L. (1956) *Science and Linguistics in Language, Thought and Reality*. Cambridge, MA, Massachusetts Institute of Technology Press.

Wilkie, M. (1866) *Northern Counties Magazine* no. 83.

World Health Organisation (1986) A traditional practice that threatens health – female circumcision. *WHO Chronicle* **40**, 31–36.

**Further reading**

Bermant, C. (1974) *The Walled Garden – The Saga of Jewish Family Life and Tradition*. Jerusalem, Weidenfield and Nicholson.

Bleich, J.D. (1991) *In Vitro Fertilisation: Questions of Maternal Identity and Conversion*. Tradition **25**, 82–102.

Fletcher, A. (1993) The Hako, a Pawnee ceremony. *22nd Annual Report of the Bureau of Ethnology*, Washington, DC.

Lupton, D. (1994) *Medicine as Culture*. London, Sage Press.

MacCormack, C. and Strathern, M. (1980) (eds) *Nature, Culture and Gender*. Cambridge, Cambridge University Press.

Palos, S. (1971) *The Chinese Art of Healing*. New York, Herter and Herter.

Pearson, R. (1982) Understanding the Vietnamese in Britain: marriage, death and religion. *Health Visitor* **55**(9).

Rankin, J., Brown, A. and Gateshill, P. (1994) *Ethics and Religions*. London, Longman.

Rosner, F. (1979) Artificial insemination in Jewish law. In: Rosner, F. and Bleich B.D. (eds) *Jewish Bioethics*. New York, Sanhedrin Press, pp. 105–118.

Tripp Reimer, T. and Anna Afifi, L. (1989) Cross cultural perspectives on patient teaching. *Nursing Clinics of North America* **24**(3), 613–619.

## CHAPTER 5

# Altered body image in children

*Sue Cluroe*

Body image may also be referred to as self-image, self-concept and by a variety of other terms. Gross (1992) sees body image as one component of self-concept, as illustrated in Figure 5.1. As children develop physically, psychologically and socially throughout their young lives and all aspects are interdependent, it is difficult to divorce body image from the other aspects. This chapter will, therefore, explore the development of the self-concept as a whole

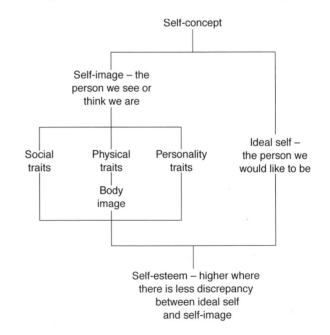

*Figure 5.1*   Relationship between body image and self-concept.

in children, how this affects their understanding of illness, hospitalization and disability, and the role of the nurse in minimizing the trauma that can result from such events.

Children are not isolated people. They are part of a family and a society where peers are an integral and important aspect. The effect of these on the child and of the child's problems on them will also be identified.

During childhood, many changes occur naturally, such as, growth in height and weight, changes in general appearance, sexual changes, which are all part of maturation that continually requires adjustments. However, some physical aspects are seen as more attractive than others, for example wide eyes and a pleasant smile, and some are dependent on another person's view, for example a girl with short, curly hair may see long straight hair as more desirable. Many problems can occur where society places value on certain characteristics, such as, when above average height is seen as desirable in boys but not in girls. This leaves boys who are short in stature prepared to endure a great deal of pain and discomfort in leg lengthening operations and procedures to achieve what is seen as preferable.

The difference between what a child would like to be and what they are partly determines our self-esteem: the greater the discrepancy the lower is their opinion of themselves. Argyle (1969) sees that this is influenced by:

1.  The reaction of others. Initially children are influenced by their immediate family, but as they get older, school and peers become increasingly important.
2.  Comparison with others. Some aspects, e.g. colour of skin is absolute, but height, weight and intelligence are variable. Children are continually looking at peers or media figures, and comparing their weight and size, which may lead to problems such as anorexia. Equally, if they decide they are not as clever as others and nothing is done to correct this, it may become part of a self-fulfilling prophecy.
3.  Social roles. As children develop, they incorporate more social roles from being part of a family, to becoming playmates, school friends and taking a part-time job, and these have an influence on self-concept development.
4.  Identification. As a child identifies with one parent or the other, with peers or other influences, this is incorporated into the ideal self and perhaps into the self-image. This is

particularly potent with media or sports persons who are seen as ideal. It can also become an important tool for the nurse who may use a personality as an example, for example Gary Mabbutt who has insulin-dependent diabetes and has played soccer for England can be a very useful role model for a soccer-mad boy newly diagnosed with diabetes with whom to identify.

The self-esteem formed in childhood remains with the child into adulthood. Coopersmith (1967) studied hundreds of boys aged 9–10 years and examined their self-esteem. Those with high self-esteem at that time continued to outperform the others in the group educationally and vocationally as adults. Whilst these were white, middle-class boys, Gross (1992) cites other research, which shows working-class and delinquent groups have a measurably lower self-esteem. In the case of the former, this again may indicate that role models are taken from areas, such as media or television with a resultant very different ideal self. It is against the background knowledge of the influences and the importance of fostering a high self-esteem, that the development of self-concept including body image should be explored.

**Stages of development in children**

The development of children is traditionally divided into age bands in recognition that they develop at different rates and, therefore, these age bands should be flexible. In the light of Argyle's (1969) idea that others affect self-concept, it is useful to use bands that reflect the varying influence: preschool (where family is the overriding domination); early school years (where teachers and peers may inspire); and adolescence (where peers and a sexually developing body are the prominent features).

*The preschool child (0–5 years)*

This period covers the first two stages of cognitive development described by the Swiss psychologist Jean Piaget: the sensorimotor stage (0–2 years); and the preoperational period (2–6 years).

In the former, children develop an understanding of their environment by relying on areas learnt through the senses, sight, touch, taste, etc. In the early months, they do not make a connection between their own actions and the outside world. However, by 4–8 months, they begin to realize that their behaviour affects the objects around them and, after the end of one year, children can imitate the actions of others around them. Towards the end of the sensorimotor stage, they appear to be able to manipulate mental images in their head and have developed a sense of perception.

Wong (1993) sees the early development of body image in a child evolving from the tactile experience. They learn about their world and themselves by touching objects and particularly as their bodies become useful for the development of motor skills, for example their hands are useful tools for grabbing a beloved teddy bear.

By the end of the first year, children have learnt that they are an object distinct from others, particularly their parents and that they can begin to operate independently, such as crawling and walking. They will desperately wish to exploit this independence in areas such as meal times. This idea of being a separate person also leads to an increased interest in his or her own image when looking in a mirror. By the age of 21 months, three-quarters of children studied by Lewis and Brooks (1978) would use their own name when looking at a photograph of themselves. This is the first time that a child will show realization that he or she has recognizable features. Soon after this the child develops self-conscious behaviours such as embarrassment (Lewis *et al.*, 1992). This can be seen as the initial stages of self-esteem, or the evaluation of the difference between self-image and ideal self.

By the time children reach 2 years of age at the time of transition from the sensorimotor to preoperational stage, they become aware of gender differences and, according to Bee (1995), are able to define themselves as big or little, good or bad. However, they see themselves as one or the other, not a mixture of both. The preoperational stage, according to Piaget (1970), is when children learns to use symbols (including words) to stand for something else. They are, therefore, able to increase the words they use to describe themselves, but still only externally. The words used may also be inaccurate, for example the child who, when told that a lady's fat tummy is due to her having a baby, asks the fat man if he is 'having a baby'.

The internal body also remains a mystery. The child sees invasive procedures, even those that do not affect the integrity of the skin, such as the taking of a temperature or examination of an ear, as traumatic. Painful procedures are as frightening as non-painful ones. It is also difficult for a child to understand how problems can be repaired, such as, how can an injection given in the buttock stop pain in the wrist, or something swallowed heal a cut foot. This makes it particularly challenging for the nurse who needs to explain to a boy why he is having surgery such as a hernia repair or orchidopexy. Children of this age are notably concerned with mutilation.

As more words are added to the child's vocabulary, along with widening experiences, they begin to recognize more qualities and differences. This can include skin colour and other features. They are particularly vulnerable to learning prejudicial views and the words to vocalize them, such as 'ugly'.

Towards the end of this period, the child is able to consider issues more concretely. Harter (1987) found that children could not take the global perspective – thinking in terms of an 'awful person' – but used visible characteristics, such as, looks or abilities rather than personality traits. This is also linked to gender perception, where external characteristics, such as, length of hair and clothing, appear to be the important cues.

Because children think concretely, they may appear cruel or rude in the remarks they make. They only see the difference from what has been learnt as the normal, with no understanding of how it could have evolved, such as, hair loss from chemotherapy. This would only be seen as 'everyone has hair, you don't, therefore you are odd'.

However, it is the feedback from primary care givers which expressly affects children with birth defects and these children are at risk of a distorted body image as a result. This importance on significant people remains with the child throughout their life.

*School age child (5–11 years)*

As the circle of friends and acquaintances widens, the child's self-concept develops through these interactions (Winkelstein, 1989). Zamberlan (1992) sees this development and that of its evaluative component, self-esteem, as one of the most important tasks of this time. Whilst parents remain important to children, the others in their lives become more significant, and Gross (1992) feels that the self-image becomes differentiated in that children believe their teachers about their school work but their parents about other issues.

Piaget describes this time as being in the third of his phases – concrete operational. The child develops a set of general rules (or concrete operations), such as, reversibility, serial ordering, classification and conservation. Children learn that actions can be reversible, for example when they go on holiday, they will return

home and the move is not permanent. Equally, they will understand more that pain from surgery will go eventually. This also
means they will become aware of permanency, that not everyone
recovers from illness and that death is permanent, as are some disfiguring marks such as scars. At this stage, the child will gradually,
therefore, become less concerned with pain and more with permanent disability.

A knowledge of classification develops through this period
which enables the child to place anything within a group, for
example, children who wear glasses, footballers, etc. Mosher and
Hornsby (1966) felt most children were able to classify by the age
of 8 years and all by 11 years. Following quickly on from this, children learn to serial order or place in a hierarchy such as tallest to
smallest. This enables a comparison with others and the developing concept of ideal self, which accounts for children as young as 7
years feeling that others are slimmer than they, with the resultant
development of anorexia at such a young age.

The ability to classify and compare also allows the child to
move to a more global perspective and include value judgments.
Research by Montemayor and Eisen (1977) found that 10–11-
year-olds could compare one aspect of themselves to another, for
example 'I am usually well behaved, but occasionally naughty. I am
good at drawing, but find sums hard'. The self-concept is, therefore, becoming more complex and, for some, difficult to understand.

As part of this complexity, children will compare themselves
with others. Differences become magnified, such as, ears that pro-
trude too much or sight problems necessitating the wearing of
glasses. This becomes particularly acute if other children make
unkind remarks. However, Wong (1993) feels the problems particularly occur if participation in activities such as sports or games
is affected. Teasing or criticism can affect the child's self-esteem
and remain a problem for life. Many children by the age of 9 or 10
have learnt mechanisms to cope with disability and fears, such as
participation in care or procedures. However, illness is still defined
in concrete terms and abstract ideas, such as psychological concerns, are difficult to comprehend. Many children will wish to
know the outcome in terms of physical issues, such as scarring,
inability to ride a bicycle, etc.

Also during this time, children are developing a knowledge of
the internal body including that some parts of the body are indis-
pensable, hence a fear of not getting better. Crider (1981) felt that

this knowledge commenced with considering bodily functions and only later progressed to the differentiation of organs. This would agree with Piaget and Inhelder's (1958) view that development occurs as a result of experiences. This would explain the apparent precociousness of some children with a chronic illness. However, this is not always the case.

Jones *et al.* (1992) state that, whilst research shows generally the increase in knowledge of internal anatomy occurs in the 8–10-year-old, studies have shown that some children with chronic illness can name less internal organs than well children. Variables could include the terms used or the quality of the interactions or communication in explaining their ill health to these children. It can be seen that children about to enter the adolescent phase have a growing idea of their body, and also their worth or value to themselves and others.

*The adolescent (11 years onwards)*

Adolescence is a time of great change. Petrillo and Sanger (1980) feel that teenagers are able to be resilient to the stress of the changes if they have a healthy self-esteem.

Piaget (1970) describes this period as the formal operational stage when the task is to develop a more powerful set of skills. Whilst previously the child had thought only about objects or facts which could be touched or seen, adolescents are thinking more abstractly, moving from the actual to the possible, imagining more and considering the consequences. School-age children would use inductive logic (using their own experience to move to a general principle) but teenagers begin to think deductively (to use a general principle to a specific case) and, therefore, increasingly can solve problems. However, many researchers, including Piaget, feel that not every child reaches this stage, and Keating (1980) estimated that only 50–60% in Western countries use formal operations. This becomes an important issue when considering the extensive research (cited by Puskar *et al.*, 1992), which identifies that, at times of stress, adolescents who attempt suicide are unable to solve problems. It may also suggest that those who are able to think systematically through an issue are able to trust their decision which in turn may be due to a higher self-esteem.

Because teenagers are more able to think abstractly, they are less bound by physical, external characteristics, although these do remain important. Montemayor and Eisen (1977) identified that 16–17-year-olds made reference to beliefs and abstract ideas, whilst Damon and Hart (1988) saw that by late adolescence, most describe themselves by referring to thought processes, standards and longer lasting traits. Their self-concept also becomes more flexible depending on their role – as a friend, a son or daughter, a student. They are also more flexible and abstract in their beliefs about gender. Rather than see male and female as very separate entities, teenagers are more able to consider the mixture of male and female traits in one person. However, peer pressure can affect which traits are displayed, as a masculine role leads to a high self-esteem owing to the approval of his friends, although Massad (1981) feels that girls with no masculine characteristics, such as assertiveness, have a lower self-esteem. This all comes at a time when sexual feelings and orientation are being explored, leading to confusion between heterosexuality and homosexuality.

Until the onset of the adolescent period, most physical changes have concerned issues such as height. However, as the teenager enters puberty, there are dramatic changes in appearances and shape, linked with very differing emotions. Wong (1993) sees this sudden growth leading to confusion and a loss of security from the familiar. As identified, adolescents think of themselves in terms of abstract traits but they have a growing awareness of appearances which are becoming more adult in nature. When asked what they did not like about themselves, Jersild (1952) found that it was the physical aspects which were listed by 60% teenagers. This widening discrepancy between what they are and what they want to be (the self-image and the ideal self) affects their self-esteem.

Teenagers are continually comparing themselves with their peers (such as when each girl first needs to wear a bra) and they feel threatened if they are too different from others. Erikson (1980) sees the area of development at this stage concerned with identity versus role confusion. The different bodily changes affect the old ideas and a new identity needs to be formed which will take account of the roles the soon-to-be adult will fulfil. In trying to identify a role for themselves, they form groups or cliques, excluding everyone different from themselves whether by colour, race or merely by dress (as in the 'Mods' and 'Rockers' of the 1960s). This group formation assists with a feeling of security, whilst their own beliefs may be examined.

Phinney (1990) found that in developing the self-concept concerning ethnic background and affiliation, adolescents work through a crisis which is often helped by having a good role model of their own culture to assist in defining the ideal self. If this is not possible, conflict may occur when the teenager takes on traits of another culture. This conflict is visible in Asian children who experience their own culture at home, but live in a Westernized culture at school.

Knowledge of the internal body shows not only increasing understanding of the whereabouts of organs but also the physiology involved. It is, therefore, only at this stage that a complete understanding of issue related to ill health can be obtained, for example, in diabetes (Bannard, 1987).

The advent of chronic disease or permanent physical disability has long-term consequences at this point in the life of the adolescent. Anything which sets them apart from their peers in the mastery of tasks or in the ability to participate is seen as a major problem, and consequently may affect their self-image throughout adulthood. Equally, because of the changing ideas about their body, issues which have been present may be viewed differently at this stage. One example is the child who has had diabetes since early childhood.

Owing to growth spurts and a changing lifestyle, the diabetes may need restabilizing. A greater understanding of the physiology has also added to the appreciation of long-term effects. Adolescents may then reassess the impact on their lifestyles and the differences that result between them and their peers, and may rebel against the situation. Further help and counselling will be required as this stage is reached.

As can be seen, the images children have of their bodies and themselves are intertwined. The ideas develop from initially only being what they can see or touch, through ideas of classification and grouping to someone who is different but wishes to be the same as others, whilst becoming a unique individual accepted by others. An increasing knowledge of what is happening to the internal body and the gender changes can cause confusion to even the most stable of lives. This is further complicated when depression, handicap, ill health or disfigurement are present.

## Assessment of body image and self-esteem

The assessment of body image, self-esteem and knowledge of body organs and working needs to be undertaken with care. This is partly due to the many aspects involved but also to the developmental process children undertake. It is generally accepted by research practitioners that a variety of tools or methods should be used, but these fall broadly into two categories, those which rely on drawings, others which require answers to questions or use unfinished statements which the child completes.

The Human Figure Drawing (HFD) has been used by many researchers. It involves examining drawings from three perspectives – the details of the body and clothing, the sizing of the figure and its placement on the page, and, finally, any differences to the drawing, such as, shading or erasing of areas. Because of the interpretation required, Offman and Bradley (1992) feel the tool is not sufficiently validated for its reliability, and needs to take more account of individual cognitive development.

The other major area where drawings are used is in the determination of knowledge of the internal body where an outline of a figure is presented to the child. The child is then asked to draw in the parts of the body.

The second category involves a list of questions, which, when the answers are analysed, give an overall score of self-concept or self-esteem. Various tools of this type exist. The Body–Self Relations Questionnaire (BSRQ) developed by Winstead and Cash (1984) assesses attitude in three areas (fitness, health and physical appearance). The Piers–Harris Children's Self-concept Scale (Piers, 1984) consists of 80 questions each requiring a Yes/No answer and has been used by many researchers to assess self-concept of a group of children with a given health problem. Zamberlan (1992) used Piers–Harris' tool along with one of her own to assess the quality of life following liver transplants in children. The Zamberlan tool consisted of 29 open-ended questions to elicit the subjective aspects of the transplant procedure, such as emotional adjustment.

It can be seen that a level of literacy is required to use these tools and they are, therefore, only appropriate for children from 8 years upwards. Even those in the younger areas of this range may need help in completing the questionnaires, which raises the issue of potential contamination of answers.

In studying the research around body image, self-esteem or self-concept in children, very few report the use of only one tool. Many consider that for validity purposes all areas should be explored.

*The effect of disfigurement*

Children are felt by some to adapt to disfigurement if it occurs early in their life (Stoddard *et al.*, 1992), although Wallace (1993) suggested that, even at this stage, without a self-concept fully developed, damage is considerable. Much of the damage occurs because the child places such enormous significance on peer-group approval, and, yet, Wallace (1993) found that the feeling was of people avoiding them and the resultant sense of isolation. The revulsion felt by others also decreased the self-esteem, even if it is only perceived revulsion rather than actual. The more significant the person showing the distaste, the more traumatic it becomes, therefore, parents are a particular influence in maintaining a positive body image.

Adolescents have a greater risk of depression, although it can occur at any age. However, Stoddard et al. (1992) found that the onset of the distress occurred after healing, the mean age at which the trauma occurred being 4.4 years with the onset of depression at a mean age of 9.2 years. This may also be precipitated by other issues such as family problems. The delay may also be due to the realization of the permanence of the blemish. Whilst most research has been undertaken in areas such as burns, accidents and major causes, it should be remembered that to a teenager the problems of acne allied to other bodily changes can be equally traumatic, and should not be ridiculed or minimized.

The effects of disfigurement last longer in teenagers, with Sutherland (1988) identifying phobic neurosis occurring four times longer than in adults, whilst Rivlin (1988) found that adolescents following burn injury had lower career aspirations. It should also be noted that, perhaps unsurprisingly, females with a disfigurement had lower self-esteem than males. This may be because such emphasis is placed in the media and society on physical attributes for girls, where boys may pass scarring off as a 'trophy'.

Children will deny the permanence of the disfigurement and may deny the cause. In this way, a form of bereavement will occur. Goffman (1963) described three coping strategies employed in these cases. Firstly, the flaw may be covered or hidden, for example, by growing hair longer. Secondly, the child may attempt to reduce the significance of the blemish. Finally, they may withdraw, thus increasing the risk of social isolation and depression.

## The effect of disability

Disability can be either learning difficulties or physical in nature, whilst the latter can be congenital (i.e. present at birth) or acquired. There has been little research into the body image or self-esteem of young people with learning disabilities, although work by Huntington and Bender (1993) demonstrated that they differ in their self-concept from normally achieving children, but difficulty occurs in measuring the variation. Huntington and Bender identified that some research suggests that adolescents with learning difficulties can show deficits, demonstrating higher anxiety levels and depression. Peck (1985) indicate those who are severely depressed tend to have a lower self-concept whilst others have demonstrated a potentially increased risk of suicide. Pfeffer (1986) suggests this is due to the inability to assess difficult situations accurately and determine a solution.

Of the physically disabled, Rousso (1984) feels those who have a congenital problem have never known themselves as existing any other way, therefore, do not think of themselves as helpless, and as a result have a higher self-esteem. This is thought to be because they see the problem as part of themselves and their identity. This is not always the case and even those with a congenital disability will have problems completing certain physical tasks which will at times lead to great frustration. If this is handled correctly, it can promote positive self-worth, but if dealt with badly can lead to increased inferiority.

These children also have increased body awareness. Anderson and Spain (1977) suggest even the more severely handicapped should undertake physical education activities, but these should be carefully planned to enhance the child's abilities. Darling (1979) would agree that not all congenitally disabled children have problems with self-esteem, particularly if the child has more positive experiences of this kind than negative.

Children with problems which would appear to be similar but with different causes may have differing outcomes, such as in those who have short stature. Fenning-Naisberg (1993) found that children with achondroplasia had poor self-concept which improved after leg elongation, whilst Drash *et al.* (1968) identified that those with dwarfism had no disturbance of their body image but saw themselves as a miniaturized version.

Rousso (1984) identifies that children with an acquired disability have a sense of loss which requires a period of mourning for the change in the body image. Keltikangas-Jarvinen (1987) agreed that, in the case of juvenile rheumatoid arthritis, a body image disturbance certainly took place.

One of the severest causes of disability is trauma resulting in serious head injury or spinal damage, which, of course, may be accompanied by disfigurement. The child has to relearn many skills and requires assistance at times. Worthington (1989) feels that this trauma is worse during adolescence when the major task is to gain independence but the injury is causing increased dependence. Inability to adapt to the new situation leads to poor self-esteem.

In the case of spinal injury without a head injury, Dewis (1989) found that adolescents would particularly attempt to maintain normalization in three areas – physical appearance (with the possibility of worrying more about this or losing interest), maintaining physical and emotional development (and thus requiring privacy), and, finally, maintaining social skills and interpersonal relationships. Coping mechanisms employed included wearing clothes which hid body changes and camouflaged bowel or bladder accidents, and adding decorations and gadgets to wheelchairs whilst talking about them like cars.

The major issue comes in interpersonal relationships. Dewis (1989) found some cut their circle of previous friends to two or three really 'close' ones whilst others cut all old friends out completely or maintained the briefest of contact. This area was also described as difficult for brain-injured adolescents. Worthington (1989) identified that these children became increasingly isolated from peers who continue to lead a normal life. This is particularly true if the brain injury results in behavioural disturbances or changes in appearance with which peers cannot cope. This isolation leads to a poor self-esteem over and above that caused by the trauma.

*Effect of chronic and life-threatening illness*

Many chronic illnesses requiring constant monitoring and medications, such as asthma and diabetes, may have little outward sign but can still affect the child's self-esteem. Indeed, Penn *et al.* (1971) observed a decreased self-concept in children with a chronic problem in the long term, whilst Park (1995) found that repeated asthma attacks led to alterations. Some of the latter cases may be due to body changes which may occur as a result of treatment with steroids or due to lack of exercise.

In part, the problem of repeated attacks may be the resultant guilt as their family's normal activities are restricted. Moen *et al.* (1977) certainly found that children with phenylketonuria displayed these emotions because of the special dietary requirements and this could equally be seen to be true of children with diabetes. Certainly, the family's acceptance not only of the problem but also the peripheral issues is as important to the child's self-esteem.

As with children with disability, the isolation from peers and repeated absences from school leading to a delay in accomplishing developmental tasks are seen by many as the major issues. Indeed, in Zamberlan's study (1992) of children following liver transplant showed, the fear of organ rejection is less than the worry of appearing different or falling behind their peers in ability. Much of the effect is related to the severity and duration of the condition. If the onset is rapid, there is little time for adjustment to the situation. Also, whilst any chance remains of a cure, a positive body image is maintained.

Burt (1995) found children immediately had a change of body image on being given the diagnosis of cancer, although Kellerman *et al.* (1980) and Jamison *et al.* (1986) both found that no difference had occurred, leading them to suspect that altered self-concept was not due solely to the diagnosis. This would agree with Mullis *et al.* (1992) who found in their research that there was no difference between children with leukaemia and those without in any area other than academic work and gender. Whilst the former could be seen as a result of missed education owing to repeated admissions and ill health, the latter issue showed that boys with chronic illness had a better self-image than girls – the opposite to that found in healthy children.

Adolescents with chronic or life-threatening illness remain dependent on parents for longer and the inability to meet this important developmental task along with uncertainty of eventual outcome adds to the isolation from peers. Kashani and Hakami (1982) found that the severest depression came from the side effects of treatment suggesting also that appearance has a great effect.

The longer term picture is also an important consideration as research by Gavaghan and Roach (1987) demonstrates that healthy children have higher aspirations for the future in areas such as career or marriage.

*The effects of abuse*    It is generally accepted that abuse lowers the body image and self-concept of children and this is shown within their drawings. They consistently omitted more body parts than children who were not abused. Young (1992) observed that sexual abuse particularly caused a lower self-esteem, which in turn increased depression and suicide. He felt this was especially so if the act was performed by a close relative as this caused the child to question their perception about themselves, others and the trust they placed. The resultant rejection they feel equates to the isolation from peers felt in cases of chronic illness. The child questions their body integrity complicated by general lack of understanding of the body with the boundary between 'inside' and 'outside' crossed. Many have talked about dissociation between mind and body at the time of sexual abuse, and this can lead to the self as being the mind with the body as the receptacle, which is damaged and hated. This in turn may lead to self-abuse of the body or anorexia.

The child feels unable to prevent the abuse, which in turn makes them hate themselves more. They may even feel that they have been so naughty that they deserve the punishment and it is all their own fault. This all causes a downward spiral of the self-esteem. However, this is not an irreversible problem as much of the work undertaken with abused young people shows it is possible to improve their self-concept.

## The influence of the parents

As already identified, children are influenced by the attitude of the significant people in their lives, particularly parents. They are often watching for non-verbal responses, the looks, the body language, which may show approval or revulsion, which in turn will inform them of the views of others concerning their body image. However, parents often have their own thought processes and difficulties.

Many parents when given a diagnosis of disability or life-threatening illness need to mourn the loss of their perfect child. As part of this bereavement process, the parents may attempt to blame others or themselves, and will certainly feel guilt at being unable to protect their child. The whole family will, therefore, be placed under great strain, which may make the child feel guilty for disrupting everyone's lives.

Parents of children with a life-threatening illness may have difficulty in balancing the fear of losing the child and fear of the required treatment. This according to Roskies (1972) forces parents to remain silent about the future as they do not know what to expect. This concern is often transmitted to the child which may explain the lower aspirations children have on issues such as a career.

Children have a need to please their parents and, in turn, parents need to display pride. However, society views disability and chronic ill health in a negative way, and this social embarrassment adds to the stress felt by all members of the family. Despite this, if children are encouraged to master tasks within the range of their ability, it enables these needs to be met and a more positive self-esteem will result.

*Result of low self-esteem in children and adolescents*

Children, just like their parents, may go through a period of bereavement as the result of loss of self-esteem. This includes displays of anger which may be directed at the family, peers, nursing staff or the person they identify as the cause of the problem. Equally, they may show signs of depression which Whitfield *et al.* (1995) identifies as manifesting in disruptive behaviour, truancy or eating disorders.

Winkelstein (1989) discusses the results of low self-esteem as involving self-destructive behaviours, such as drug or solvent abuse, and this may particularly occur as a result of the anger being directed inwards. Reder *et al.* (1991) also identifies self-harm occurring as a result of the loss of self-esteem or due to a problem in a relationship. This may occur because of the sense of isolation from significant people in their life and will be further complicated if these are people who have previously enhanced self-concepts. This self-harm may result in a suicide attempt following when a negative attitude from the nurse may add to the downward spiral.

Puskar *et al.* (1992) actually see suicide occurring as a result of an inability to solve problems. Lack of skills in this area may in turn be due to lack of confidence in their own ability as a result of low self-esteem. This illustrates the lack of coping mechanisms which the child possesses both owing to the level of cognitive development and poor self-concept. As part of the anger, the long-term feeling of hopelessness and the self-harm activities, non-compliance in treatment can occur, which Price (1994) sees as a potential of altered body image. This may also be the only method the child has to demonstrate some control over their situation and needs to be recognized as such.

The long-term effects, as already identified, may be chronic substance abuse or low career aspirations. However, if provided with coping mechanisms and empowerment, the child can demonstrate a positive role with acceptance of the situation. These are often the young people honoured in the annual 'Children of Courage' or similar awards who show the personality to meet and overcome their problems with high self-esteem. Nurses should be aware that even these children may have periods of depression.

*The role of the nurse*

Nurses working with children and adolescents must firstly have an understanding of the normal development of their patient in all aspects – physical, psychological, social and spiritual, including development of body image and self-concept. This will also assist in understanding internal body image, which enables explanations to be given in a way the child will understand. In attempting to assess the child, the nurse should be aware of a low self-concept and the causes, but without specific training should not attempt to 'read' the child's drawings as part of this assessment.

Self-esteem is certainly linked to the quality of any interaction, particularly with significant people. Peers should be encouraged to visit the patient and talk openly, as should the family. The nurse must help them deal with anxiety, showing empathy for their fears. Also, in discussing the issues in an honest manner with the child, the nurse may act as a role model for parents who are afraid of their child's reactions or of hurting them even though they may realize that silence is worse.

One way to establish the trust required to build a therapeutic relationship is to reduce the number of nurses who work with the child and family. Neff and Beardslee (1990) certainly felt that the specialist oncology nurse prevented too great a loss of self-esteem in the children. Equally, in a more general area this should be within the sphere of the primary nurse.

Good communication skills should be a requirement of all nurses with non-verbal aspects needing specific attention. As already identified, children are aware of revulsion and isolation, and will watch the face of the nurse for any cues. Children also need to talk through their feelings, therefore, listening with full attention is essential, with a response which is acceptable but honest. Verbal communication is also important with praise given for achievements without condescension. One very positive way to help the child is the promotion of humour about the situation, although timing of this is vital, as the child will not accept this if still angry or depressed. Listening is also necessary for children who have been abused, as this shows belief in what they are saying which in itself is therapeutic. Being believed will raise their opinion of themselves and, therefore, their self-concept, and removes the feeling of isolation.

The other major role of the nurse is, according to Dewis (1989), the teaching of coping mechanisms. This can be achieved in a variety of ways but perhaps the initial target should be empowerment of the child, assisting them to achieve assertiveness and a feeling of self-worth. This has been particularly successful in cases of abuse and is the method used, for example, by helplines. By considering the child holistically, positive aspects and abilities can be highlighted and praised.

Promoting self-care and reducing the dependence, particularly in adolescents, is vital according to Worthington (1989), with assistance required in developing a new role. This may need the skills of a trained counsellor working as part of the multidisciplinary team, but is important if the child is to maintain expectations for the future. As part of this the nurse should promote hope whilst being honest and realistic. This may also require the potential example of a famous role model, appropriate to the child's situation.

The nurse can also help the child to challenge negative attitudes both in themselves and others, including society. This gives the child a positive feeling about themselves and their ability to act as a role model for others.

**Summary**

This chapter has explored the development of the concepts of body image, self-concept and self-esteem in children and adolescents. It can be seen that all are interlinked. Research has shown the impact of illness, disability and abuse on the fragility of the child can have far-reaching effects. The nurse has a vital role in prevention of harm and this should be seen as of as great an importance as other aspects of safety, health promotion and nursing care.

**References**

Anderson, E. and Spain, B. (1977) *The Child with Spina Bifida.* London, Methuen and Co Ltd.

Argyle, M. (1969) Cited in Gross (1992).

Bannard, J. (1987) Children's concepts of illness and bodily function: implications for health service providers caring for children with diabetes. *Patient Education and Counselling* **9**, 275–281.

Bee, H. (1995) *The Growing Child.* London, Harper Collins.

Burt, K. (1995) The effects of cancer on body image and sexuality. *Nursing Times* **91**(7), 36–37.

Coopersmith, S. (1967) Cited in Gross (1992).

Crider, C. (1981) Children's conceptions of the body interior. In: Bibace, R. and Walsh, M. (eds) *Children's Conceptions of Health, Illness and Bodily Functions*. San Francisco, Jossey-Bass.

Damon, W. and Hart, D. (1988) *Self Understanding in Childhood and Adolescence*. Cambridge, Cambridge University Press.

Darling, R. (1979) *Families against Society. A Study of Reactions to Birth Defects*. London, Sage.

Dewis, M. (1989) Spinal cord injured adolescents and young adults: the meaning of body changes. *Journal of Advanced Nursing* **14**, 389–396.

Drash, P., Greenberg, N. and Money, J. (1968) In: Cheek, D. (ed.) *Human Growth, Body Composition, Cell Growth, Energy and Intelligence*. Philadelphia, Lea and Febiger. pp. 568–581.

Erikson, E. (1980) *Identity and the Life Cycle*. New York, W.W. Norton.

Fennig-Naisberg, S., Fennig, S., Ganel, A., Sack, J. and Tyano, S. (1993) Body image of achondroplastic children before and after leg elongation. *Israel Journal of Psychiatry and Related Sciences* **30**(1), 33–39.

Gavaghan, M. and Roach, J. (1987) Ego identity development in adolescents with cancer. *Journal of Pediatric Psychology* **12**, 202–212.

Goffman, E. (1963) *Stigma – Notes on the Management of Spoiled Identity*. Englewood Cliffs, NJ, Prentice Hall.

Gross, R. (1992) *Psychology, The Science of Mind and Behaviour*, 2nd edn. London, Hodder and Stoughton.

Harter, S. (1987) The determinations and mediational role of global self-worth in children. In: Eisenberg, N. (ed.) *Contemporary Topics in Developmental Psychology*. Chichester, Wiley-Interscience.

Huntington, D. and Bender, W. (1993) Adolescents with learning disabilities at risk? Emotional well-being, depression, suicide. *Journal of Learning Disabilities* **26**(3), 159–166.

Jamison, R., Lewis, S. and Burish, T. (1986) Psychological impact of cancer on adolescents: self-image, locus of control, perception of illness and knowledge of cancer. *Journal of Chronic Disease* **39**, 609–617.

Jersild, A. (1952) *The Psychology of Adolescence*, 2nd edn. London, Macmillan.

Jones, E., Badger, T. and Moore, I. (1992) Children's knowledge of internal anatomy. *Journal of Pediatric Nursing* **7**(4), 262–268.

Kashani, J. and Hakami, N. (1982) Depression in children and adolescents with malignancy. *Canadian Journal of Psychiatry* **27**, 474–477.

Keating, D. (1980) Thinking processes in adolescence. In: Adelson, J. (ed.) *Handbook of Adolescent Psychology*. Chichester, Wiley.

Kellerman, J., Zeltzer, L. and Ellenberg, L. (1980) Psychological effects of illness in adolescence. *Journal of Pediatrics* **97**, 126–131.

Keltikangas-Jarvinen, L. (1987) Body image disturbances ensuing from juvenile rheumatoid arthritis. *Perceptual and Motor Skills* **64**, 984.

Lewis, M. and Brooks, J. (1978) Self knowledge and emotional development. In: Lewis, M. and Rosenblum, L. (eds) *The Development of Affect*. New York, Plenum.

Lewis, M., Allesandri, S. and Sullivan, M. (1992) Differences in shame and pride as a function of children's gender and task difficulty. *Child Development* **63**, 630–638.

Massad, C. (1981) Sex role identity and adjustment during adolescence. *Child Development* **52**, 1290–1298.

Moen, J., Wilcox, R. and Burns, J. (1977) PKU as a factor in the development of self-esteem. *Journal of Pediatrics* **90**, 1027–1029.

Montemayor, R. and Eisen, M. (1977) The development of self-conceptions from childhood to adolescence. *Developmental Psychology* **13**, 314–319.

Mosher, F. and Hornsby, J. (1966) On asking questions. In: Bruner, J., Olver, R. and Greenfield, P. (eds) *Studies in Cognitive Growth*. Chichester, Wiley.

Mullis, R., Mullis, A. and Kerchoff, N. (1992) The effect of leukaemia and its treatment on self-esteem of school age children. *Maternal–Child Nursing Journal* **20**(3,4), 155–165.

Neff, E. and Beardslee, C. (1990) Body knowledge and concerns of children with cancer compared with the knowledge and concerns of other children. *Journal of Pediatric Nursing* **5**(3), 179–189.

Offman, H. and Bradley, S. (1992) Body image of children and adolescents and its measurement: an overview. *Canadian Journal of Psychiatry* **37**(August), 417–422.

Park, S. (1995) Psychological aspects of the management of asthma in children. *Clinical Paediatrics* **3**(2), 419–427.

Peck, M. (1985) Crisis intervention treatment with chronically and acutely suicidal adolescents. In: Peck *et al.* (eds) *Youth Suicide*. New York, Springer-Verlag.

Penn, I., Bunch, D., Oleniik, D. and Abouna, G. (1971) Psychiatric experience with patients receiving renal and hepatic transplants. *Seminars in Psychiatry* **3**(1), 133–144.

Petrillo, M. and Sanger, S. (1980) *Emotional Care of Hospitalised Children*, 2nd edn. Philadelphia, Lippincott.

Pfeffer, C. (1986) *The Suicidal Child*. New York, Guilford Press.

Phinney, J. (1990) Ethnic identity in adolescents and adults: review of research. *Psychological Bulletin* **108**, 499–514.

Piaget, J. (1970) Piaget's theory. In: Mussen, P. (ed.) *Manual of Child Psychology*. Chichester, Wiley.

Piaget, J. and Inhelder, B. (1958) *The Psychology of the Child*. New York, Basic Books.

Piers, E. (1984) *Piers–Harris Children's Self-concept Scale: Revised Manual 1984*. Los Angeles, Western Psychological Services.

Price, B. (1994) The asthma experience: altered body image and non-compliance. *Journal of Clinical Nursing* **3**, 139–145.

Puskar, K., Hoover, C. and Miewald, C. (1992) Suicidal and non-suicidal coping methods of adolescents. *Perspectives in Psychiatric Care* **28**(2), 15–20.

Reder, P., Lucey, C. and Fredman, G. (1991) The challenge of deliberate self-harm by young adolescents. *Journal of Adolescence* **14**(2), 135–148.

Rivlin, E. (1988) The psychological trauma and management of severe burns in children and adolescents. *British Journal of Hospital Medicine* **40**(3), 210–215.

Roskies, E. (1972) *Abnormality and Normality – The Mothering of Thalidomide Children*. Ithaca, Cornell University Press.

Rousso, M. (1984) Disabled yet intact: guidelines for work with congenitally physically disabled youngsters and their parents. *Child and Adolescent Social Work* **1**(4), 254–269.

Stoddard, F., Stroud, L. and Murphy, M. (1992) Depression in children after recovery from severe burns. *Journal of Burn Care Rehabilitation* **13**(3), 340–347.

Sutherland, S. (1988) Burned adolescents' description of their coping strategies. *Heart Lung* **17**, 150–156.

Wallace, E. (1993) Nursing a teenager with burns. *British Journal of Nursing* **2**(5), 278–281.

Wong, D. (1993) *Whaley and Wong's Essentials of Paediatric Nursing*, 4th edn. St Louis, Mosby.

Whitfield, W., Leeming, M. and Papworth, P. (1995) Stemming the rising tide. *Paediatric Nursing* **7**(4), 16–17.

Winkelstein, M. (1989) Fostering positive self-concept in the school-age child. *Pediatric Nursing* **15**(3), 229–233.

Winstead, B. and Cash, T. (1984) Cited in Offman, H. and Bradley, S. (1992).

Worthington, J. (1989) The impact of adolescent development on recovery from traumatic brain injury. *Rehabilitation Nursing* **14**(3), 118–122.

Young, L. (1992) Sexual abuse and the problem of embodiment. *Child Abuse and Neglect* **16**, 89–100.

Zamberlan, K. (1992) Quality of life in school-age children following liver transplantation. *Maternal-Child Nursing Journal* **20**(3,4), 167–229.

CHAPTER 6

# Altered body image and disability

*Jan Dewing*

**Introduction**

Traditional medical explanations would suggest that disabled people have an altered body image stemming from visible or non-visible physical impairment. Drench (1994), Gillies (1984) and others suggest that anyone who becomes ill or sustains an injury experiences change and loss, including an alteration in body image. It is also widely assumed that disabled people find it difficult to achieve and maintain psychological wellness owing to their physical impairments (Noh and Posthuma, 1990). However, most of the literature on illness and altered body image has not specifically considered physical disability or the experience of disability in its wider context. There is literature on altered body image associated with certain illnesses or conditions, such as, breast cancer and following mastectomy, bowel disease and stoma formation, and following facial disfigurement. There is little literature on body image with motor neurone disease, multiple sclerosis, spinal injury, muscular dystrophy and cerebal palsy, for example.

It is necessary to examine the literature critically that is generally available to consider if it applies to disability, especially, as will be argued in this chapter, given that the social and cultural experiences of people with disabilities can be very different from non-disabled people. Body image and the experience of disability must not be solely considered from the context of the body image but from the context of the disability experience, which in itself is socially and culturally determined.

It would, on first inspection, appear obvious that, if individuals have an altered body presentation, such as many people with a physical disability have, then they would experience an altered body image. This may be true in many cases. However, this must not be assumed. For example, Sammonds and Cammermeyer (1989) found that some people with multiple sclerosis (MS) had a high degree of satisfaction with their body image and sometimes people with more advanced MS had higher degrees of satisfaction than those with less severe manifestations of MS. If nurses and other health care workers are to offer a non-discriminating service to disabled people, then they must be aware of their own views about disability and against what 'norm' disabled people are being compared with or fitted into. Why should it automatically be assumed disabled people have an altered body image? Wassner (1982), amongst others, suggests that one of the variables influencing adjustment to a change in altered body image is the knowledge, attitudes and behaviours of health care workers. This variable has more prominence where the health care worker has a relationship with the patient that is regarded by the patient as being significant. Given this is true, then it is important nurses and other health care workers are knowledgeable about body image in the context of the patient's health, social and cultural experiences.

This chapter aims to:

- Consider body image in the context of disability.
- Provide an overview of some of the factors that may influence body image in people with physical disability.
- Raise some questions about the applicability of existing knowledge in the context of altered body image and disability.
- Offer some suggestions about the areas of knowledge and skill nurses may need to develop.

**The experience of disability**

It is extremely difficult and somewhat naive to believe we can imagine what it is like to be disabled, but we can begin to think about what it must be like for disabled people to experience disability within our culture. There is a plethora of literature, especially by disabled people, that describes their experiences of disability. This literature offers a variety of perspectives on the experience of disability and how physical disability and people with disabilities are perceived by non-disabled people. Evans cited in Morris (1991 p. 19) has identified a number of assumptions abled bodied people hold about disabled people. Several of these refer to the body. For example:

- Disabled people feel ugly, inadequate and embarrassed.
- Disabled people crave to be normal.
- Disabled people desire to emulate abled bodied people in appearance.
- Disabled people have been affected psychologically because of physical impairment.

The normal that is being referred to is that of non-disabled or abled bodied. Most non-disabled people can be very sensitive about suggestions that they are prejudiced, let alone actively discriminate against disabled people. This is especially so now that awareness of disability issues is becoming more common both in society and in nursing education. Nurses are no exception to this. The experience of disability is not one that can be understood by thinking only about the physical pathology or impairment. Non-disabled people can begin to come to an understanding of the experience of disability when they refer to and take account of the historical processes that have led to the current cultural images of disability and disabled people (Oliver, 1990 p. 76). Often non-disabled people have views about disability and the disabled that have become embedded in our individual and social consciousness. Given the position of nurses, the power and influence they can have with disabled people, it is essential nurses examine their own views, both as non-disabled members of society and from the context of health workers.

One of the things most of us take for granted is that we are generally like everyone else. Often small differences, such as, our height, weight or body shape, can seem overwhelming and yet more often than not, without being conscious of it, we know we are reasonably normal. We become more aware of this when we notice others who are dissimilar to a greater degree than the social and cultural norms allow for. These *others* stand out as being different in some way. They may make us feel uncomfortable because it reminds us that we are 'normal' and they are not. The body presentation and appearance is reflected in and is a reflection of social norms. At its most basic, physically disabled people are seen as having bodies that are of little or no value. As our society places a high value on the body, especially its physical presentation, disabled people are not considered part of what is normal. The concept of spread then comes into action. Because negative values are ascribed to the physical presentation of the disabled, the same or similar negative values are then attached to psychological, emotional and intellectual characteristics of disabled people. Thus the disabled person becomes worthless and redundant socially and culturally.

There are social and cultural norms about what is acceptable and about what can be considered as ideal in terms of body image. Disabled people may find that their actual body presentation is considered less than acceptable against non-disabled norms, therefore, it becomes impossible for disabled people to achieve anywhere near to an ideal when judged by non-disabled norms. Achieving an acceptable appearance is very important in our society. We know that Goffman (1963), cited in Janelli (1993), identifies physical difference as one form of stigma. Price (1986) states that, in our society, the ideal is based around images of youth, beauty, vigour, intactness and good health. All of these attributes carry physical implications. Many factors interact to influence the creation and reproduction of these social and cultural norms, including the media, clothing and fashion industries. Where do disabled people see themselves represented in these images and, if there are any images, are they positive representations?

Non-disabled people perhaps strive to fall somewhere between what is acceptable and what is ideal, both on an individual level and a social/cultural level. Assuming we hold the view that disabled people have an altered body image because of their physical differences, what then do they strive to achieve, in terms of body image? Do they aim to achieve what is considered acceptable by a non-disabled society or do they aim for an ideal as well, and is that ideal a non-disabled one or something else of their own creation? How much does the cultural *norm* of non-disabled society influence ideals and expectations in disabled people? Does this differ between people with congenital and acquired disabilities? These are some of the questions that need to be considered if nurses are to be confident that existing ideas and theories about body image can be applied to people with physical disabilities. No doubt there are also other questions that can be put forward for consideration. Asking questions like this will serve a dual purpose as it helps nurses to raise awareness about their own unexplored attitudes to disability, and to uncover just how deeply socialization processes have discounted disabled people or discriminated against disability and disabled people.

In a review of a number of empirical studies, Bordieri *et al.* (1983) demonstrate the importance of physical attractiveness in impression formation. They refer to studies that show a positive correlation between physical attractiveness and impressions in success with job interviews, college work and social popularity. Social norms such as this still operate in the context of the nurse–patient relationship and delivery of health care.

Nordholm (1980) has demonstrated that the degree of physical attractiveness influenced first impressions health workers had of patients. Using photographs, a sample of 289 workers, of whom approximately 25% were nurses, were asked to give their impressions about a range of people of different ages and with different physical characteristics. The more attractive individuals were ascribed more positive personality attributes. They were described as probably being more co-operative, approachable and motivated. They were thought to be less complaining, less aggressive, more intelligent, responsible, pleasant and trusting.

Other authors (such as Stockwell, 1972) have identified the concept of the popular and unpopular patient. The nurses basing their value judgements on a variety of personal and physical characteristics held by the patients. Disabled people can also be included in this framing and perhaps they may be doubly disadvantaged. Bordieri *et al.* (1983) found that physically attractive victims following car accidents were perceived to have a better prognosis for recovery than were physically unattractive victims. This research was based on verbal information and not the use of photographs. The study demonstrates that, simply from hearing verbal information, the subjects formed images and made impressions about the victims. Being influenced in this way does not necessarily mean that nurses would behave in discriminatory ways towards disabled people, although it is possible that unless nurses were self-aware and reflective about themselves and their practice that they could be influenced by first impressions to the point that it would in some way influence how they behaved with patients. One of the interesting points is to consider what it is that enables first impressions to take hold so easily. It could be supposed that earlier socialization processes, of which we are not always fully aware, have influenced us. Once again this highlights the need for nurses to develop their self-awareness in relation to their attitudes and beliefs about disability.

Morris (1993) states:

'. . . *disabled people are not normal in the eyes of non–disabled people. Our physical and intellectual characteristics are not "right" or "admirable" and we do not "belong". Having given such a negative meaning to abnormality, the non-disabled world assumes that we wish to be normal, or to be treated as if we were. It is supposedly progressive and liberating to ignore our differences because these differences have such negative meanings for non-disabled people. But we are different. We reject the meanings that the non-disabled world attaches to disability but we do not reject the differences which are such an important part of our identities'.*

In this quotation, Morris appears to be reclaiming the right to be different and to have pride in that difference. Furthermore, she is arguing that it is disabled people who will redefine and give new meanings to the differences. Therefore, non-disabled people will need to learn from disabled people. These assertions are very similar to those made by the lesbian and gay rights movement. Morris's quote would also suggest that existing theories do not fully explain the meaning of disability from the perspective of disabled people.

In his book *The Politics of Disability*, Oliver (1990 p. 63) argues that disability is an ideological construction and that the construction has been undertaken by non-disabled people from within their own social and cultural norms. Oliver uses the concepts of adjustment and stigma as examples to demonstrate how some successive theories have been built on established ideologies that do not provide a useful or accurate description of disabled people. It is interesting to note how frequently nurses refer to models of adjustment, coping and stigma when trying to make sense of changes owing to illness and disability. Perhaps we need to re-examine the validity of these ideas and theories. There is growing evidence to suggest that supposedly research-based knowledge used in an attempt to explain features and implications of disability has in fact never been researched directly with disabled people (Oliver, 1990 p. 66). It has instead been collected by anecdotal means, such as the research by Daniel (1976, cited in Noh and Posthuma, 1990) in which the author suggested disabled people had a significantly higher rates of depression than non-disabled people.

It has been argued that the experience of disability is fundamentally influenced by social and cultural factors. Any serious consideration of body image within the context of physical disability must give due acknowledgment to two important points.

Firstly, the literature on body image that is generally available to nurses is written by non-disabled people who, therefore, present a view of disability and body image from the outside in. There is nothing intrinsically wrong with writing from the outside in (as I am doing), but it must be taken into account that the view may be distorted or at least limited in terms of its usefulness. This approach needs to be balanced with academic work produced by those on the inside (i.e. people with disabilities). Secondly, disability is not a medical, nursing or individual problem, but instead it is more of a social and cultural construction. Nurses must be critical of existing perspectives about disability, especially where the literature considers aspects of impairment and disability in reductionist ways.

How disabled people see themselves can affect the way in which they identify problems in their life (Finkelstein, 1993 p. 9). Some disabled people, given the immense social pressures to appear young, intact and beautiful, must desire to look and feel differently, as indeed many non-disabled people do. It must be considered that the pressures faced by disabled people could be more intense. Craving to be normal is likely to result in greater dissatisfaction with body image, whilst an acceptance and pride in difference may lead to a greater satisfaction with existing body image. Rage and anger against society for its attitude to people with disability may be wrongly interpreted by nurses as a failure by the patient to adapt to their disability.

Non-disabled people often begin from the assumption that disabled people want to conform to a 'normal' image based on non-disabled norms. This assumption can filter into nursing and health care. Finkelstein (1993 p. 14) argues that rehabilitation and the publicity surrounding it promotes the aim of normalizing disabled peoples' appearances and behaviours. Sutherland cited by French (1993 p. 46) believes that disabled people are put under pressure to conform. Sutherland goes on to say that this is one of the main reasons for the manufacture of elaborate prosthetic limbs and other technological devices. The use of surgical cosmetics could also be included. Take an example of an adult who having had a mid thigh amputation declined to use a prosthesis and aimed instead to make use of a wheelchair to achieve his mobility. How might nurses respond to this approach by the patient? The wearing of prostheses and cosmetics is an extremely contentious and deeply personal area. I am not arguing that people with an altered or changing body image should not use cosmetics or prostheses if this is what they want, and I am certainly not suggesting it is in any way wrong to do so. Instead, I am raising awareness of the pressures put upon disabled people and people with any form of altered body image, by a non-disabled society, to conform to non-disabled norms, in all aspects of their lives, including body presentation and body image. Non-disabled people, especially nurses, need to consider other and different perspectives than the current existing ones which tend to stem from an able-bodied view.

There are many ways in which non-disabled norms or culture can pervade the lives of disabled people once they come into contact with health care services. Blackwood (1978) commented that hospitals can cure illnesses but often at great expense to the disability. There are accounts written by disabled people that show how many hospital staff and hospital environments can not cope with the needs of disabled people. There are several accounts that describe traumatic rehabilitation programmes where disabled people have been expected to fit into prescribed norms. Finkelstein (1988 p. 4) describes how, following a spinal cord injury, he spent 'endless soul-destroying hours' trying to approximate to able-bodied standards by 'walking' with calipers and crutches when he would rather have made use of a wheelchair and spent his energy on other activities. Yet many nurses would perhaps take a dim view of someone who wanted to use a wheelchair when, with effort, they could walk. Nurses hold great store in physical independence, so this being the norm, it is applied to disabled people. Therefore, disabled people must attempt to achieve our norm despite the effort and loss of energy it may take. In a study about the experiences of physically disabled people in acute hospital wards, Atkinson and and Sklaroff (1987) found that less than 1% of nurses had any special preparation of nursing people with physical disabilities. This often meant that disabled people became more disabled as a result of being nursed in poorly adapted environments by nurses with poor awareness and knowledge. The study suggested that nurses would benefit from a greater awareness of the practical difficulties faced by disabled people.

**Body image and disability**

It has been discussed why it can not be assumed that disabled people have an altered body image. There is also a need to clarify what is meant by an altered body image or at least to be clear that an altered body image is not considered as an abnormal body image. This is especially important in the context of physical disability, given the dominance of negative social and cultural images of disability. The use of the word 'altered' is misleading because it seems to suggest that some state or condition has been arrived at, and that something has been completed. It could also suggest that there has been a mutation or deterioration of some sort. It is important that nurses do not have any of these ideas about body image in the context of physical disability. Whereas it would seem more positive to perceive the baseline of body image as always altering throughout the course of life as part of the usual life and ageing processes regardless of disability or non-disability (Fitzgerald-Miller, 1992 p. 138; Grunbaum, 1985; Janelli, 1986). Then body image can further alter with illness, injury and disability (Gillies, 1984; Drench, 1994). It may be more useful to consider body image in terms of the alterations, diversities, variations or changes that can be experienced rather than perceiving it as altered.

The literature contains competing information about body image changes and the experience of disability which leads to the conclusion that it can not be assumed disabled people have an altered body image by virtue of being disabled, either by acquired or congenital means. Stensman (1989) looked at individuals with acquired disabilities and those with congenital disabilities, all of whom were wheelchair users and all of whom required assistance with activities of daily living, and found no differences regarding body image. Furthermore, when compared with a non-disabled control group, the degree of satisfaction or dissatisfaction with the body was not significantly different.

In multiple sclerosis (MS), there can be a range of physical and psychological changes that take place in the body that can affect body image. So it can be assumed that people with MS will experience an altered body image as Gould (1983) suggests. Despite the abundance of medical research on MS, there is little research on MS and body image. Samonds and Cammermeyer (1989) carried out a descriptive study to examine the perceived body image of persons with MS, and the relationship between body image and the severity of physical disability. Satisfaction with the body was established by using Secord and Jourard's Body-cathexis Scale and the Self-cathexis Scale. Kurtzke's Status Disability Scale was used to measure the degree of physical disability. There are limitations to the methodology which should be considered, in that the subjects were all elderly males ($n = 20$), although the authors do indicate that no inferences should be drawn from their small-scale study. The results of this study show that the majority of subjects (55%) were satisfied with their bodies. Subjects who were satisfied with their bodies and selves were older, had had MS longer and were more disabled. It could be assumed that, the greater the physical changes occurring in the body, then the more dissatisfaction there would be with the body image. However, it may be that there are other psychological changes that offset the effects of altered body image. The Samonds and Cammermeyer study shows that it is not necessarily the actual changes that occur in the body or the body image, but the way in which they are perceived by the individual that matters. Lacey and Birtchnell (1986) also support this assumption.

As Salter (1988) states, what constitutes a change in body image for one person may not be the same for another. Research by Janelli (1993) indicates that different tools show different results in body image between men and women. Other authors would suggest this is due to gender and age differences. Young adults with spinal cord injuries tend to have intense feelings about appearing normal and achieving normal physical functioning according to Dewis (1989), whilst these were not so important for the spinal-injured subjects in Stensman's study. Different aspects of body image may be important for people with different disabilities or impairments, for example, Maycock (1988) describes the importance of appearance of the hands and face for people with rheumatism. Furthermore, when body image is considered alongside issues of sexuality (homosexuality and heterosexuality), self-esteem and self-concept, it becomes more or less clear how to isolate body image.

Gould (1983) asserted the most common nursing diagnosis in a cohort of 15 people with MS was a disturbance of self-esteem caused by an altered body image. There were only seven subjects who were diagnosed as having a disturbance of self-esteem and these diagnoses originated from the nurses' assessment rather than directly from the disabled persons' own perceptions. How did the nurses assess the patients' body image? Did they obtain information directly or indirectly? Was it from what the patients said or did? Was it a general comment made by the patient or specifically in the context of the nurse discussing with the patient their feelings about their body? It could be argued that assessing body image could be likened to assessing patients' sexuality. It is not really done because it is a tricky area for nurses to feel comfortable and confident with, so information is gleaned indirectly. Often a casual comment made on a single occasion by patients can be given too much significance. On the other hand, patients may say things about their bodies and their feelings towards their bodies that are an indicator of their body image.

Many disabled people in their writings about disability show a highly positive regard for their bodies, whilst acknowledging the difficulties a physically impaired body can cause. It may be that work written by disabled people about their own experiences has a lot to offer nurses. The perspectives offered by disabled people writing from the inside may challenge nurses, and the theories they use and apply to disability.

**The disabled body and body image**

According to Helman (1990 p. 12) there are three key concepts to body image:

- Beliefs about the optimal shape and size of the body.
- Beliefs about the body's inner structure.
- Beliefs about how it functions.

The ideal shape and size of the body is cultural and socially determined and, therefore, it can change over time (Helman, 1990 p. 14). Quite often, fashion can dictate frequent changes. Disability may constrain the range of change that is possible. Because the body has social meaning, the adornments to the body communicate information about the position of the wearer. If the body is adorned with exclusive designer jewellery, it communicates meaning to others. If the body is adorned with a prosthesis or a head restraint, it communicates meaning to others. Quite often, physically disabled people come with a range of attachments, such as wheelchairs and their accessories, other mobility aids, communication devices, restraining straps and pads to their bodies which can communicate messages about the lack of intactness and control. These attachments can influence the person's view of their own body and of the nurses viewing the body. If the body smells pleasant or unpleasant, it communicates meaning to others. Lawler (1991) offers a fascinating analysis of the body, its social significance and how nurses deal with the problems associated with people's bodies. Freudian theory suggests that certain body functions are invested with psychological meaning. London (1977 p. 169) emphasizes the importance of smell because it is usually associated with body products or excreta. The presence of an unpleasant smell is associated with lack of physical control, and this can then be applied or spread to the psyche.

The way in which the body's internal organs are structured and function can be perceived differently by individuals. An example of this can be found in the findings from a study by Pearson and Dudley (1982). A total of 81 adults (male and female) were questioned about their knowledge relating to body organ location. From a total of 729 responses, 48% were inaccurate, 14% were vague and only 28% were correct. In relation to the functioning of organs, 65% were inaccurate, 23% were vague and 12% were correct. At a very basic level, this study highlights the description of body image as the mental picture one has of one's body and how it works. Subjects in this study obviously had their own impressions of where their internal organs lay and what they did. The authors of this study do not state if any subjects were disabled.

It can be assumed that disabled people have their own mental picture of how their bodies are structured, where their organs lie and what functions they perform. Given that most of our knowledge about the internal organization of the body is based on non-disabled norms, it must be difficult at times for disabled people to form a clear picture in their minds of their own bodies. As most charts and pictures in books are based on non-disabled ideals, disabled people may experience confusion in trying to understand their own bodies. The mismatch can create a distortion that influences how disabled people understand the workings of their bodies. This may also go some way to understanding why there are many publications written by disabled people or representative organizations explaining what happens to the body with different disabilities.

Sometimes, the way in which disabled people need to carry out certain functions or activities of daily living can be different from that of non-disabled people. This difference is often seen as a problem or difficulty by non-disabled people. Some nurses have a low acceptance of disabled people because they are perceived to have an unnecessarily high level of dependency (Atkinson and Sklaroff, 1987 p. 73). For example, some disabled people may need to make frequent use of a toilet to empty their bladder. If they are told they have a 'weak bladder' then this can influence how they see their body and its functions. Furthermore, if there are not accessible toilets or nurses willing to provide the necessary assistance, then disabled people can easily become frustrated either with others or with themselves, which in turn may contribute towards a negative image of the body. Disabled people who experience a lack of motor control and co-ordination often require frequent assistance with activities, or with achieving suitable seating and lying positions. Often nurses do not appreciate the necessity of such needs or that they are in fact the norm, and not just the patient being difficult or demanding of attention.

In summary, Mairs (1988 p. 124) eloquently describes some of the issues surrounding body image and disability in the following way:

'. . . as I entered adolescence, I believed myself unpopular because I was homely: my breasts too flat, my mouth too wide, my hips too narrow, my clothing never quite right in fit or style. I was not, in fact, particularly ugly, old photographs inform me, though I was well off the ideal; but I carried this sense of self-alienation with me into adulthood, where it regenerated in response to the depredations of MS. Even with my brace I walk with a limp. . . . My shoulders droop and my pelvis thrusts forward as I try to balance myself upright. . . . When I think about how my body must look, especially to men, to whom I have been trained to display myself, I feel ludicrous, even loathsome.

At my age, however, I don't spend much time thinking about my appearance. The burning egocentricity of adolescence, which assures one that all the world is looking all the time has passed, thank God, and I'm generally too caught up in what I'm doing to step back, as I used to, and watch myself as though upon a stage. I'm also too old to believe in the accuracy of self-image. I know I'm not a hideous crone, that in fact, when I'm rested, well dressed and well made up, I look fine'.

Mairs perhaps demonstrates that disabled people can acknowledge their body reality in comparison with something else, either their previous self or with the expectations or ideals of others. This reality can be integrated into a self-concept in a way that is both acceptable and healthy.

**Attribution and body image**

Regardless of the physical signs and symptoms associated with disability, people wonder about the causes of their disability and seek to find explanations. Individual explanations may vary from the biological, natural, lifestyle, work, social to divine causation (Herzlich and Pierret, 1986). Attribution theory helps us to understand how people attribute beliefs, causes or reasons for occurrences in either the self or others (Hall, 1982 p. 80). Morrison (1994 p. 37) states that much of our communication with others is based on assumptions and these assumptions are often the result of the attributions made about ourselves and other people. The way in which attributes are developed has been said to involve three factors (Morrison, 1994 p. 38):

- The characteristics of the person perceiving.
- The features of the object, behaviour or person being perceived.
- The social setting in which the behaviour occurs.

In order to value attribution theory, we need to accept that, as part of our everyday life, we constantly try to make sense of ourselves, others and situations by seeking common-sense reasons and causes for things happening or being the way they are. The conclusions reached may or may not be scientific in their construction or outcome. Attribution theory is useful because it can help nurses to reflect critically on their own attitudes and assumptions, to make conscious how they may be attributing cause to disabled people, either as individuals or a group, and to different types of disabilities.

Attribution theory is also a useful framework to assist nurses in their understanding of why some disabled people may have come to hold specific beliefs or reasons, some of which may be labelled as naive or nonsensical about the cause of certain features or behaviours associated with their disability. Attribution stems from the cognitive model of psychology and, as such, it can be seen by some as an objective method of focusing on the mind and its dysfunctions (Hall, 1982 p. 79).

Attribution theory should be considered alongside other theories, for example, those on physical attractiveness, locus of control and learned helplessness (Morrison, 1994 p. 30). It can also be considered alongside emotional response to disability (Brennan, 1994) and beliefs about justness (Bordieri et al., 1983). In a paper by the latter authors, they suggest levels of physical attractiveness can influence how attributions are made concerning the cause of a disability and the prognosis. Physically attractive individuals are considered to have more control over their lives and are, therefore, assumed to be more at fault if they acquire a disability through an accident. But the 'just world' belief (Lerner *et al.*, 1976) states that people believe that tragedy does not happen at random and, in order to come to an understanding (and reduce anxiety), they attribute causes for the tragedy based around a belief in 'the just world'. Thus, if an attractive person acquires an injury, although it may be believed that they acted in such a way to deserve the injury, the consequences become unjust. People also excuse the behaviour as perhaps being daring or brave. From this we can begin to see how it is some disabled people are considered brave and heroic (Morris, 1991). Furthermore, people believe, if it could happen to someone with highly attractive physical characteristics, then it could happen to anyone (including the perceiver), thus it seems even more unjust.

Conversely, if tragedy affects an unattractive person, there is not such a great threat to the perceiver and the disabled person is often regarded as an unfortunate victim, to be regarded with sympathy. Their physical unattractiveness makes people susceptible to tragedy so it is 'not their fault'. Physically unattractive people are considered not to have control over their bodies and their lives, and can, therefore, be excused their disability. Again, it can be seen how these psychological processes contribute with other social and cultural processes to the view that some disabled people are figures of tragedy or victims (Morris, 1991).

It is possible to see a variety of ways, either directly or indirectly, in which ideas about attribution can influence disabled people's understandings about their bodies and their internal structuring and workings. This in turn can influence body image. It is also possible to see how non-disabled people, including nurses, having formed their own attributions, can hold beliefs and attitudes or behave in ways that can influence disabled people, and either affect their self-esteem, self-concept or their body image. Influencing any one of these parts of identity may influence any other part (Gillies, 1984; Drench, 1994).

**The nurse's role**

It would seem that body image is a composite of many factors. It is difficult to isolate body image from other aspects of self-identity, such as, sexuality, self-esteem and self-concept in non-disabled people, let alone disabled people with the additional differences in social and cultural experiences. How then do nurses develop a feeling and thinking understanding of body image in the context of disability and how can they incorporate reliable knowledge-based strategies into their care with disabled patients?

Before even considering the nurse–patient interface and putting into practice strategies, nurses must critically reassess their own attitudes, beliefs and knowledge. Self-assessment of our own attitudes is often quite problematic as we like to assume our attitudes are positive and non-judgemental to begin with.

As Oliver (1990 p. 64) states

'. . . *professionals are clearly influenced by cultural images and ideological constructions of disability as an individual, medical and tragic problem. The issue of adjustment, therefore, became the focus for professional intervention and reinforced these very images and constructions by rooting them in practice'.*

Nurses must acknowledge disabled people as having expertise about how their bodies feel to them, also how they feel and understand its functions. Nurses need to accept the aids and equipment that disabled people often require as an extension or attachment of the body. When coming into a health care setting, disabled people are often concerned about their equipment and aids to daily living on several counts (Atkinson and Sklaroff, 1987 p. 69). Firstly, nurses will remove it. Secondly, they will not treat the equipment or aid with care and it will become broken, and also the nurses will either not use the equipment or use it incorrectly owing to a lack of knowledge. If equipment and aids are regarded by disabled people as vital to maintaining their abilities, they can often be regarded as extensions of themselves. It is important that nurses recognize this and treat equipment and aids with as much care and consideration as possible. Alternatively some people with disabilities choose not to make use of aids and equipment that nurses think they should. One of the many reasons for this may be that aids and equipment can cause blurring of the body boundaries, leading to feelings of loss of control and intactness. The issues surrounding equipment and aids are provided as an example. Disabled people are generally knowledgeable about the management of their disability; nurses should not expect disabled people to hand over the management of their disability simply because they come into contact with nurses (either in hospital or in the community) for other health care needs.

It was previously argued that nurses need to critically review the appropriateness of literature that can be applied in practice.

Literature taken from psychology, sociology and nursing can discriminate against disabled people. Having considered carefully what and how the literature is applied, it is necessary for nurses to reflect on their own beliefs and attitudes, and to develop processes of making conscious unquestioned assumptions that may be held about disability and disabled people. In order to practise competently when working with people who are physically disabled, there is a requirement for nurses to consider critically their own knowledge of disability experiences and disability culture. How much knowledge comes from literature researched and written by disabled people, and how much comes from able-bodied professional fields? Over-reliance on one set of ideas or theories which are then routinely applied cannot be recommended as good practice.

The assessment of body image exposes many practical problems for nurses, least of all because there do not appear to be any assessment tools or frameworks that are quick and easy to use in practice. However, as Price (1990 p. 76) states any assessment tools, when they do become available, will only assist the nurse's holistic assessment and not supplant it. Patients need to be viewed as individuals within the context of their own social and cultural experiences, including their experience of disability. Probably one of the most unhelpful actions nurses can undertake is to isolate altered body image as a problem for the patient (Price, 1990 p. 91). All the evidence suggests that body image is one of many components that make up self-concept. It cannot be pulled out, dealt with like a pain or a headache, and put back in place. Nurses who want to assist disabled people to change or in some ways improve their body image must truly work in a holistic way with patients and other members of the health care team.

Working with disabled people who experience difficulties in dealing with changes in their body image takes time and energy. Coming to an acceptance or resolution about changes in body image can take disabled people a long time to achieve. Therefore, when planning interventions, nurses should be realistic about the time required to achieve successful outcomes. This also means that one or two brief interactions with patients are not likely to produce significant outcomes. Theoretically, every interaction the nurse has with patients can affect the body image. This is quite a significant thought to bear in mind. That working together must begin from the basis that all patients already have coping methods for dealing with changing body image (Gould, 1983).

Nursing work with disabled people necessarily involves the application of a variety of technical and practical skills. If disabled people are to feel safe and confident with their care, then nurses need to perform their work with reasonable competence. There is also the need for nurses to develop a range of holistic interventions. These interventions can be used to work towards achieving several goals that the nurse and patient may be trying to fulfil. These interventions, which have been adapted from Fitzgerald-Miller (1992 p. 321) would include:

- Modifying the environment.
- Increasing the awareness and sensitivities of nurses and other health care workers to disability issues.
- Expanding and understanding the patient's experiences within context.
- Working with the patient to achieve *their* goals.
- Identifying and accepting the patient's coping behaviours and strategies.
- Using positive interventions to modify coping behaviours where they are not achieving health-orientated outcomes for the patient.
- Promotion of self-control.
- Advancement of empowerment.
- Working with others regarded as significant by the patient.

This range of interventions requires nurses to draw on a wide range of knowledge and skills. The strategies are interdependent and holistic in nature, and will influence body image. Many of the interventions require nurses to focus on assisting patients to build up positive self-esteem, and confidence in themselves and their abilities in the widest sense. The mobilization of this energy can enable patients to manage their changing body image more positively amongst other needs they may have.

## Conclusion

Body image and disability must be considered in parallel. The experience of disability is influenced by social and cultural variables as is the formation and development of body image. Nurses have begun to apply to disabled people, ideas and theories based on able-bodied experiences. This has obvious limitations. Disabled people, and their bodily and social experiences, therefore, become constrained within able-bodied norms, compared with these norms and judged against them. Existing literature does not always accurately portray disability, which means nurses do not come closer to understanding disability. However, it has been suggested that there are alternative sources of literature available for nurses to inform them of different perspectives in relation to disability. This is literature researched and written by disabled people themselves.

Body image cannot be considered in isolation from other aspects of self-concept such as sexuality and self-esteem. If nurses want to incorporate interventions for dealing with developing and changing body image into their work with disabled people, then they need to ensure they are providing holistic attention to patients' needs and that they have a range of interventions available that work towards several needs in an individualistic manner. Working with people who have physical disabilities should be challenging for nurses given the experiences of able-bodied people and disabled people are different. Nurses cannot assume they understand the experiences of disabled people until they have consciously explored their own beliefs and views about disability and disabled people.

## References

Atkinson, F.I. and Sklaroff, S.A. (1987) *Acute Hospital Wards and the Disabled*. London, Royal College of Nursing.

Blackwood, M. (1978) Disability without handicap: a cry from the heart. *Nursing Times* **74**(33), 22–23.

Bordieri, J.E., Sotolongo, M. and Wilson, M. (1983) Physical attractiveness and attributions for disability. *Rehabilitation Psychology* **28**(4), 207–215.

Brennan, J. (1994) A vital component of care. *Professional Nurse* **9**(5), 298–303.

Dewis, M.E. (1989) Spinal cord-injured adolescents and young adults: the meaning of body changes. *Journal of Advanced Nursing* **14**, 389–396.

Drench, M.E. (1994) Changes in body image secondary to disease and injury. *Rehabilitation Nursing* **19**(1), 31–36.

Evans, P. (1991) Cited in Morris, J. (1991) *Pride Against Prejudice*. London, The Women's Press.

Finkelstein, V. (1988) Cited in Oliver, M. (1990) *The Politics of Disablement*. Basingstoke, Macmillan.

Finkelstein, V. (1993) The commonality of disability. In: Swain, J., Finkelstein, V., French, S. and Oliver, M. (eds) *Disabling Barriers – Enabling Environments*. Milton Keynes, The Open University, pp. 9–16.

Fitzgerald-Miller, J. (1992) *Coping with Chronic Illness Overcoming Powerlessness*, 2nd edn. Philadelphia, F.A. Davis.

French, S. (1993) Disability, impairment or something in between? In: Swain, J., Finkelstein, V., French, S. and Oliver, M. (eds) *Disabling Barriers – Enabling Environments*. Milton Keynes, The Open University, pp. 17–25.

Gillies, D.A. (1984) Body image changes following illness and injury. *Journal of Enterostomal Therapy* **11**(5), 186–189.

Goffman, E. (1963). Cited in Janelli, L.M. (1993) The reality of body image. *Journal of Gerontological Nursing* **12**(10), 23–27.

Gould, M.T. (1983) Nursing diagnosis concurrent with multiple sclerosis. *Journal of Neurosurgical Nursing* **15**, 339–345.

Grunbaum, J. (1985) Helping your patient build a sturdier body image. *Registered Nurse* October, 51–55.

Hall, J. (1982) *Psychology for Nurses and Health Visitors*. London, Macmillan.

Helman, C.G. (1990) *Culture, Health and Illness*, 2nd edn. London, Butterworth Heinemann.

Herzlich, C. and Pierret, J. (1986) In: Currer, C. and Stacey, M. (eds) *Concepts of Health, Illness and Disease*. Leamington Spa, Berg.

Janelli, L.M. (1986) The reality of body image. *Journal of Gerontological Nursing* **12**(10), 23–27.

Lacey, J. and Birtchnell, S.A. (1986) Body image and its disturbances. *Journal of Psychosomatic Research* **30**(6), 622–631.

Lawler, J. (1991) *Behind the Screens Nursing, Somology, and the Problem of the Body*. Edinburgh, Churchill Livingstone.

Lerner, M., Miller, D. and Holmes, J. (1976) Deserving and the emergence of forms of justice. *Advances in Experimental Psychology*. New York, Academic Press.

Loudon, J.B. (1977) On body products. In: Blacking, J. (ed.) *The Anthropology of the Body*. London, Academic Press.

Mairs, N. (1988) In: Saxon, M. and Howe, F. (eds) *With Wings: An Anthology of Literature by Women with Disabilities*.

Maycock, J. (1988) The image of the rheumatic disease. In Salter, M. (ed.) (1988) *Altered Body Image: The Nurse's Role*, 1st edn. Chichester, John Wiley, pp. 117–136.

Morris, J. (1991) *Pride Against Prejudice*. London, The Women's Press.

Morris, J. (1993) Prejudice. In: Swain, J., Finkelstein, V., French, S. and Oliver, M. (eds) *Disabling Barriers – Enabling Environments*. Milton Keynes, The Open University, pp. 101–106.

Morrison, P. (1994) *Understanding Patients*. London, Baillière, Tindall.

Noh, S. and Posthuma, B. (1990) Physical disability and depression: methodological consideration. *Canadian Journal of Occupational Therapy* **57**(1), 9–15.

Nordholm, I.A. (1980) Beautiful patients are good patients. *Social Science and Medicine* **14A**, 81–83.

Oliver, M. (1990) *The Politics of Disablement*. Basingstoke, Macmillan.

Pearson, J. and Dudley, H. (1982) Bodily perceptions in surgical patients. *British Medical Journal* **284**, 1545–1546.

Price, B. (1990) *Body Image Nursing Concepts and Care*. London, Prentice Hall.

Price, B. (1986) Keeping up appearances. *Nursing Times* **82**, 30–32.

Salter, M. (ed.) (1988) *Altered Body Image: The Nurse's Role*. Chichester, John Wiley.

Samonds, R.J. and Cammermeyer, M. (1989) Perceptions of body image in subjects with multiple sclerosis: a pilot study. *Journal of Neuroscience Nursing* **21**(3), 190–194.

Stensman, R. (1989) Body image among 22 persons with acquired and congential mobility impairment. *Paraplegia* **27**, 27–35.

Stockwell, F. (1972) *The Unpopular Patient*. London, Royal College of Nursing.

Wassner, A. (1982) The impact of mutilating surgery or trauma on body image. *International Nursing Review* **29**(3), 86–90.

CHAPTER 7

# An oncological perspective

*Jacquie Woodcock*

The diagnosis of cancer no longer necessarily results in a rapid decline in the condition leading to an inevitable death. It is now recognized that cancer is often a chronic disease with which people will continue to live and to which they will need to adapt. This recognition by health care professionals has led to an awareness of the importance in maintaining an acceptable quality of life for patients during these longer disease-free intervals.

Changes in physical appearance are known to have a negative effect on an individual's quality of life (Die-Trill and Straker, 1992; Mock, 1993) and it has been recognized that receiving a cancer diagnosis may also result in a lowering of self-esteem (Rosenburg, 1979; Waltz, 1986). This chapter will, therefore, explore the alterations in body image that patients with a cancer diagnosis may experience, and how nurses may assist in the patient's adaptation to these changes in order that an acceptable quality of life is maintained.

**Receiving a cancer diagnosis**

Changes in self-esteem and body image will often occur as a result of receiving a cancer diagnosis. A study carried out by Carpenter and Brockopp (1994) on women prior to and following chemotherapy concluded that their self-esteem fell following the diagnosis of cancer and subsequent treatment. This is often due to fear of the disease itself, but may also be related to feelings of guilt, which can be associated with such a diagnosis (Cassileth and Cassileth, 1979). Uncertainty regarding the future can adversely affect an individual's feelings about themselves and the role that they had expected to fulfil in life. These negative influences on self-esteem and body image can to lead to feelings of loss of control and patients describe feeling of being taken over. Many of

the fears associated with a cancer diagnosis are due to the consequences of disease, such as, disfigurement, pain, increased dependency and physical changes to the body. Patients with a chronic
illness, such as cancer, experience many losses, such as an active
lifestyle and activities that are unable to be maintained (Benoliel,
1971). The individual may grieve for future losses and the uncertainty of further changes in appearance and role. Indeed, Price
(1990) states that one of the greatest problems for individuals
experiencing changes in body image owing to a pathological
process is the uncertainty as to whether further changes may
occur, leading to a continual state of insecurity. It is important for
health care professionals to carry out a thorough assessment of the
impact of a cancer diagnosis on each individual's self-esteem and
body image before moving on to consider alterations that are
likely to occur either as a result of the disease process or as a
sequelae of treatment.

## Alterations in body image associated with surgery

The majority of cancer patients will undergo surgery at some stage
in their cancer experience. This may range from diagnostic procedures and the insertion of long-term methods of venous access,
such as Hickman lines or porta-caths, to potentially curative procedures, and emergency and palliative care. Alterations in body
image that arise as a result of this treatment modality may be
either temporary in nature, for example, the insertion of intravenous infusions, catheters, drains and nasogastric tubes, or result
in permanent changes in function and appearance, such as the formation of stomas, amputation, or reconstructive surgery for head
and neck cancers and breast cancer. The needs of patients undergoing procedures for the formation of a stoma and breast surgery
are dealt with elsewhere in this text, therefore, the issues to be discussed here are those relating to general surgical procedures and
others relating to a site-specific cancer diagnosis.

Ritualistic practice may continue to form a large part of the preoperative preparation of patients. For example, skin preparation
prior to surgery still often includes shaving despite research that
questions the usefulness of this procedure (Fairclough, 1987). This
clearly demonstrates the lack of consideration given to the impact
of such procedures on an individual's body image. Hair removal
may threaten an individual's sexual identity or may be contraindicated for cultural reasons, and can result in distress.

Nurses' attitudes to preparing patients may not take into account the distress caused by even temporary alterations in body image, as they may feel that, compared with the need to treat the underlying disease, these are minor inconveniences. However, the wearing of hospital gowns and the removal of dentures and other prostheses can lead to feelings of loss of individuality, dignity and respect. Sensitive nursing care can help to reduce the anxiety these procedures may cause by providing privacy and minimizing the length of time the patient has to spend like this.

Immediate postoperative alterations in body image include the presence of intravenous infusions, nasogastric tubes, drains and urinary catheters. Nursing measures that may lessen the impact of these alterations include the correct positioning and camouflaging of such equipment, for example, intravenous infusions should be sited in the least used arm, thus allowing the patient to maintain some movement and independence, which will help in enabling a sense of control. Drains and catheters should be positioned discreetly and to maximize comfort. The use of bags, etc. may be utilized, if appropriate. If tape is used to secure tubes, especially nasogastric tubes, this should be changed regularly and not allowed to become soiled.

Concern over the size and appearance of scars is often experienced by patients. Again, these concerns may not be valued by health care professionals whose goal may be to cure. This can be a major concern for patients undergoing surgery for the removal of malignant melanoma, where it is often necessary to excise the full thickness of skin and a margin of tissue between 3 and 5 cm (Roses et al., 1985). This can leave large indented areas of scar tissue, which may be difficult to disguise with clothing. The use of camouflaging makeup may be appropriate in such a situation and it is important that nurses caring for such patients are able to provide the information regarding how such services may be obtained. Cancer patients may also be distressed at the presence of other scars even though these may be well covered and do not obviously alter body image. It is important for the nurse to understand that the patient may feel a sense of violation both by the cancer itself and, indeed, by the surgical procedure, and that these feelings may occur even when the surgery is thought to be curative.

Surgery may also cause unseen effects to a patient's body image and self-esteem. For example, women who undergo surgical treatment for gynaecological cancers may perceive this as a threat to their feminine identity owing to the potential that the disease has to damage or destroy the patient's genitalia and fertility. Derogatis (1986) recognized that these cancers have a very negative effect on a patient's body image, sexual functioning and self-esteem. Also men undergoing surgical procedures, such as radical prostatectomy, may have hidden effects on the perception of their body image. During a radical prostatectomy, autonomic nerves that lie just below the prostate may be severed or damaged, leading to an inability of the patient to achieve an erection. Although, wherever possible, nerve-sparing surgery will be performed, this may also result in a temporary inability to achieve an erection. As a result of these problems, men may well experience feelings of loss and emasculation (Bachers, 1985).

Surgical intervention remains the primary treatment for patients with head and neck cancer. Head and neck cancers and their treatments not only affect facial appearance, but may also produce speech disabilities and difficulties in swallowing, eating and drinking, and interfere with adequate respiration (Die-Trill and Straker, 1992). Shapiro and Kornfield (1987) suggest that these alterations in function often cause feelings of repugnance in others and lead to demoralization of the patient. It is difficult to see how one may be able to promote positive body image in these circumstances. However, Mulgrew and Dropkin (1991) identified a supportive network of hospital staff as of great importance in the patient's adaptation to their deformity. Social support has also been identified as important for successful adaptation to occur. In a study carried out by West (1977) of 152 head and neck cancer patients, 68% had successfully adapted to their disfigurement. This group all had effective social support.

Assessment of a patient's ability to cope with this amount of disfigurement and dysfunction is imperative in order to identify those individuals at greatest risk of developing depression. Dropkin (1989) developed a scale (the disfigurement/dysfunction scale), which can be used to aid assessment. This scale assesses the patient's coping abilities by observing the level of self-care activity and social interaction in which they engage. They noted that those patients who by the sixth postoperative day were beginning to participate in self-care activities and social interaction were utilizing their coping mechanisms effectively, whilst those patients who had not resumed such activity by this time were often denying their situation and were likely to develop depression. On this basis, relevant intervention could be introduced to those patients requiring it.

Surgery is the oldest of the cancer therapies and, as such, is sometimes given less consideration than other therapies. It is important for nurses caring for cancer patients undergoing surgery not to forget the uncertainty and insecurity they face due to potential alterations in body image, and not to assume that these are acceptable for the patient in return for a chance of extended survival. Quality of life is a subjective concept that may not only be measured in terms of extended survival. This may be forgotten by health care professionals at times when they are dealing with newly diagnosed patients for whom they see cure as the main aim of treatment.

## Alterations in body image associated with chemotherapy

Chemotherapy is a systemic treatment which can produce a multiplicity of side effects, some of which may have an adverse effect on the patient's body image. Again, before discussing the physical alterations that can occur, it is necessary to address issues that may contribute to a lowering of self-esteem within this patient group. The administration of chemotherapy will often take place over a period of months, each course separated by 3–4 weeks. This pattern of administration can cause major disruption to the patient's lifestyle, resulting in an inability to maintain their previous role and causing a subsequent lowering in self-esteem (Morris, 1985).

Many patients will have venous access established via a tunnelled central venous catheter, such as a Hickman line or portacath. Whilst this will provide the patient with safe long-term access (Reymann, 1993), it may cause some patients considerable distress, owing to the catheter exiting through the chest wall causing disturbances to function, for example, swimming and also acting as a constant reminder of their disease status (Reymann, 1993).

One of the more obvious alterations to body image, which is caused by the administration of certain cytotoxic drugs, is alopecia. Freedman (1994) acknowledges that, throughout history, hair has been symbolic of cultural and social climates. Indeed, in some societies, a hair style will indicate the social standing, gender, occupation and religious convictions of an individual. It can, therefore, be seen that the loss of one's hair can have negative effects on self-concept, self-identity and body image. Baxley *et al.* (1984) studied 40 patients receiving chemotherapy and noted that the body image of patients experiencing alopecia was significantly lower than those patients not experiencing alopecia. Freedman (1994) states that 'the loss of hair as a symbolic loss of self creates an alienation from the self and from others' (Freedman, 1994 p. 339). It is such a public statement of the individual's situation that it forces them to acknowledge the presence of their illness constantly. Society's attitudes are such that patients are then often channelled into recreating some normality by wearing wigs, hats or headscarfs, however uncomfortable or unflattering these may be, in order that they feel more accepted in social situations. This typifies the attitudes of a society where great value is placed on an individual's physical appearance.

Other side effects of chemotherapy that may give rise to alterations in body image include nausea and vomiting. Developments in antiemetic therapy and, in particular, the development of the 5-hydroxytryptamine (5HT) antagonists have reduced the severity of this unpleasant side effect. However, some patients may still suffer from the embarrassment of this symptom and the restrictions that it may impose on their normal routine. Anorexia may also be associated with fear of the possibility of nausea and vomiting, and may result in weight loss. Linked to both of these issues is the problem of mucositis. This is a common side effect following the administration of chemotherapy and produces discomfort, anorexia and a reluctance to participate in normal activities, such as talking and kissing, owing to concern over halitosis and difficulty in controlling saliva production. All of these side effects can have a profound effect on the patient's confidence to interact with individuals outside of his or her immediate circle.

The effects of cytotoxic drugs on the haemopoietic system can have a life-threatening effect on the patient and, therefore, the effect of these alterations on an individual's body image may not be given due consideration. However, limitations to patients' lifestyles that may occur as a result of a neutropenic state can be immensely restricting for the patient and indeed negatively affect their quality of life. Thrombocytopenia may manifest itself with bleeding gums and epistaxis, again a constant reminder to patients of the presence of their disease. Patients may also develop anaemia, leading to pallor and lethargy. If left untreated, this may lead to the patient experiencing increased levels of fatigue and dyspnoea, which, in turn, will lead to reduced mobility and the patient may be unable to carry out their normal activities. Again, these changes in role can cause a lowering of self-esteem.

Issues arising from alterations in sexual function may be twofold. The libido of patients may be lowered during this time and they may feel ambivalent about participating in sexual activity. This may also be reflected in the anxiety of a partner who does not wish to cause any harm. If these issues are not discussed, they may give rise to longer term problems, and feelings of rejection and lack of self-worth both for the patient and the partner involved. As previously stated, many patients will receive their chemotherapy via a Hickman line, which will remain *in situ* for long periods of time. These devices, whilst being very useful for patients, may also cause them anxiety both as an alteration in body image and also, in a very practical sense, they may be frightened of engaging in any sexual activity for fear of damaging or dislodging the device. Therefore, reassurance needs to be given and tips on securing the exposed line can be useful. Other side effects that may occur include a lack of vaginal lubrication and a reduced orgasmic response (Derogatis, 1986). Again it is important that patients are aware that these side effects may occur and that they receive information on the use of other lubricants that may be helpful, and sexual positions that may maximize their sexual response. Fertility following treatment may also be of concern to patients. Careful counselling should be available in these circumstances and, whenever possible, patients should be offered preservation of sperm or ova prior to the commencement of treatment. Camp-Sorrell (1991) states that women who experience amenorrhea as a result of chemotherapy may also experience menopausal symptoms, such as hot flushes, osteoporosis and vaginal atrophy. These symptoms may lead women to feel a loss of femininity. If not contraindicated by their underlying diagnosis, some of these women may benefit from hormone therapy and certainly require advice on the management of these unpleasant symptoms.

The term chemotherapy is often used in cancer care to refer to treatment with cytotoxic drugs. However, other drugs commonly used in cancer care may also bring about alterations in body image. The most obvious example of these is the use of corticosteroids used as part of cytotoxic treatment regimen. These drugs may cause weight gain, changes in skin coloration and integrity, and bruising (Burt, 1995). Other drugs that may bring about alterations in body image include antidepressants, which may affect the patient's ability to reach orgasm, and hormonal treatments, which may cause a lowering of libido. These, again, have negative effects on the individual's gender role and feelings of self-worth, leading to a negative effect on their quality of life. Hormonal manipulation for men with a diagnosis of prostatic cancer may involve a bilateral orchidectomy. This can cause significant damage to their feelings of masculinity. Patients undergoing this type of surgery are often older men and this may lead to presumptions by health care professionals that the impact of such surgery may be less than it would be for a younger man with a testicular tumour. These assumptions may lead to the issues of alterations in body image not being adequately addressed for these men. Whether hormonal manipulation is carried out surgically or pharmacologically, these men will also experience sexual dysfunction, including loss of libido, erectile dysfunction and gynaecomastia (Waxman, 1993), which are all alterations in body image that may lead to a lowering of self-esteem and affect the man's close relationships. These effects on their quality of life need to be clearly explained to patients and informed consent gained prior to such treatment being commenced.

**Alterations in body image associated with radiotherapy**

As with the previous treatment modalities discussed, radiotherapy treatment may induce both physiological and psychological side effects, which may, in turn, lead to an alteration in the patient's body image and self-esteem. The environment in which radiotherapy treatment is given, for example, in basement areas, and the nature of the treatment, necessitating that patients are left alone lying under large frightening machines, often on uncomfortable couches, can lead to feelings of loss of control and isolation. Radiotherapy needs to be given accurately day after day, and this means that the treatment area is often marked on the patient's skin either in ink or by using tatoos. These marks can cause patients considerable distress and act as an indicator to all that treatment is being given. The side effects of radiotherapy are usually site specific as radiotherapy is a localized treatment. However, there are some systemic side effects that may lead to alterations in body image and, therefore, need consideration. These are thought to arise through the release of the metabolites of tumour breakdown into the systemic circulation. They include anorexia, nausea and vomiting, and fatigue.

Anorexia may limit the individual's ability to take part in socialization during meal times and may lead to weight loss, causing a physical alteration in body image. Whenever possible, patients should be encouraged to maintain their nutritional status by including nutritious drinks and supplements into their dietary pattern. These patients may well need support and advice from nutritional experts.

Nausea and vomiting can be experienced by patients having radiotherapy to the gastrointestinal tract and may occur in others, as already mentioned, owing to the release of metabolites as a result of tumour breakdown. This side effect is also often exacerbated by the patient's fear and anxiety regarding the radiotherapy treatment they are having, and may be relieved by clear explanations and reassurance regarding the treatment process and the expected side effects and outcomes.

Fatigue is a symptom experienced by many cancer patients but, in studies carried out by King *et al.* (1985) and Kobashi-Schoot *et al.* (1985), fatigue was documented as a symptom experienced by patients receiving radiotherapy. They noted that increased levels of fatigue occurred as treatment progressed and as the cumulative dose of radiation increased. This symptom can affect the patient's body image by limiting their ability to function in their normal role and, therefore, consolidate feelings of loss of control and isolation.

Other alterations in body image may occur as a result of localized skin reactions. Although the use of megavoltage linear accelerators and cobalt machines that deliver the maximum dose of radiation below the level of the skin has led to a reduction in the amount and severity of skin reactions, these may at times still occur. Skin reactions can range from a mild erythematous reaction to moist esquamation. Certain areas of the body, such as skin folds in the groin and perineal areas, axilla and behind the ears, are known to react most severely and require special attention. Patients having radiotherapy to head and neck cancers need to be advised to wear loose-fitting collars or cravats. These will help decrease friction and also camouflage any erythematous reaction. Longer term skin reactions may cause permanent alterations in body image, for example, telangiectasia, changes in pigmentation and fibrosclerotic changes.

Site-specific side effects that may result in temporary alterations in body image are disturbances of the gastrointestinal tract leading to nausea and vomiting, or diarrhoea, which may restrict a patient's activity and cause embarrassment and lowering of self-esteem. Effects on sexual functioning that may occur as a result of radiotherapy include vaginal fibrosis and dryness following inter-cavity treatment, and in rare cases the development of fistulae.

Men receiving extended beam radiation therapy to the prostate gland and adjacent lymph nodes have an erectile dysfunction rate of 40%. Radiation therapy may also cause pain on ejaculation resulting from irritation caused to the posterior urethra; semen volume will be permanently reduced (Waxman, 1993).

**Alterations in body image as a result of the disease process**

Alterations in appearance as a result of the disease process may present themselves even prior to diagnosis and may, indeed, have been the symptom that took the patient to the doctor in the first place. The pathology of cancer may cause substantial alterations in body image, one of the most distressing of which is cancer cachexia, a syndrome of malnutrition involving progressive loss of body weight, fat and muscle. Kern and Norton (1988) report that one-half to two-thirds of all cancer patients experience cachexia. It is difficult to assess which patients may be at greatest risk of developing this syndrome as little connection has yet been made between cachexia and type or extent of tumour (Skipper et al., 1993). However, this syndrome will cause severe alterations in body image and, indeed, may consolidate patients' feelings of loss of control.

Pain is another symptom that can be experienced as a direct result of the disease process. Twyford and Lack (1988) state that pain is experienced by one-third of all cancer patients and often manifests itself in more than one site. The patient who has pain may experience alterations in body image related either to the sensory dimension of their pain that is the location and sensation of pain itself, which can cause restriction to mobility, which leads to changes in that individual's ability to perform their normal role. Also related to the affective dimension of pain, the patient may experience associated anxiety and depression leading to a lowering of self-esteem. Ahles et al. (1983) reports on a study showing that two-thirds of patients interviewed believed that their pain was related to progression of their disease, and that were suffering from anxiety and depression related to this. Other symptoms experienced as a result of the pathology of cancer include the accumulation of ascitic fluid. This occurs in approximately 6% of patients, in whom it creates severe abdominal distension, leading to problems of ill-fitting clothes and only being able to wear loose articles, and may also affect comfort and mobility.

Further alterations in body image relate to less obvious symptoms, for example, dyspnoea, which, according to Regnard and Tempest (1992), occurs in 51% of cancer patients. The limitations that this has on an individual's lifestyle again result in a lowering of self-esteem and compromises body image.

Unfortunately, some cancer patients may have to cope at some stage of their disease with a fungating wound. Whilst the management of such wounds has improved greatly, they still present a major alteration in the patient's body image and often produce an odour and an exudate.

Non-specific effects of the pathology of cancer, such as feelings of fatigue, again often mean that the patient is no longer able to carry out normal activities and this may lead to a lowering of self-esteem.

**Alterations in body image associated with biological therapies**

Side effects of biological therapies are unlikely to cause patients to experience major permanent alterations in body image. Patients experience similar side effects of flu-like symptoms, nausea and vomiting, headaches following administration of various biotherapies, including tumour necrosis factor and interleukin-4 and interleukin-6.

Side effects associated with interleukin-2 include multisystem toxicity, which can be life-threatening. However, these side effects are rapidly reversible. Patients will need reassurance concerning the nature and duration of the side effects. Fatigue may persist and affect the patient's ability to return to normal activity. Central nervous system toxicity resulting in agitation and confusion has been reported but this usually recedes on completion of the administration of therapy. However, patients may experience feelings of loss of control during this time.

Weight gain between 5% and 10% of total body weight is associated with both interleukin-2 and interleukin-4. Jassak (1993) states that 32% of patients experience weight gain of 10% or more of their normal weight. This weight gain may cause significant alteration in body image, and patients will need advice and help in adapting to this change.

**The implications for nursing practice**

This chapter has identified alterations in body image that can affect all cancer patients at some stage of their disease process. However, it is important that nurses do not apply a blanket diagnosis of altered body image to all cancer patients. It must be appreciated that alterations will be of greater significance to some patients and that many patients will adapt to these alterations, while others will need intervention to aid them with the adaptation process. Price (1993 p. 17) acknowledges the need to recognize 'subjective, perceptual and interpretive dimensions of body image . . . in an attempt to identify those variables that most strongly threaten a satisfactory body image'. In order to identify the patients at greatest risk, accurate assessment of the patients and their families needs to be carried out; various frameworks can be utilized to facilitate this assessment.

Price (1990) presents a framework consisting of three concepts: *body reality*, the way the body physically is; *body ideal*, the way one would wish the body to be; and *body presentation*, the way in which one tries to achieve the body ideal. This framework identifies an individual's coping mechanisms and social support networks as two important variables in the patient's ability to adapt to alterations in body image.

Norris (1978) identified similar variables affecting a person's ability to adapt to alterations in body image. These may also be used as a framework on which to carry out a detailed nursing assessment and comprises:

1. The nature of the threat.
2. The meaning that the individual attributes to the change.
3. The person's coping ability.
4. Responses of others significant to the individual.
5. The support available to the patient and family.

Dewing (1989) identifies four stages that patients experiencing alterations in body image pass through. He identifies *impact*: the initial shock and anger, depression and pessimism regarding recovery. Patients then may *retreat* into a state of mourning for the affected part. This may include a period of denial and withdrawal. Eventually, the patient may confront the problem and engage in activities to maximize their coping responses. This is described as *acknowledgement*; eventually *reconciliation* occurs – this involves the patient adapting to the alteration and becoming involved in future plans.

Attributions theory as described by Abramson and Martin (1981; cited in Brennan, 1994) may also be useful for nurses to consider when assessing patients' responses to altered body image. They suggest that an individual's response to a physical change in appearance or function depends to a great extent on the causative factors behind that change. Abramson and Martin (1981) carried out a study examining the attributions leading to depression in patients with altered body image. They found that depression occurred in patients who associated the causes of their physical changes with internal factors with permanence and perceived them as affecting other areas of their life.

Many cancer patients feel some guilt involved in the development of their disease. This can highlight their emotions as identified by Abramson and Martin (1981). Therefore, the application of attribution theory to the care of the cancer patient with altered body image can also be useful in answering an individual's adaptation. These frameworks can act as guides for nurses to assess, plan and deliver appropriate intervention for those patients experiencing alterations in body image.

Researchers have developed tools to measure people's reaction to changes in body image. Secourd and Journard (1953) developed the Body Cathexis–Self-concept Scale to measure satisfaction and dissatisfaction with body parts.

Other scales, for example, the Body Esteem Scale and Body–Self Relations Questionnaire have also been used to assess the ability of individuals to adapt to changes in body image (Groenwald *et al.*, 1993). However, these measurement scales, whilst useful for research purposes, are often long and time-consuming to complete, and the perceived benefits of their use in clinical practice are not necessarily apparent. One model that has been adapted well to assess patients' need for sexual counselling is the PLISSIT model. This model consists of four levels of intervention: permission, limited information, specific suggestions and intensive therapy.

In order to plan the care of patients facing alterations in body image successfully, nurses need to continue to explore models and frameworks that may be adapted and used to assess, plan and evaluate the care that these patients receive in order that their quality of life is satisfactory throughout their disease experience.

**References**

Abramson, L.Y. and Martin, D.J. (1981) A vital component of care. The nurse's role in recognising altered body image. *Professional Nurse* February, 298–303. (Cited in Brennan, 1984).

Ahles, T.A., Blanchard, E.B. and Ruckdesdel, J.C. (1983) The multidimensional nature of cancer-related pain. *Pain* **17**, 277–288.

Bachers, E.S. (1985) Sexual dysfunction after treatment for genitourinary cancers. *Seminars in Oncology Nursing* **1**, 18–24.

Baxley, K.O., Erdman, L.K., Henry, E. and Roof, B.J. (1984) Alopecia: effect on cancer patients' body image. *Cancer Nursing* **7**, 499–503.

Benobiel, J.C. (1971) Assessment of loss and grief. *Journal of Thanatology* **1**, 182–194.

Burt, K. (1995) The effect of cancer on body image and sexuality. *Nursing Times* **91**(7), 36–37.

Camp-Sorrell, D. (1991) Controlling adverse effects of chemotherapy. *Nursing* **91**(4), 34–42.

Carpenter, J.S. and Brockopp, D.Y. (1994) Evaluation of self-esteem of women with cancer receiving chemotherapy. *Oncology Nursing Forum* **21**(4), 751–757.

Cassileth, P. and Cassileth, B. (1979) Learning to care for cancer patients; the student dilemma. In: Cassileth, B. (ed.) *The Cancer Patient*, p. 313. Philadelphia, Lea and Febiger.

Derogatis, L.R. (1986) The unique impact of breast and gynaecology cancers on body image and sexual identity in women: a reassessment. In: *Body Image. Self-esteem and Sexuality in Cancer Patients*, 2nd edn. Basel, Karger.

Dewing, J. (1989) Altered body image. *Surgical Nurse* **2**(4).

Die-Trill, M. and Straker, N. (1992) Psychological adaptation to facial disfigurement in female head and neck cancer patients. *Psycho-Oncology* **1**, 247–251.

Dropkin, M.J. (1989) Coping with disfigurement and dysfunction after head and neck cancer surgery. A conceptual framework. *Seminars in Oncology Nursing* **5**, 213–219.

Fairclough, J. (1987) Skin shaving: a cause for concern. *Journal of Royal College of Surgeons of Edinburgh* **62**(2), 76–78.

Freedman, T.G. (1994) Social and cultural dimensions of hair loss in women treated for breast cancer. *Cancer Nursing* **17**(4), 334–341.

Groenwald, S., Frogge, M., Goodman, M. and Yasko, C. (1993) *Cancer Nursing Principles and Practice*. Boston, Jones and Bartlett.

Jassak, P. (1993) Biotherapy. In: Groenwald, S.K., Frogge, M.H., Goodman, M. and Yarbro, C. (eds) *Cancer Nursing Principles and Practice*, 3rd edn. Boston, Jones and Bartlett.

Kern, K.A. and Norton, J.A. (1988) Cancer cachexia. *JPEN* **12**, 286–298.

King, K.B., Nail, L.M., Kreamer, K., Strohl, R. and Johnson, J.

(1985) Patients' descriptions of the experience of receiving radiation therapy. *Oncology Nursing Forum* **12**(4), 55–61.

Kobashi-Schoot, J.A.M., Hanewald, G. and Van Dam, F. (1985) Assessment of malaise in cancer patients treated with radiotherapy. *Cancer Nursing* **8**(6), 306–313.

Mock, V. (1993) Body image in women, treated for breast cancer. *Nursing Research* **42**(3), 153–157.

Morris, C.A. (1985) Self-concept as altered by the diagnosis of cancer. *Nursing Clinics of North America* **20**, 611–630.

Mulgrew, B. and Drapkin, M.J. (1991) Coping with craniofacial resection. A case study. *Journal of Publ. Soc. Otorhinolaryngeal Head and Neck Cancer* **8**, 10.

Norris, C.M. (1978) Body image: its relevance to professional nursing. In: Carlin, C.E. and Blackwell, B. (eds). *Behavioural Concepts and Nursing Interventions*, 2nd edn. Boston, Jones and Bartlett, pp. 218–231.

Price, B. (1990) A model for body image care. *Journal of Advanced Nursing* **15**, 585–593.

Price, B. (1993a) Dignity that must be respected. Body image and the surgical patient. *Professional Nurse* July, 670–672.

Price, B. (1993b) Profiling the high risk altered body image patient. *Senior Nurse* **13**, 17–21.

Reymann, P.E. (1993) Chemotherapy: Principles of administration. In: Groenwald, S.K., Frogge, M.H., Goodman, M. and Yarbro, C.H. (eds) *Cancer Nursing Principles and Practice*, 3rd edn. Boston, Jones and Bartlett, pp. 293–330.

Rosenburg, M. (1979) *Concerning the Self.* New York, Barni Books.

Roses, D.F., Harris, M.N. and Gumport, S.L. (1985) Surgery for primary cutaneous melanoma. *Dermatology Clinic* **3**, 315–326.

Secourd, P. and Journal, S. (1953) The appraisal of body cathexis and the self. *Journal of Consulting Psychology* **17**, 343–347.

Shapiro, P.A. and Kornfields, D.S. (1987) Psychiatric aspects of head and neck cancer surgery. *Psychiatric Clinics of North America* **10**, 87–100.

Skipper, A., Szeiluga, D. and Groenwald, S. (1993) Nutritional disturbances. In: Groenwald, S., Frogge, M.H., Goodman, M. and Yarbro, C.H. (eds) *Cancer Nursing Principles and Practice.* Boston, Jones and Bartlett, pp. 621–643.

Twyford, R.G. and Lack, S.A. (1984) *Therapeutics in Terminal Cancer.* London: Pitman.

Waltz, M. (1986) A longitudinal study on environmental and dispositional determinants of life quality; social support and coping with physical illness. *Social Indicators Research* **18**, 71–93.

Waxman, E.S. (1995) Sexual dysfunction following treatment for prostate cancer: nursing assessment and interventions. *Oncology Nursing Forum* **20**(10), 1567–1571.

West, D.W. (1977) Social adaptation patterns among cancer patients with facial disfigurements resulting from surgery. *British Phys. Med Rehabilitation* **58**, 473–479.

CHAPTER 8

# Whole or partial breast loss and body image

*Ann Tait and Mavis Wing*

**The cultural significance of breasts**

There has never been a time since Adam and Eve when a woman's breasts were not important. Through the ages, the ways in which they were portrayed have changed, but the message remains essentially the same. The female breast is regarded as the symbol of intrinsic femininity, sexual desirability, and maternal comfort and succour. Whether breasts are alluded to in a subtle and evocative way or explicitly exhibited, they are central to many peoples' views about 'being a woman'. It is small wonder, therefore, that any real or potential threat to a woman's breast is stressful. Men's breasts can also be threatened sometimes, with the resultant feelings that masculinity is challenged. However, because only 1% of all breast cancers affect men, the major focus of this chapter is on women.

Culturally, the significance of the breast can vary and reflect the values of differing societies, so that the general notion of body image, as portrayed in Chapter 1, can partly be seen as a social construction (Norris, 1978). In the eye of a Moslem family, for instance, where the roles of daughter, wife and mother are of supreme importance, the threat to such a symbolic organ as the breast can be devastating. This occurs regardless of whether the breast is exposed or hidden from view. For many women the mere thought, let alone the reality, of exposing their breasts, perhaps to a male doctor, is extremely traumatic (Sampson, 1982). Dobson (1983) argues that nurses need to be aware of these issues and to do everything possible to alleviate embarrassment.

**Individual perception of whole or partial breast loss**

The threat of surgery to the breast is not dependent merely on the cultural values of the society to which the patient belongs but also on the significance that the breast holds for each individual (Bard and Sutherland, 1952). In addition, individual perceptions can change over time and so may require continual assessment from nurses.

Breast surgery may be required for cosmetic adjustment, or in order to identify and treat benign or malignant breast disease. With the latter condition, the threat to a woman is double-edged. Not only may a part or all of her breast be removed, but she has to live with the fear that she has a potentially life-threatening disease as well. However, the view that women are worried either by whole or partial breast loss, cancer or both, may be somewhat simplistic. As Rosser (1981) has shown, women are threatened mainly because they know that the treatments for breast cancer are often unpleasant and yet may well not be effective in prolonging life or necessarily contribute to an improved quality of life.

**Diagnosis of breast disease**

It is known that one woman in four will experience some kind of abnormality in her breasts (Stanway and Stanway, 1982). However, nurses can encourage women to develop breast awareness throughout their adult lives and participate in The National Breast Screening Programme when they are in the appropriate age group.

*Breast awareness*

Breast awareness has replaced breast self-examination because the latter had become either synonymous with a lump hunt or was seen as a medical examination that the average woman was unable to do properly. Encouraging breast awareness allows women to become familiar with their own breasts and aware of any changes that occur. Any new symptom, especially a unilateral one that persists throughout one menstrual cycle should be investigated. Changes such as thickenings, dimpling or changes in the skin, inversion or soreness of the nipple, swelling or pain as well as lumps should always be noted. Leaflets explaining breast awareness are produced by the National Breast Screening Programme and several other charities.

*Breast screening*

The National Breast Screening Programme (NBSP) was implemented in the UK in 1988 following the Forrest Report (Forrest,

1987). The NBSP invites all women between the ages of 50 and 65 years to have a mammogram every 3 years. Any abnormality noted then requires the woman to be assessed at a Breast Screening Assessment Centre. Assessment entails further mammograms and possibly an ultrasound scan of the breast, a clinical examination and a fine needle aspiration (FNA). The woman can be reassured after any one of these procedures and recalled for rescreening in 3 years. The preliminary report of the NBSP (Vessey and Gray, 1991) indicates that anticipated targets of women recalled, biopsies done and cancers detected have been reached. It is as yet too soon to know whether the anticipated 25% reduction in mortality will be achieved.

*Biopsy*

A biopsy is the removal of: a piece of breast tissue; a piece of the lump; or the whole lump for histopathological examination.

- Tru-cut biopsy or core biopsy is done under local anaesthetic using a needle to remove some tissue from the abnormal area.
- Excision biopsy is the removal of the abnormal area, usually under a general anaesthetic, requiring a day visit to hospital or sometimes an overnight stay.
- Ultrasound-guided biopsy is an excision biopsy, of the impalpable abnormal area that has previously been located by the radiologist using ultrasound and indicated with a mark on the skin.
- Wire-guided biopsy is an excision biopsy, of the impalpable abnormal area that has been located by the radiologist inserting a fine wire into the breast with mammographic control.

Women need to understand that they will have a small scar on the breast following an excision biopsy.

Symptomatic women attending a hospital breast clinic may generally expect to be investigated by clinical examination, mammography and/or ultrasound scan, and FNA. Any of these investigations may embarrass and upset the patient. Careful explanation of these procedures and an indication of what patients may reasonably expect (mammography is momentarily painful; FNA or a tru-cut biopsy may result in bruising) is often helpful. In addition, patients should be kept warm and attention should be paid to modesty avoiding unnecessary exposure of the patient. The patient should also be chaperoned if being examined by a male doctor.

**Preoperative care**  Once the diagnosis of breast cancer has been made, it is extremely important that the woman and her partner understand what the implications of surgery may be on her body image. They must have the opportunity to voice their feelings about the surgery with the doctors and nurses involved in their care. It is now known that the long-term mortality rates following mastectomy, or wide local excision as the treatment for primary and localized breast cancer are similar (Fisher *et al.*, 1985). In 1994 concerns were raised about the validity of some of the data in Fisher's trial but, even when the suspect data are excluded, the overall conclusions of the trial remain unchanged (Wuethrich, 1994). Therefore, patient choice becomes an essential criteria when considering two equally successful treatments.

An assessment of the patient's main concern prior to surgery is vital. Fallowfield *et al.* (1990) showed that there was a significant effect of surgeon type on the incidence of depression, with patients treated by surgeons who offered a choice showing less depression than those treated by other surgeons. Morris and Royle (1988) also found that involving the patient in the decision-making process had a positive effect on anxiety and depression scores. Both these patients and their partners had improved scores, up to 6 months postoperatively regardless of whether they had chosen mastectomy or breast conservation. A woman who has strong negative feelings about mastectomy may wish to conserve her breast, but equally a woman who will be anxious about cancer in the remaining breast tissue may prefer a mastectomy. In both instances the patient can benefit from discussion about treatments with a nurse. This discussion will also give her the opportunity to express and clarify her feelings.

Denton and Baum (1983) found that women whose prime concern prior to surgery was breast loss rather than having cancer were more likely to require psychiatric referral later. However, if a woman has a malignant tumour behind the nipple, she may well need help from the nurse to understand the likely adverse cosmetic effect of a wide excision as opposed to a mastectomy. There has been a distinct trend towards breast conservation as the preferred treatment for early breast cancer in recent years (Morris *et al.*, 1992). This usually necessitates a 5–6-week course of radiotherapy following surgery. The patient needs to be aware of the time involved and the side effects of radiotherapy when making her choice.

Preoperatively, it is also important for women to know what can be done to alleviate their potential asymmetry following surgery. They should be informed about temporary and semipermanent prostheses and about the possibility of breast reconstruction (see later). Misconceptions about the scar often exist. For instance, some women think they will have a gaping hole in their chest wall following mastectomy. A drawing, picture or explanation of a neat flat scar on the chest wall may alleviate their worst fears.

'Frozen section and proceed' (to mastectomy) is not now recommended practice. Although some women say they would prefer to cope with the uncertain outcome in order to have only one operation, it is now thought to be in the woman's best interest to know the diagnosis prior to definitive surgery (King's Fund, 1986).

**Postoperative care**

Sensitive handling by the nurse is of the utmost importance as women start to adjust to their altered body image. Removal of the dressing for the first time, when the woman is exposed to the reality of her loss can be traumatic and should never be done on a ward round. Nurses can prepare the woman for this event by assisting her to bathe and dress in day clothes prior to the removal of the dressing. The presence of an empathetic nurse during these simple tasks can make a major contribution to the patient's subsequent adjustment. When the dressing is removed for the first time (usually when a redivac drainage tube is removed), the patient should be gently encouraged to look quickly at the wound, before it is recovered. However, forcing the issue can be counterproductive and some women continue to cope by using avoidance tactics. They may raise the height of mirrors or decide to shower rather than have a bath. A nurse can help a patient to realize the limitations of such practices by empathetic discussion and permission to show distress and emotion about her loss. However, the decision about whether to look at the scar or not must belong to the patient. It is never helpful to tell her she has a lovely scar, but it can be helpful to ask her how she feels about it. Sensitive care at this stage will facilitate adjustment to a significantly altered body image.

**Assessment: perceptions and needs**

This is a continuing process and necessary throughout the course of diagnosis and treatment of breast cancer. Of course, in the patient's mind, her notion of altered body image may not be separated from the reasons for which the operation took place, i.e. having cancer. The stigma and fear of cancer 'eating the body away', 'invading the good cells' and causing body wastage and pain are common. In addition, misconceptions about the cosmetic effects of common treatments for breast cancer, such as radiotherapy, chemotherapy and hormone therapy, are often frightening. For some women who have chemotherapy, the thought of undergoing breast loss and subsequently hair loss (even when the latter is of a temporary or minimal nature), can be the last straw. Likewise, oophorectomy can be viewed as a further assault on her femininity.

It is estimated that one in five patients will have problems with altered body image following mastectomy (Maguire, 1985). In order for the nurse to realize the impact of altered body image on a woman, she needs to have some baseline assessment of how much body image mattered to that woman prior to her diagnosis and treatment. The structure of assessment and the methods used to manage this, are described by Tait *et al.* (1982). With body image issues, it helps if the nurse asks general questions initially and, then, depending on the answers by the woman, tentatively begins to ask more personal questions as the patient's trust develops. A general question might be: 'Generally speaking, are you someone who is figure-conscious or worries about how you look?' If the patient answers 'yes', the nurse might then ask: 'How important would you say that your breasts are?'. If the patient answers that her breasts are important, the nurse can ask specific questions such as: 'Do you normally wear low necklines?' or 'Do you normally wear clothes that reveal your figure?'. If the patient does, it can be helpful to ask if she is a sun worshipper. Many women now go topless when sunbathing. The impact of mastectomy on such a practice could be devastating, though some women are confident enough to continue doing this.

It is estimated that one in three women will develop sexual problems following mastectomy, and that one in four will develop a clinical depression or anxiety state within the year following surgery (Maguire *et al.*, 1978). The evidence suggests that such problems become chronic unless recognized and treated. Nurses can invite discussion about sexuality and sexual relationships by asking the patient such general questions about a relationship as: 'Do you think you will be able to let your partner see your scar?', 'Does your partner usually see you undressed?'. Even if the answer is 'no', it should not be assumed that there is no physical relationship. Some women express enormous relief when these issues are raised and are only too pleased to discuss their fears with an understanding nurse (Fallowfield, 1992). Discussion with a nurse may enable the patient to discuss these things with her partner or help her find the courage to allow the relationship to resume. Involving the partner in these discussions may be beneficial to both the patient and her partner, but must always be with the permission of the patient. However, some women are unable or unwilling to discuss such topics, so the nurse must be very aware and sensitive to the patient's responses at the outset of such discussions. Assessment of a patient's morale, as well as her feelings about sexuality, are important as these are linked with her feelings about body image.

Unfortunately, the incidence of depression and anxiety in women undergoing partial breast loss and radiotherapy as a primary treatment appear to be similar, so these are not solely issues related to mastectomy (Fallowfield *et al.*, 1990). Any scar on the breast can result in the perception of an altered body image. A nurse involved in counselling of this nature can enable a woman to control her own situation better and promote the process of rehabilitation, as Watson *et al.*'s (1984) and McArdle *et al.*'s (1996) studies have shown. In another study, where patients undergoing mastectomy were randomized to routine care alone or routine care plus the services of a specialist nurse, the results were similar. There was a threefold reduction in psychiatric problems in the group seen by the specialist nurse (Maguire *et al.*, 1980). In addition, women who had seen the specialist nurse returned to work more quickly, showed a greater sense of social recovery, and adapted better to breast loss and a prosthesis (Maguire *et al.*, 1983).

**Provision of temporary and semipermanent breast prostheses**

Although it cannot be assumed that all women will want a breast prosthesis (Lorde, 1980), this important aspect of care has often been neglected (Simpson, 1985; Pendleton and Smith, 1986) and in the UK has only in recent years begun to improve. It is now accepted that every woman after breast surgery should have a breast prosthesis of her choice if she so wishes (Royal College of Nursing of the United Kingdom, 1994).

A soft fibre-filled 'cumfie' should be offered postoperatively to a woman to replace her lost shape as soon as she wants to wear it. These days, women are encouraged to dress in comfortable day clothes and wear a bra within 2 or 3 days of the operation. Pope (1981) has shown how 'cumfies' can be pinned into a nightdress if the patient prefers.

It is helpful if women understand what is likely to happen to them before they are fitted with their semipermanent prosthesis. Many of them appreciate having relevant literature depicting breast prostheses. Some may wish to see and feel a sample breast prostheses before leaving hospital but many are not ready at this stage to cope with a realistic replacement. They may find the mere thought of a prosthesis, let alone the feel of one, very upsetting, and so the nurse must show great sensitivity when introducing the subject. Not all women want a prosthesis and its use should never be forced on them. Women should be told when they could be fitted prior to their hospital discharge and have a contact telephone number of the appliance officer if the fitter is other than the breast care nurse. The patient should understand that the prosthesis can be changed whenever necessary. When being fitted it may be helpful for someone else to accompany the patient so that moral support and constructive criticism can be given. A woman should, if possible, wear garments that reveal her figure when being fitted, such as a thin jumper or a well-fitting T-shirt. Before any semipermanent prosthesis can be fitted, the patient must have a well-fitting bra and it is surprising how few women bother, in the normal course of events, to have one fitted. Pockets to hold prostheses can be fitted into her usual bras free of charge via the hospital surgical appliance service.

A semipermanent breast prosthesis is usually made of silicone and can be fitted as soon as the patient's wound has healed, normally between 1 and 2 months after the operation. If a course of radiotherapy is given, the skin may be too tender during or immediately after treatment, so a temporary prosthesis can be worn. There is now a good selection of whole or partial breast prostheses available through the National Health Service, including some self-adhesive prostheses. These use hypoallergenic adhesive and work very well for some women. However, there is a caution with self-adhesive prostheses for women who have had a course of radiotherapy to the chest wall. They must seek individual advice from their radiotherapy consultant before use, because damage to irradiated skin can present difficult healing problems. These are also problems which may not improve with time.

Breast Cancer Care is a charitable organization which provides support and information to women with breast cancer. It also has a comprehensive range of breast prostheses available for fitting purposes and for inspection for women who feel they are only being given a limited choice locally.

**Breast reconstruction**

This can be an important part of a patient's total treatment. Women should be aware of the possibility of reconstruction at the time of their initial surgery. It is especially important for women who continue to feel upset by their breast loss. It is increasingly accepted that reconstruction is available within the NHS and it is recommended that this should continue as part of the total treatment for breast cancer (King's Fund, 1986). Women should be aware that the position, size, shape and feel (and sometimes the temperature) of a reconstructed breast may not be the same as the original. A consultation with a plastic surgeon is necessary to discuss the most suitable reconstruction for each individual patient. In the case of a large-breasted woman, a reduction mammoplasty on the normal side may be necessary to achieve a good cosmetic result. Concerns have been raised in the United States about the use of silicone implants, but the Department of Health in the UK has found no cause for concern at present has but set up a central register at the Salisbury Plasic Surgery Unit to monitor the continuing use of silicone implants. The patients concerned must be informed of any risks but, at present, the Department of Health policy is that the benefits outweigh the risks for women who want a reconstruction.

Psychologically a woman needs to be realistic about what a reconstruction may offer. Some women hope it may improve their relationship with their partner but this is seldom the case. If a woman realizes that she is not, in fact, obtaining another breast but a shape that will at least give her a cleavage, she is more likely to adapt. It can be helpful when a woman has doubts about a reconstruction if she can be shown photographs of good and bad cosmetic results. She may also benefit from meeting someone who has already had a reconstruction. The nurse can help by making information available and giving support when the woman makes her decision.

*Types of implant*

The following types are available:

- Inflatable implants. These are filled with a saline solution after insertion.

- Silicone gel implants. These come in different shapes and sizes.

With both types leakage can be a problem.

| | |
|---|---|
| *Subcutaneous mastectomy* | This involves a mastectomy in which all the internal breast tissue is removed, leaving the nipple and areolar with its blood supply intact. An implant is inserted into the cavity. This operation can only be considered for women with non-invasive carcinoma, for example, intraduct or lobular carcinoma *in situ*. It is sometimes recommended as a prophylactic treatment for women with a high risk of developing breast cancer. |
| *Subpectoral implant* | This is a silicone implant which is placed under the pectoralis muscle on the chest wall. |
| *Latissimus dorsi musculocutaneous* | The latissimus dorsi musculocutaneous skin flap from the woman's back is passed through a skin tunnel under the axilla and brought out on to the mastectomy wound. The latissimus dorsi muscle and pectoralis major muscles are sutured to allow a silicone implant to be inserted. |
| *Rectus abdominus* | The transverse rectus abdominus musculocutaneous flap from the lower abdomen is lifted on to the chest wall at the site of the mastectomy. The muscles are sutured to allow a silicone implant to be inserted. |
| *Nipple and areola reconstruction* | There are many difficulties in attempting to duplicate a nipple. When a nipple is free of tumour it may be saved by being sewn to a temporary site. However, inadequate projection and lack of erectile properties pose many problems. Silicone nipples are available commercially and can on occasion be made to measure (Priestley, 1992). |
| *Postoperative nursing care* | This can vary according to the operative procedure used. Women need to wear a well-supporting bra or a mammary vest immediately following surgery. They are often instructed not to raise their |

arms above shoulder height for at least 3 weeks postoperatively. When the wound has healed, massaging the breast may help to keep it soft but it is important that the breast should not be pressed downwards towards the suture line. Postoperative complications can include sepsis, haematoma, implant encapsulation and sloughing of skin edges with resulting necrosis.

**Lymphoedema**

Lymphoedema has, until a few years ago, almost been ignored together with its effect on body image. It has been considered an inevitable side effect of breast cancer treatment, for which little or nothing could be done. Much of the interest and expertise now being developed in this field, has been inspired by the palliative care movement and their attention to symptom control.

Brennan (1992) stated that lymphoedema occurs when lymphatic vessels fail to keep up with the normal demands of tissue homeostasis. This results in accumulation of protein-rich fluid in the interstitial spaces of affected tissues. It can be a chronic wearying condition and can be an added threat to a woman's feelings about her body image. A large and heavy arm can impede normal functioning to a significant degree. Mobility is often impaired and many items of clothing may be difficult, if not impossible to wear.

Lymphoedema is a potential side effect for any breast cancer patient who has an intervention of either surgery or radiotherapy in the axilla, or has a progression or recurrence of her disease. The incidence is high in women who require both treatments.

Hoe *et al.* (1992) and Ivens *et al.* (1992) both found that a third of patients undergoing axillary clearance in their unit complained of arm swelling and 8% said it interferred with everyday life. Lymphoedema is a chronic progressive disorder and increasingly interferes with perceived body image. There is much that the nurse can do to enable the patient to minimize its occurrence. This includes:

- The early mobilization of the affected arm.
- Education and information about the potential risk.
- The need for prompt treatment when it occurs.

Patients, following an intervention in the axilla, should be advised to:

- Use the arm normally.
- Use rubber gloves or gardening gloves when necessary.

- Use a thimble when sewing.
- Use depilatory cream or a battery razor for underarm hair removal.
- Use insect repellent cream when necessary.
- Avoid vaccinations, inoculations and injections in the affected arm.
- Avoid sustained carrying.
- Be aware that any inflammation or swelling in the hand or arm needs medical advice.

*Treatment*

When considering treatment, screening should exclude active disease, venous occlusion, pathological fracture and infection because appropriate treatment as well as, or instead of, may be required. A treatment programme is likely to include assessment, exercise, a specific massage regimen, compression sleeves, use of intermittent or graduated compression pumps and bandaging. If lymphoedema is treated at the outset, when first noted, it can be controlled without the use of compression pumps and bandaging, which is time consuming both for the patient and the carer. Patient compliance is essential with all of these treatments, and nurses have a role to play in explaining, advising and monitoring progress. The British Lymphology Interest Group was formed in 1985 to co-ordinate interest, encourage research and provide a multidisciplinary forum for those treating lymphoedema (Badger, 1986). Both this group and Breast Cancer Care provide patient literature explaining and advising about this condition.

**Lay and professional resources**

The charity Breast Cancer Care, as well as the prosthesis service already mentioned, provides literature, practical information, a free telephone helpline, and an individual and trained volunteer service. The volunteer service allows a woman who has undergone surgery for breast cancer to meet someone who has had a similar experience at least 2 years previously. Such a person can be a positive example of survival, adjustment and the ability to cope, and can greatly encourage a patient who is facing the stress of diagnosis and treatment.

The charities Bacup and Cancerlink are also able to provide written and helpline information and support for these women and their families.

Among many committed carers, lay and professional, there are increasing numbers of specially trained breast care nurses in the UK now, who can help the patient to cope with the fear and distress of breast cancer and begin the adaptation process to an altered body image. In some cases, nurses and volunteers can liaise, complementing each other in the care that is given.

Nurses also need to know what self-help groups exist locally and how patients and professionals evaluate them. Breast Care Nurses, if they do not fit breast prostheses, need good and close liaison with appliance officers and commercial representatives. They are also likely to need good liaison with clinical psychologists, psychotherapists, psychiatrists, community psychiatric nurses, sex therapists and physiotherapists for referral when necessary.

The most important resource of all, however, is the patient herself (Tait, 1985), her family and her friends, for with a sensitive and caring nursing team, she can be helped to work towards adequate management of her body image problems. A woman with breast cancer may face an uncertain future, but a competent nurse can help give her the confidence to cope, always bearing in mind that referral to others may be necessary.

**Case study**

*Ann was diagnosed with breast cancer when 34 years old. At presentation, because her lump was small and situated away from the nipple, she was given treatment options, i.e. wide excision and radiotherapy, or mastectomy. Both treatments included axillary clearance. Ann opted for breast conservation, with very little hesitation.*

*Ann was slim, attractive, and fashionably-dressed, with long dark hair, which she wore in a variety of styles. Her husband, John, accompanied her to all her hospital appointments and was caring and supportive. They had one 6-year-old son and had recently decided to 'to try for another baby' having miscarried during a pregnancy when James was 3 years old. Ann enjoyed aqua-aerobics and working out at the gym. They were a close, energetic, outdoor family. After an initial discussion with the surgeon, Ann and John discussed the proposed treatment of wide excision, axillary clearance and radiotherapy with the Breast Care Nurse, including the effects that these treatments would impose on their lifestyle. Ann was advised not to go swimming during the course of radiotherapy and that tiredness might limit her working out initially and some of her more energetic family activities. She was reassured that all those activities could resume as soon as she was able and once treatment was completed. Though Ann had a modest 34 B* bust size, she expressed fears that she did not know how she or John would have coped with mastectomy, and was very relieved to have been able to conserve her breast.

Ann's postoperative recovery was uneventful, other than her expressing her anger about her 'loss of fertility and this disease invading every aspect of her life', for she had been advised not to contemplate another pregnancy for at least 2 years. Although she had not desperately wanted another child (it was more John's idea) prior to the diagnosis, she now felt that the most female parts of her being, her breast and her capacity to bear a child, had been assaulted. Her discussion with the breast-care nurse related to her loss, bereavement and loss of control, also that body image was perhaps something that is perceived by the individual rather than being visually apparent to someone else.

When the pathology report following the operation was available, Ann's cancer had spread to two lymph nodes and a course of adjuvant chemotherapy was recommended. Though Ann had been aware of this possibility, she had hoped it would not occur. Losing her hair was the final insult and, although Ann did not become completely bald, she was extremely distressed by the degree to which her hair thinned. Her remaining long hair was cut short and, although she would not tolerate a full wig, she was creative with the use of 'hairpieces', scarves, hats and earrings. On good days, she looked stunning but on the bad, she did not look like the old Ann at all.

It was summer time throughout her course of radiotherapy and she hated having to cover up her radiotherapy planning marks. Her limited choice of clothing interfered with her perception of herself and her loss of control over her body image. John was attentive and caring and managed to find earrings, scarves and silk underwear to surprise her in an effort to lift her mood and soothe her battered image. Despite these problems, one year later, Ann had resumed all her usual activities. Her hair had regrown curly and somewhat streaked with grey, but as Ann said positively 'I would never have had a short and curly hair style if it hadn't been for chemotherapy'. She and John had come to believe that perhaps they were better with only one child; materially they could provide so much more for him.

Three years later, to the month, as Ann tearfully reminded the medical team, she was aware of discomfort in the same breast. An almost impalpable thickening was proven by fine-needle aspiration and mammogram to be carcinoma. During the following traumatic 2 weeks, Ann's disease was restaged by blood tests, chest X-ray, bone scan and liver scan, all of which were normal. Ironically, Ann was relieved to accept that her worst nightmare, a mastectomy, was the only course of action. John, as before, was by her side. Following the operation Ann expressed her revulsion about her 'one-sidedness' and her fears about John seeing the scar. So on the day before hospital discharge it was agreed that the dressing should be changed while John was present, discreetly but in a routine matter of fact way. John was invited to stay and readily agreed to when the nurses came to change the dressing. It was a neat flat scar, in which the sutures needed to remain for 3 weeks because of Ann's previous radiotherapy. They both cried and held each other and John said 'It wasn't as bad as he had expected'.

Ann was soon up and about the ward, wearing her 'cumfie' and taking care of her appearance. She was constantly concerned that her cumfie was the right size and in the right place and needed constant reassurance. When she came to be fitted for her semipermanent prosthesis she was pleased by the range of choice and was very positive, after an initial reluctance about the choice available. She brought bras and swimsuits to try on and was encouraged by the fact that few of these items needed to be discarded or required only minor adjustments. She discussed reconstruction readily and was aware that, because of the previous radiotherapy, a delay time of 2 years was recommended. Ann also revealed that she had been embarrassed to be naked after her breast conservation operation, so was not sure that reconstruction was what she wanted. She knew it made no difference to John but also knew that she had lost the carefree, comfortable confidence that she had felt when undressed prior to her breast surgery.

Ann quickly resumed her usual activities again including her aqua-aerobics, for which she felt most secure wearing a mastectomy swimsuit. She was able to enjoy and share her son's comments about 'mummy's bionic boobie'.

Some 3 years on, Ann remains fit and well, she still swims a lot but decided she had become too old for the aqua-aerobics. She does not think she will bother with reconstruction, neither she nor John need it. She has adapted to her altered body image; she does not like it, but accepts that is how she is now. She likes to see any new prostheses that become available but tends to be very attached to the one which was fitted first. Ann recently offered to become a volunteer and talk to other women undergoing surgery for breast cancer saying 'I've coped when I never ever thought I would', so she is in touch with Breast Cancer Care to do some volunteer training.

**References**   Badger, C. (1986) The swollen limb. *Nursing Times* **82**(31), 40–41.

Bard, M. and Sutherland, A. (1952) The psychological impact of cancer and its treatment. Adaptation to radical mastectomy. *Cancer* **8**, 656.

Brennan, M. (1992) Lymphoedema following the surgical treatment of breast cancer. *Journal of Pain Management* **7**(2), 110–116.

Denton, S. and Baum, M. (1983) Psychosocial aspects of breast cancer. In: Margolese, R. (ed.) *Breast Cancer*. Edinburgh, Churchill Livingstone.

Dobson, S. (1983) Bringing culture into care. *Nursing Times* **79**(5), 53–57.

Fallowfield, L. (1992) The quality of life: sexual function and body image following cancer therapy. *Cancer Topics* **9**(2), 20–21.

Fallowfield, L., Hall, A., Maguire, G. and Baum, M. (1990) Psychological outcomes of different treatment policies in women with early breast cancer outside a clinical trial. *British Medical Journal* **301**, 575–580.

Fisher, B., Redmond, C., Fisher, E. *et al.* (1985) 5-year results of a randomized clinical trial comparing total mastectomy with or without radiotherapy in the treatment of breast cancer. *New England Journal of Medicine* **312**(11), 674–681.

Forrest, P. (1987) *Breast Cancer Screening*. London, HMSO.

Hoe, A., Ivens, D., Royle, G. and Taylor, I. (1992) Incidence of arm swelling following axillary clearance for breast cancer. *British Journal of Surgery* **79**, 261–262.

Ivens, D., Hoe, A., Podd, T., Hamilton, C., Taylor, I. and Royle, G. (1992) Assessment of morbidity from complete axillary dissection. *British Journal of Cancer* **66**, 136–138.

*King's Fund Consensus Conference on the Treatment of Primary Breast Cancer* (1986) London, King's Fund.

Lorde, A. (1980) *The Cancer Journals*. London, Sheba Feminist Publications.

Maguire, P. (1985) The psychological impact of cancer. *British Journal of Hospital Medicine* August, 100–103.

Maguire, P., Lee, E. and Bevington, D. (1978) Psychiatric problems in the first year after mastectomy. *British Medical Journal* **April**, 963–965.

Maguire, P., Tait, A., Brooke, M. and Sellwood, R. (1980) The effect of counselling on the psychiatric morbidity associated with mastectomy. *British Medical Journal* **2**, 1454–1456.

Maguire, P., Brooke, M., Tait A., Thomas, C. and Sellwood, R. (1983) The effect of counselling on physical disability and social recovery after mastectomy. *Clinical Oncology* **9**, 319–321.

Markowski, J., Wilcox, J. and Helm, P. (1981) Lymphoedema incidence after special post-mastectomy therapy. *Archives of Physical Rehabilitation* **62**, 449–452.

McArdle, J., George, W. and McArdle, C. (1996) Psychological support for patients undergoing breast cancer surgery: a random study. *British Medical Journal* **312**, 813–817.

Morris, J. and Royle, G. (1988) Offering patients a choice of surgery for early breast cancer: A reduction in anxiety and depression in patients and their husbands. *Social Science and Medicine,* **27**(11), 1257–1262.

Morris, J., Farmer, A. and Royle, G. (1992) Recent changes in the surgical management of T1/2 breast cancer in England. *European Journal of Cancer* **28A**(10), 1709–1712.

Norris, C. (1978) Body image – its relevance to professional nursing. In: Carlson, C. and Blackwell, B. (eds) *Behavioural Concepts and Nursing Intervention.* Philadelphia, Lippincott.

Pendleton, L. and Smith, G. (1986) Provision of breast prostheses. *Nursing Times* **82**(22), 37–39.

Priestley, M. (1992) Breast reconstruction following mastectomy. *British Journal of Nursing* **1**(3), 118–121.

Pope, B. (1981) After the mastectomy, prosthesis and clothing. *Nursing Times* **77**(6), 314–318.

Rosser, J. (1981) The interpretation of women's experience – a critical appraisal of the literature on breast cancer. *Social Science and Medicine* **15**(E), 257–265.

Royal College of Nursing of the United Kingdom (1994) *Breast Care Nursing Standards.* London, Scutari Press.

Sampson, C. (1982) *The Neglected Ethic, Religious and Cultural Factors in the Care of Patients.* London, McGraw Hill.

Simpson, G. (1985) Are you being served? *Senior Nurse* **2**(6), 14–16.

Stanway, A. and Stanway, P. (1982) *The Breast – What Every Woman Needs to Know from Youth to Old Age.* London, Granada.

Tait, A. (1985) *The Mastectomy Experience. Two Interviews Examined. Studies in Sexual Politics.* Sociology Department, University of Manchester.

Tait, A., Maguire, P., Faulkner, A., Brooke, M., Wilkinson, S., Thomson, L. and Sellwood, R. (1982) Improving communication skills. The use of a standardised assessment for mastectomy patients. *Nursing Times* **78**(51), 2181–2184.

Vessey, M. and Gray, M. (1991) *Breast Cancer Screening 1991: Evidence and Experience since the Forrest Report.* Sheffield, NHSBSP Publications.

Watson, M. (1984) The effectiveness of specialist nurses as oncology nurses. In: Watson, M. and Greer, S. (eds) *Psychosocial Issues in Malignant Disease. Proceedings of the 1st Psychosocial Oncology Conference.* Oxford, Pergamon Press.

Wuethrich, B. (1994) Trials on trial. *New Scientist* 28 May, 14–15.

CHAPTER 9

# The gynaecological perspective

*Tonia Dawson*

**Introduction**

Body image, self-concept and sexuality are intrinsically linked with the definition of who and what we are. Despite the Women's Independence Movement and the sexual evolution of women, the traditional view of femininity and womanhood represented by childbearing, motherhood and family life, is still apparent in society today. The issues such as abortion, lesbianism and infertility challenge these expectations and can have a profound effect on how we feel about ourselves and ultimately the quality of our lives.

Dickson (1990) points out that, long before puberty, most of us are aware of the importance and the significance of our appearance. Although individuals may refuse to conform, we still know that girls are expected to be graceful, attractive and to stay clean. Similarly, women are expected not only to bear and nurture their children but also to extend their 'maternal' qualities of caring, nurturing and self-sacrifice to one and all. Dickson (1990) highlights the media's portrayal of women and the use of women's bodies to add decorative appeal to whatever is for sale from soap powder to cars. With so much importance vested on outward appearance, it is no wonder that some women ask themselves 'How do I look?' instead of 'Who am I?'. Gynaecological disorders bring with them a real threat to femininity. It is this threat that results in a loss of self-esteem leading to a feeling of worthlessness.

The following chapter emphasizes the need for sensitive informed nursing within a gynaecological setting. Many of the issues raised are of an intimate nature and may remain unresolved and unspoken if not brought to the surface. There will be feelings of guilt and embarrassment. The overriding priority for the nurse is to generate feelings of acceptance and self-esteem.

**Surgery**

A gynaecological operation, whether it be large or small, involves the organs of a system that is, or has been, of special significance in a woman's concept of herself as a female. All women should be seen by a nurse prior to surgery. They should be admitted early so that the nurse can utilize this time to develop an open considerate relationship and to prepare them for pre- and postoperative experiences. If the woman wishes, her partner should be present.

The surgical treatment obviously differs for each organ site as does the extent of surgery but the physical consequences of certain gynaecological surgery can be quite damaging to a woman's image of herself. For instance, the loss of emotive organs, the disappearance of menstruation, loss of femininity and hormonal disturbances. Young women often view themselves as less desirable as a marital or sexual partner, and many women have misconceptions about their anatomy and physiology. Nurses, therefore, need to devote uninterrupted time to these women to offer them correct information and reassurance. Unfortunately, many of the psychological problems do not manifest themselves until many months postsurgery, which is why nurses need to be forward thinking in offering support and advice. No woman should suffer because of ignorance about her operation or its effects.

Hysterectomy is one of the most frequently performed operations on women. Research findings have often appeared contradictory as to its effect on women, perhaps reflecting inherent methodological problems and confusions over the type of hysterectomy performed. Early studies emphasize the adverse psychological sequelae, which have not been confirmed by prospective studies. Ryan *et al.* (1989) in their prospective study on psychological aspects of hysterectomy found, in their 60 women, that there was a high prevalence of preoperative psychological morbidity (55%), which reduced to 31.7% afterwards. There was no evidence that hysterectomy led to a greater psychological distress.

Webb and Wilson-Barnett (1983) conducted a comprehensive study of 142 patients recovering from a hysterectomy for benign disease. The results of the interview conducted 4 months after surgery indicated that depression was not caused by hysterectomy as suggested by previous research but was in fact reduced. Anxiety and fatigue were also reduced, while vigour and hostility levels were increased, and self-concept appeared relatively unchanged. Women generally felt healthier than before the operation and, within 4 months, were back to their previous activity levels. Delayed recovery seemed to be related to unresolved physical symptoms, mainly infections, and there were some indications that social support was related to outcome.

Hysterectomy operations are performed for numerous reasons, therefore, it is important that we learn, as tactfully and as thoroughly as we can, what meaning the reproductive organs have for the individual patient and how they feel about the forthcoming surgery (Price, 1990). It cannot be assumed that all patients will grieve the loss of their uterus. For every patient who says it saddens me to lose my 'baby cradle', there seems to be another who is glad to be rid of symptoms from their disease and enjoy a new-found freedom.

Whilst hysterectomy remains the classic hidden surgery, not all gynaecological surgery is hidden. Extensive surgery for cancer, such as vulvectomy or pelvic exenteration, produces extreme visual disfigurement. For many women, this surgery is an incredible threat to their femininity. Anderson and Hacker (1983) empirically documented body-image disruption in patients with vulvic cancer. They concluded that, although patients adjusted socially and within their partnerships, body image and sexual function appeared to undergo 'major disruption' even if patients were able to have sexual intercourse. Likewise, Sewell and Edwards (1980) propose that sexual dysfunction in women undergoing radical vulvectomies approaches 100%. The cosmetic changes resulting from a vulvectomy causes alterations in self-image that can preclude sexual intimacy for many of these women. Springer (1982) cites that socially, the woman's age, length of time in a relationship and her perception of the feminine role will affect the quality of her adjustment to a radical vulvectomy. The need for continuing support, education and realistic sexual counselling is great.

Pelvic exenteration, in which the bladder, vagina, uterus, rectum and associated structures are removed *en bloc*, with ostomies created for urinary and faecal excretion is the recommended treatment for some advanced pelvic cancers. Obviously, such radical surgery entails a major psychological adjustment. Dempsey *et al.* (1975) found that, whilst the surgery offers a significantly improved prognosis and that quality of life is satisfactory, it is sexual function that is compromised. However, Morley *et al.* (1973) reports that construction of a neovagina, with the special attention to sexual rehabilitation entailed, enhances the sexual outcome significantly. Anderson and Hacker's (1983) study stated that the role of a caring partner and the patient's own motivation cannot be underestimated in rehabilitative efforts.

**Menopause**

One of women's greatest fears of gynaecological surgery is the fear of hormonal changes and early menopause. It is important to distinguish between two words here, 'climacteric' and 'menopause'. 'Climacteric' refers to the cessation of ovarian function. The specific symptoms that occur at this time owing to the lowering of oestrogen levels are the climacteric symptoms. The cessation of menstruation is one of the most significant symptoms and this is known as the 'menopause'. Other physical changes are atrophy of the reproductive organs, hot flushes, osteoporosis (a condition in which there is a reduction of the total amount of bone material in the bones) and an increase in androgens, which can increase hair in unwanted areas and the skin may become slightly coarser (Farrer, 1987).

Epidemiological studies on the climacteric performed in the USA, Europe and South East Asia reveal that typical and atypical climacteric symptoms are more severe and result in greater use of medicaments in Western cultures. The psychological impact of the menopause is also much less of a problem in Asia than in Western countries.

The ideal situation for women is for their general practitioners (GPs) to deal with the 'uncomplicated' climacteric symptoms and to have the back up of a menopause clinic available for the referral of women who need specialized counselling, treatment or screening for predisposing factors to the longer term consequences of oestrogen deficiency. Unfortunately, Garnett et al. (1990) showed that 75% of all women attending a menopause clinic had referred themselves and that 38% of those women had suffered from climacteric symptoms for more than 5 years, so there is still a long way to go before these women are taken seriously.

Exercise has been reported to alleviate climacteric symptoms. Preliminary evidence indicates that both hot flushes and depression are less severe in women who exercise regularly (Short, 1990; Hunter, 1990). Short observed that the exercise factor could be the key to suffering less at the menopause.

Finally, it must be mentioned that, for women having adjuvant treatment of radiotherapy or chemotherapy, information and counselling are critical so that they understand the degree of ovarian failure involved and are given correct information on hormone replacement therapy. Body image problems can be avoided if they are given adequate support and treatment for their symptoms. At present, unless there are reasons for withholding oestrogen and progesterone treatment from women, hormone replacement therapy is the preferred choice of treatment, especially for the pre-vention of osteoporosis and heart disease.

**Screening**

Politics determine that future health initiatives lie in preventive screening, health education and counselling with a greater com-mitment to community initiatives. Perhaps the most pervasive limitation of this is that it holds the individual responsible for her health with an analysis that takes no account of those social factors that are beyond an individual's control.

This is relevant when we review the worldwide figures for cer-vical cancer of 465 000, accounting for 15% of all cancers diag-nosed in women. However, only 20% of these occur in developed countries with 80% occurring in developing countries, yet the assumption is made that individuals can control their own lifestyle and improve their health. The 'victim blaming' attitude is high-lighted in Bos's study of gynaecological cancer patients. A total of 53 women were asked what they perceived to be the cause of their cancer. It is striking that two-thirds of this group ascribed the cause to themselves experiencing extreme guilt (Bos, 1984).

This guilt is brought on by the media and medical literature linking cervical cancer with promiscuity and early sexual experi-ence, so that cervical intraepithelial neoplasia (CIN) and cancer can be seen by some as punishment for real or imagined sexual behaviour, leading to shame and embarrassment. Studies have highlighted how these feelings can prevent people attending screening programmes (McKie, 1993).

Other real fears of women attending screening programmes are that an abnormal pap smear is indicative of invasive cancer and the younger women fear the possible loss of reproductive function (McDonald et al., 1989). Few studies exist to determine the fears and concerns of patients being screened for gynaecological can-cers. McDonald et al. (1989), however, looked at 20 women with CIN and how the diagnosis and treatment of this affected self-esteem and body image. Concern for cancer overrode all the con-cerns except during the postsurgery visit, at which time loss of attractiveness was paramount. Loss of sexual functioning ranked high in all visits. As might be expected, self-esteem was lowest and anxiety highest during the initial and postsurgery visits. The study concluded that health care specialists must be cognizant of the complex issues involved, and devote special attention to fluctua-tions in self-esteem and body image as the patient progresses through treatment in order to expediate her follow-up and recovery. Campion *et al.* (1988) reinforces this idea by stating in their study that the threat posed to life, fertility and future childbearing by the diagnosis of CIN is a source of anxiety which influences most aspects of the woman's sexuality, and stresses the need for supportive and informative counselling.

Screening for ovarian cancer is still a medical and economical issue. For patients who are at high risk with a strong familial history, they should have a blood test to measure for CA 125 antigen and a transvaginal ultrasound (Department of Health, 1991). At present, because the technique is invasive and not proven to be economically effective, there are no mass screening programmes outside the realm of research.

It is important when screening a healthy population not to cause morbidity in a large number of people while trying to prevent major morbidity in a small minority of them. The general public have little understanding of the significance of abnormal results and this leads to many women becoming anxious disproportionate to the real risks.

## Infertility and sterility

Infertility is commonly defined as the failure of a couple to conceive after one year of unprotected coitus. Sterility is when completed investigations show that the couple have no chance of conceiving. Both have a major impact on self-esteem.

For couples, the anxiety of not being able to have a baby and the grief of coming to terms with this can become a major life crisis (Pfeffer and Woolett, 1983). They then have to learn to cope with this in a society that places an emphasis on parenthood. For most women the links between femininity and fertility are very strong, and the woman may feel incomplete if she is unable to produce her own child.

Although little attention has been given to infertility due to cancer, coping with infertility has proven to be even more complicated when it occurs in connection with life-saving treatment (Bos, 1984). In Bos's study on infertility problems of survivors of gynaecological cancers, it appeared that more than 70% of the women in the age group of 21–30 years had severe problems.

There is a role for the nurse as counsellor in infertility. Couples should be seen together and be given accurate honest information. If embarking on treatment, they need to know about the traumas as well as the possible aspects of therapy. Data on reproductive alternatives enable the couple to make informed decisions throughout and may support their efforts to regain control (McCormack, 1980).

## Miscarriage

The experience of miscarriage is physically and psychologically painful. To add to this confusion, the medical terminology of 'spontaneous abortion' is upsetting to a woman's self-image because of the connotations evoked from the word 'abortion'. This was a baby very much wanted, so much so that it can cause a depression equal to postnatal depression (Lewis, 1992). These feelings can be present for a long time, often being reawakened by the birth date of the baby or the sight of other women with babies.

The nurse should encourage her to express her feelings and acknowledge her loss. It is important also that her partner should be involved and allowed to express his grief (Wilkinson, 1987). All women, with or without their partner according to their choice, should have a follow-up visit either with a midwife or GP. After the miscarriage, women are often too shocked to gather the information and support they need (Helmstrom and Helmstrom, 1987), but they still have feelings of anger, guilt and a sense of failure which lowers their image of themselves. Helmstrom and Helmstrom (1987) looked at information and emotional support for women after miscarriage and found that 62% of women thought that support following miscarriage could be better, and many suggested that contact with a midwife for counselling would be helpful. Support for a woman's confidence in further pregnancies is also essential.

## Sexual violence against women

Rape, sexual harassment and indecent assault are acts of violence against women, which create an atmosphere of fear and powerlessness for women. These acts abuse women both physically and psychologically, violating their self-respect and denying them the right to have control over their own sexuality. Sexual violence can have a profound impact on a woman's life, affecting her lifestyle, present and future relationships, how she feels as a woman and her role in society, both at work and at home.

Women who are victims of sexual violence can experience a myriad of emotions and reactions. Feelings of shame and guilt, that somehow women bring it on themselves, may be experienced. Humiliation, embarrassment, disgust, anger and horror are feelings that can induce reactions that range from numbness to disbelief. A supportive and sensitive approach, regardless of one's own reactions, is necessary to enable women to share the burden they carry and to express emotions they are experiencing. Identifying support and resources available, such as partners, close friends, counsellors or local rape crisis centres is essential to ensure women are supported not only in hospital but at home when they are expected to return to their 'normal' lifestyle and role in society.

**Abortion**

Despite the Abortion Act in 1967 legalizing the termination of pregnancy, abortion remains surrounded by moral, social, political as well as medical and psychological issues. These form the basis for the ongoing debate of pro-life versus pro-choice. There is little evidence to suggest that abortion is psychologically or physically harmful. However, this does not mean that women will not react adversely. Decision-making for individuals has the potential for causing distress, although those women who lack social support and understanding for their position, and those who have abortions for fetal abnormalities are more likely to suffer psychological distress.

Fear of being alone, not being wanted by families, the prospect of motherhood, guilt inbred by moral upbringing that abortion is wrong and anger may be experienced by women. Alternatively, the decision may be a positive and powerful affirmation of independence and a tremendous relief from an unwanted pregnancy.

Wanted pregnancies, which are terminated owing to the risk of bearing a handicapped child, can cause intense grief and depression as well as guilt, anger and relief. Women may also feel a loss of femininity as represented by their ability to bear children and failure in womanhood. An environment where these women are able to make decisions free of value judgements and where equal access to resources are available is the ideal situation in which women can be supported and enabled to come to terms with their decision and loss.

**Female circumcision**

This chapter would not be complete without mentioning the devastating effects of female circumcision on a young girl's image of herself as she grows up. Over 100 000 000 girls and women in the world are affected by this practice, a figure which is steadily increasing by 2 000 000 procedures each year. It has previously been a taboo subject but, today, national committees, international organizations and non-governmental organizations address the vast, complex problem which damages the health of so many girls and women (Ismail, 1994).

Female genital mutilation was made illegal in Britain with the Prohibition of Female Circumcision Act 1985, which made it an offence in Britain to excise, infibulate or otherwise mutilate the whole or any part of the labia majora, or labia minora or clitoris of any person. This Act does not, however, make provisions to prohibit children being taken out of the country to have the procedure performed.

The problem for nurses who tackle the issues surrounding female circumcision is the fear they may be regarded as racist (Robson, 1994). They do, however, have an obligation to educate women about the complications involved. These are many, ranging through shock from pain and haemorrhage, accidental trauma to nearby organs, retention of urine, infections, anaemia, lack of sexual enjoyment, failure to consummate marriage, and damage to the mother and child at the time of childbirth (Ismail, 1994). Apart from obvious psychological effects, there are many personal accounts of the terror and unbearable pain, and the subsequent sense of humiliation and of betrayal by parents (Robson, 1994).

**Nursing gynaecology patients**

Guidance for nursing gynaecology patients can be drawn from the literature. Derogatis (1986) states from his research on gynaecology and breast patients that there is evidence that certain patient characteristics appear to have a significant influence on the quality of the patients' adjustment. For instance, a sound psychological posture prior to diagnosis, with evidence of satisfactory resolution of previous life crises and challenges, is usually a good indication that the individual will effectively cope with the stresses of illness. Similarly, good sexual functioning prior to the illness tends to predict a satisfactory sexual adjustment after treatment. Likewise, individuals less invested in sexuality prior to illness are usually in a position to be more graceful concerning its compromise by disease or its treatment (Pfefferbaum et al., 1978)

A woman's attitude is also important and, if her expectations match those of medical personnel, typically the patient will have less difficulty adjusting. Two areas that strongly affect adjustment are how important a woman's outward appearance is to her self-concept and sense of well-being, and how 'feminine' she sees her role in society. Her age plays a vital role but the quality of the patient's relationship with her primary partner and her network of social supports is more important. This is frequently identified as determining the quality of psychological adjustment (Anderson and Hacker, 1983; Wortman, 1984). There is no doubt from research that meaningful and supportive relationships with family, friends and colleagues can substantially deflect the stress inherent in illness.

Whilst the above stand out as the psychosocial variables they can not be isolated from the physical effect caused by the illness and its treatment, interventions have to take the individual's needs and social environment into account. Therefore, a counselling rather than a teaching approach is more appropriate (Webb and Wilson-Barnett, 1983). This allows the nurse to tailor information and support to meet the specific needs of a particular woman. Webb and Wilson-Barnett (1983) found that the quality and quantity of social support in women undergoing hysterectomy for a benign condition was low, and many women were dissatisfied with the amount and type of information given by health care professionals. Webb (1986) in a later paper provides nurses with a guide for their interventions, with hysterectomy patients believing that lay and professional people can learn the supportive role more adequately. She believes that interventions should be mixed relating to factual information as well as coping strategies. Venting emotions can be constructive whilst blanket reassurance is not beneficial. The system identifies housewives as having fewer opportunities to mix and gather information, and, therefore, they may need greater support from health care professionals.

Other people have shown that the woman's preoperative outlook is a good indicator of the problems that will arise postsurgery (Williamson, 1992). She states that alleviating a woman's misconceptions about hysterectomy and counselling her early, can prevent manageable inconveniences from becoming major sexual dysfunctioning. She believes that nurses should include at the minimum a list of what will and will not be removed by surgery, a discussion of the physical and emotional feelings that may change, and an exploration of tangible ways to adjust sexually. Patients should be given privacy and the nurse should address all subjects that the patient would want to hear about but would be too embarrassed to ask.

Postsurgery, the use of vaginal dilators can be beneficial in women with vaginal tightness or scarring, or for those for whom there is concern about the integrity of the vaginal vault. They are also necessary for women undergoing pelvic radiotherapy. Following radiotherapy to the pelvic area, the tissues in the genital area can lose their elasticity and become fibrotic, resulting in a stenosed vagina. Dilators can preserve vaginal patency if used regularly; this needs to be at least three times a week for approximately 5–10 minutes. With regular use, which should be comfortable, vaginal circumference and length can be maintained. Left unaddressed, problems can lead to difficult examination experiences and possibly sexual problems. It is much harder to treat than to prevent and can result in far-reaching effects on relationships.

Finally, for nurses wanting a comprehensive guide on how to assess patients who are having relationship or sexual difficulties, Auchincloss (1989) provides a step-by-step approach. She suggests that the chief complaint is ascertained first by a series of questions using the model of desire, excitement, orgasm, thus establishing where the initial problems lie. This is then extended to cover relationship history, medical treatment and psychiatric history, followed by summarizing and making recommendations. Provision of such supportive interventions and assessment can enhance self-esteem and return control. It should help women to adjust and cope, and ultimately improve their quality of life.

**References**

Anderson, B.L. and Hacker, N.F. (1983) Psychosexual adjustment after vulvar surgery. *Obstetrics and Gynaecology* **62**, 457–462.

Auchincloss, S.S. (1989) Sexual dysfunction in cancer patients: issues in evaluation and treatment. In: Holland, J.R. and Rowland, J.H. (eds) *Handbook of Psychooncology. Psychological Care of the Patient with Cancer*. New York, Oxford University Press, pp. 383–413.

Bos, G. (1984) Psychological aspects of gynaecological surgery. In: Heintz, A.P.M., Griffiths, C.T.H. and Trimbos, S.B. (eds) *Gynaecological Oncology*. The Hague, Martinus Nijhoff, pp. 307–315.

Campion, M.S., Brown, J.R., McCance, D.S. *et al.* (1988) Psychosexual trauma of an abnormal cervical smear. *British Journal of Obstetrics and Gynaecology* **95**, 175–181.

Dempsey, G.M., Buchsbaum, H.J. and Morrison, H. (1975) Psychosocial adjustment to pelvic exenteration. *Gynaecologic Oncology* **3**, 325–334.

Department of Health (1991) *Current Clinical Practices. Management of ovarian cancer*. Report of the Standing Medical

Advisory Committee of the Department of Health. London, HMSO.

Derogatis, L.R. (1986) The unique impact of breast and gynaecological cancers on body image and sexual identity in women: a reassessment. In: Vaeth (ed.) *Body Image: Self Esteem and Sexuality in Cancer Patients*, 2nd edn, pp. 1–14.

Dickson, A. (1990) *The Mirror Within: A New Look at Sexuality*. London, Quartet Books.

Farrer, H. (1985) *New Growths in Gynaecological Care*. Edinburgh, Churchill Livingstone.

Garnett, T., Leather, A., Watson, N.R., Henderson, A. and Studd, S.S. (1990) Patterns of referral to a menopause clinic. *Proceedings of the 6th International Congress of the Menopause*, Bangkok.

Helmstrom, L. and Helmstrom, V.A. (1987) Information and emotional support for women after miscarriage. *Journal of Psychosomatic Obstetrics and Gynaecology* **7**, 93–98.

Hunter, M. (1990) Reduced quality of life during the menopause: who is at risk? *Proceedings of 6th International Congress of the Menopause*, Bangkok.

Ismail, E. (1994) Female genital mutilation. *Midwifery* **10**(3), 123–180.

Kaplan, H.S. (1983) *The Evaluation of Sexual Disorders*. New York, Brunner/Mazel.

Lewis, S. (1992) Recognising the emotional effects of miscarriage. *Professional Care of Mother and Child* November/December, 331–333.

McCormack, T.M. (1980) Cited in Sherrod, R. (ed.) (1988) Coping with infertility: a personal perspective turned professional. *American Journal of Maternal and Child Nursing* **13**, 191–194.

McDonald, T.W., Nentens, J.J., Fischer, L.M. and Jessee, D. (1989) Impact of cervical intraepithelial neoplasia diagnosis and treatment, on self esteem and body image. *Gynaecology Oncology* **34**(3), 345–349.

McKie, L. (1993) Women's views of the smear test: implications for nursing practice. *Journal of Advanced Nursing* **18**, 972–978.

Morley, G.W., Lindenauer, S.M. and Youngs, D. (1973) Vaginal reconstruction following pelvic exenteration: surgical and psychological considerations. *American Journal of Obstetrics and Gynaecology* **116**, 996–1002.

Pfeffer, N. and Woollett, A. (1983) *The Experience of Infertility*. London, Virago.

Pfefferbaum, B., Pasnau, R.O., Jamison, K. and Wellisch, D.K. (1978) A comprehensive program of psychosocial care for mastectomy patients. *International Journal of Psychiatry in Medicine* **8**, 63–72.

Price, B. (1990) Body image – the hysterectomy challenge. In: Price, B. (ed.) *Body Image Nursing: Concepts and Care.* Prentice Hall, New York, pp. 223–234.

Robson, R. (1994) The issue of unspoken abuse. *Nursing Standard* **8**(32), 16–17.

Ryan, M.M., Dennerstein, L. and Pepperell, R. (1989) Psychological aspects of hysterectomy. *British Journal of Psychiatry* **154**, 516–522.

Sewell, H.H. and Edwards, D.W. (1980) Pelvic genital cancer: body image and sexuality. *Frontiers of Radiation Therapy and Oncology,* **14**, 35–41.

Short, R. (1990) Feminine forever or forever feminine? *Proceedings of the 6th International Congress of the Menopause,* Bangkok.

Springer, M. (1982) Radical vulvectomy: physical, psychological, social and sexual implications. *Oncology Nursing Forum* **9**(2), 19–21.

Webb, C. (1986) Professional and lay support for hysterectomy patients. *Journal of Advanced Nursing* **11**, 167–177.

Webb, C. and Wilson-Barnett, J. (1983) Self concept, social support and hysterectomy. *International Journal of Nursing Studies* **20**, 97–107.

Wilkinson, S. (1987) Hidden loss. *Nursing Times* **83** (15 March), 30–32.

Williamson, M.L. (1992) Sexual adjustment after hysterectomy. *Journal of Obstetric, Gynaecologic and Neonatal Nursing* **21**(1), 42–47.

Wortman, C.B. (1984) Social support and the cancer patient. Conceptual and methodologic issues. *Cancer* **53** (10 Suppl.): 2339–2362.

## CHAPTER 10

# Stoma care and its effect on body image

*Mave Salter*

**Introduction**

Walsh *et al.* (1995) suggest that clinical studies have found that patients with a stoma are a group facing multiple adjustment demands. One of these adjustment demands is altered body image. One's visual image is an important part of life, and society places an enormous significance on having an attractive body (Salter, 1992a). This chapter will address the body image concerns in clients with a stoma or continent alternative.

Some people react with shock and disgust when told they may require a stoma, for this type of surgery has a profound effect on the mind as well as the body. It reverses the healthy body image people usually have of themselves. This reaction can occur at any age and it may not be just to the stoma itself, red swollen and unsightly, but also the connotations that go with it. No wonder research into techniques either to do away with wearing a bag or to eliminate the need for a stoma have been in progress for many years.

Much has been said and written about the nursing process and seeing the patient holistically. This is particularly applicable to a stoma or potential stoma patient, and the aim of this chapter is to suggest ways in which the carer can enhance the life of stoma patients. Stoma surgery, whilst sometimes temporary, is mostly permanent and, whilst some patients may have had adequate time for preparation, others will present as an emergency with only a few days' or hours' notice.

**Types of stoma**

There are four main types of stoma (Figures 10.1 and 10.2):

- An end (usually permanent) colostomy.

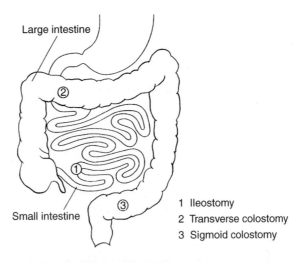

1 Ileostomy
2 Transverse colostomy
3 Sigmoid colostomy

Large intestine

Small intestine

*Figure 10.1*   The positions of bowel stomas.

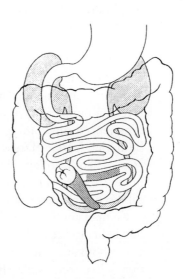

*Figure 10.2*   A diagram of an ideal conduit.

- A transverse (usually temporary) colostomy.
- An ileostomy.
- A urostomy/ileal conduit.

A stoma can be raised for a variety of reasons, but the following conditions are the most common.

| | |
|---|---|
| *Colostomy* | • Cancer of the rectum.<br>• Diverticular disease.<br>• Trauma.<br>• Fistulae (e.g. recto-vaginal).<br>• Past radiotherapy treatment.<br>• Hirschsprung's disease. |
| *Ileostomy* | • Inflammatory bowel disease, e.g. ulcerative colitis and Crohn's disease.<br>• Familial polyposis coli (a hereditary disease where there are multiple polyps that undergo cancerous change). |
| *Urostomy/ileal conduit* | • Cancer of the bladder.<br>• Patients in whom the bladder fails to function, e.g. congenital or acquired damage to nerve supply.<br>• Multiple sclerosis.<br>• Small-capacity bladder. |

**The patient with a stoma**

The literature relating to the experiences of patients with a stoma and their subsequent adaptation to perceived body-image changes reveals a number of common themes, for example, the difficulties experienced in coming to terms with an ostomy (Dyk and Sutherland, 1956; Druss *et al.*, 1968; Devlin *et al.*, 1971; Eardley *et al.*, 1976; Carolan, 1984). Devlin *et al.* (1971) suggest that an immense price is paid for cure, and this price incorporates physical discomfort and psychological and social trauma.

Kelman and Minkler (1989) investigated the impact of a stoma on quality of life and self-esteem in 50 stoma patients by means of a questionnaire and two assessment tools: Rosenberg's ten-question self-esteem scale (Rosenberg, 1965); and Padilla's 28-scale quality of life tool (Padilla and Grant, 1985). The study indicated that there is a relationship between quality of life and self-esteem among individuals with ostomies, and the outcome of the study showed that quality of life and self-esteem were indicative that the overall population had positive perceptions of their stoma. However, in contrast, MacDonald and Anderson (1984) suggest that individuals with stomas often have poor psychosocial outcomes that range from failure to return to occupations, and withdrawal from social and intimate contact, to depression and anxiety.

Wade (1990) suggests that a temporary stoma has a psychological impact on the patient and his or her acceptance and ability to cope will depend on careful explanations, and care and support from health care professionals. Emotional and social effects include feelings of degradation, damage, isolation, restriction and mutilation (Klopp, 1990). Many studies (Devlin *et al.*, 1971; Druss *et al.*, 1968; Kelticangus-Jarvinen *et al.*, 1984; Orbach and Talent, 1974) use psychiatric labels to characterize behaviours observed among individuals with stomas. Common labels include phobic, ritualistic, obsessive, compulsive and fetishist.

Wade (1990) suggests that a patient facing stoma surgery also faces the prospect of a change in appearance and loss of control of elimination. The loss of control over elimination delivers a severe blow to self-esteem and gives rise to fears of rejection by friends and of being ostracized by society. There is also fear of rejection by sexual partners or of marital breakdown.

Druss *et al.* (1968) used questionnaires on 36 patients who had a stoma to elicit their feelings regarding the stoma. The initial reaction of two-thirds of the group was depression. Subcategories included under the depression state were reaction to the loss of a body part, shame at being unable to avoid soiling, fear of being repugnant to others and anger that the surgeon had mutilated their body. Orbach and Talent (1965) sent questionnaires to 48 patients with a stoma 5–10 years after their operation. All believed that their body form had been altered in a destructive way and the passage of time had not changed their feelings.

There are significant disadvantages associated with a stoma. Church (1986) suggests that many patients are restricted in their work, hobbies and travel, while most are limited in their choice of clothing and athletic activities. In addition to these lifestyle restrictions, an end ileostomy may cause physical problems, such as skin irritation due to leakage, and psychosexual and emotional problems due to its effect on body image. The bleak picture that Church paints could be disputed as many patients do not experience the restrictions he suggests. He does, however, admit that, despite this list of drawbacks, most people with stomas, with the aid of a stoma-care nurse and and a well-fashioned stoma, adapt to their body image change and live normal lives.

In the writer's qualitative study (Salter, 1992b) of seven patients, which explored the perceptions of body image in patients with a conventional stoma followed by a continent pouch, it was found that patients with a stoma on the whole expressed difficulties in coming to terms with an ostomy, with perceived negative feelings of body image. In contrast, patients with a continent pouch, provided they were not experiencing difficulties with the pouch, were of the opinion that such a procedure enhanced their lives over that of an ileostomy. However, in examining the respondents' feelings, it was found that the majority still considered their (recent) stoma experience traumatic. This implies that the benefits of a continent pouch, in the early days after stoma reversal, were not so obvious, as body image changes of stoma surgery still had a perceived negative effect on the patients.

A further qualitative study (Salter, 1995), using a semistructured interview of ten patients, explored the perceptions of body image and sexuality in patients with a conventional stoma. The outcome of the study reflected the problems faced by patients undergoing stoma surgery as cited in the literature (e.g. Cahoon, 1973). Patients with a stoma, on the whole, expressed difficulties in coming to terms with an ostomy, with perceived negative feelings of body image and sexuality. However, the respondents had adopted coping mechanisms to adjust to life with a stoma and this is why other literature (e.g. Kelman and Minkler, 1989) suggests that ostomists manage well.

If one can try to imagine the repulsion felt by an ostomist, perhaps it is easier to understand the kind of complex problems faced by stoma patients. Salter (1980) states 'The anus is conveniently and appropriately hidden in the "normal" person; it is functional and effective, usually needing little more than basic toiletry attention. Stoma surgery totally reverses this situation. The anal equivalent is placed on the abdomen in a prominent position, a reminder to the patient that he [or she] can never be cured, for while many surgical procedures leave a scar and memories of an unhealthy part of the body having been removed, a stoma demands continual attention. It can act, sometimes quite audibly, in public and overwork at the wrong, intimate moments. It is subject to various complications and can become a dominant part of the person's daily life'.

Some patients coming to stoma surgery may not have heard of the operation before, or may know someone who has a stoma and, as a consequence, be filled with horror. Others just do not want to know or discuss the subject until the stoma is a reality. Stomas are perfect agents with which to alienate patients from social activity, to encourage them to become reclusive and to create real depression. Yet, to the general public and those relatives and friends to whom they choose not to tell their personal and embarrassing secret, they are, to all intents and purposes, normal healthy human beings. The loss of part of their internal organs and the creation of an external one is a loss that needs to be mourned, and a patient may well go through the various stages of grief (Salter, 1980).

## Stigma

Stoma patients may feel stigmatized by family, society or employers. This is particularly true within some ethnic groups where a young girl with a stoma is not considered acceptable for marriage (Whitethread, 1981). People living in bedsitters and sharing a communal bathroom may go to great pains to ensure their flatmates do not know about their stoma in case they are ridiculed or asked to leave. Incontinence is socially unacceptable – a fact that is instilled into us in childhood. Thus, part of the grieving process stoma patients have to go through is not only the loss of part of their bodies, but of their bladder or bowel control too. In Coe and Kluka's (1988) study, stigma-related sensory phenomena (odour, sound, appearance) was associated with a decreased satisfaction with the body. Furthermore, as this concern increased, satisfaction with self and body decreased.

## Different age groups

Stomas can be raised at any age – from the baby with, for example, imperforate anus, to the child with spina bifida, the adolescent involved in trauma, to the young married with inflammatory bowel disease, the middle aged with cancer of the rectum, or the elderly with diverticular disease.

## Paediatric care

In considering some of the different age groups, what particular problems do patients have? A young baby will not have the problems of body image, but his parents have to face the fact that their child is different from their friend's offspring. Not many appliances are made with the tiny neonate in mind, and it must be disturbing for parents to see their new arrival in an incubator with a bag that is almost as big as he or she is. How will these parents learn to cope with their offspring and this peculiar red bowel protruding on their abdomen?

It may be that, if the nurse's face, words and actions show acceptance of both the stoma, the baby and the parents' feelings, and the nurse gives them time to express their emotions, they will grow to accept it too. If the nurse can be there, giving support when a friend or other family member first sees the stoma, it is a source of help and support to the parents. Much is spoken about bonding these days and this, too, is important to establish where a baby with a stoma is concerned, especially if the mother is worried that she will damage the stoma when caring for her baby. A mother should be encouraged not to be fearful of touching her baby or hurting the stoma. It should be pointed out that the stoma itself does not have any feeling and that, whilst she should be careful when undertaking skin care and changing the bag, she can touch, cuddle and, therefore, bond with her baby as she would normally.

## Childhood stomas

Children with stomas may well have grown up with them, so they will not feel too different until they go to school. It is a well-known fact that children can be cruel to each other at times, but again, if children with stomas are accepted by those caring for them, they will learn to have a positive regard for themselves. Children often feel that being ill or having to go into hospital is a form of punishment, and it is important to point out that this is not so, that they are loved and wanted.

## Normal or special schools?

Many parents are overprotective towards their children, yet others are fighting to have their children treated as equals. If a spouse or siblings are being neglected because a mother feels guilty and is, therefore, concentrating all her time on her 'sick' child, family therapy may well be required. In such a situation it may be necessary for the nurse to act as the family's advocate. The primary health care team, particularly the school nurse or health visitor, has an important role to play and can suggest to the mother that she takes time off from caring for her sick child to be with the rest of her family. Volunteers in the community could be asked to help to enable the parents to have a break.

Parents and children may have questions regarding, for example, sports, communal showers, managing school trips away for a few days and the importance of establishing self-care at an early age. The United Ostomy Association in the USA has produced literature to cover the period of childhood and adolescence, and whilst intermittent self-catheterization and 'undiversion' of urinary stomas (reconnecting the urinary tract so that the urostomy is no longer needed) are in vogue at present, there are still many children who come to stoma surgery and need help to adjust. Indeed, children who have had a stoma raised in early childhood, and for whom it has been decided a urostomy is not necessary, will require assistance as their urinary tract is reconnected. Many children learn how to catheterize themselves at regular intervals during the day.

It is becoming more of a common practice to integrate handicapped children into the normal school environment, where possible, and this is of benefit and importance to the child with a stoma. If the stoma is the only 'handicap' the child has, there need be few problems, and careful liaison between home, school and hospital can enable the child to manage the emptying or changing of the appliance at school. Thus, if they are taught to be independent, they can usually manage with help from one of the school staff, if required.

If a child has an added handicap, such as spina bifida, parents and the caring team need then to decide what school is best. It may be that a child with calipers or a wheelchair cannot manage the stairs or steps, but many obstacles can be overcome by discussing the situation with the medical officer, school nurse or teaching staff, and then a decision can be made on the best course of action to take. The child's welfare is of prime importance and teaching staff may need to have their fears allayed by having explained to them the needs of the child. Obviously, the more independent children are in their own care, the more readily they will be accepted for normal school placement. This reaffirms them as equal with their peers and helps other children to accept them as being on the same level as they are. As well as being cruel, children show remarkable powers of adaptation and acceptance. Therefore, if a child with an appliance shows no embarrassment when showering or changing for gym, a simple explanation by a teacher is often all that is needed.

## The adolescent

If body image is constantly changing, adolescence must, indeed, be a difficult time for a person with a stoma to live through. One has to look at this age group in two categories – those who have grown up with a stoma and those who come to surgery in their adolescence. Often with inflammatory bowel disease, surgeons put off creating a stoma during this traumatic period. Sadly, growth may be stunted as a result of this deferment; conservative treatment fails and there becomes no alternative but to raise a stoma.

Yet, postoperatively, these young people often thrive, put on weight, grow and declare that they wish they had had a stoma before! This is not so with everyone, however, for whilst patients with Crohn's disease and ulcerative colitis are often treated conservatively for a number of years, they may not welcome stoma surgery, even if it means an end to the misery of their diarrhoea and pain. Although many are warned that it may be necessary to have stoma surgery one day, others come to surgery with a very short history of disease and are emotionally shocked and unprepared, especially as it is questionable whether a young teenager has yet established a healthy body image at this traumatic age.

Familial polyposis is a hereditary condition where careful follow-up of teenagers in families known to have the disease often show cancerous or precancerous changes in the colon, thus necessitating the need for a colectomy. Although it is possible to undertake surgery to create a perineal pouch with a temporary, covering ileostomy, there is still much conflict in families, coupled with tension and guilt feelings on the part of parents because of the hereditary nature of the disease.

It is interesting to note that, whilst one school of thought considers it better for adolescents not to have stomas and to reverse temporary stomas as early as possible, another viewpoint is that delay in raising a stoma may mean body image change anyway in the way of stunted growth, and, therefore, it is kinder to raise a stoma when needed. In one instance, a 16-year-old girl showed grave psychiatric disturbance when her stoma was reversed. To her it had become a crutch, and she saw the loss of her stoma as loss of sympathy, and dependence on others; her mother in particular.

Some points that need specific mention are swimwear and the ability or otherwise to wear a bikini, what to tell their friends, and how parents and the caring professions can diplomatically help teenagers in their conflict. Whilst it is possible to wear a two-piece swimsuit, a bikini does present problems with concealing the appliance. One patient managed to overcome this by wearing an indian scarf tied at the side of the stoma, thus concealing the bag. As one-piece swimwear seems to be in vogue at present, wearing a patterned costume means that the appliance will be less noticeable underneath and, if an appliance requires emptying whilst one is, for instance, sunbathing, a towel can be draped over the arm, just as when in public a handbag or coat can conceal a full bag until it is convenient to empty the appliance.

Although it may be thought unwise that a teenager should go around telling everyone that they have a stoma, they may well be advised to confide in their closest friends, who it is hoped would have visited them whilst they were in hospital and learnt something of the type of surgery they had undergone. However, if this has not been the case, in order to reduce the element of shock or surprise, a young person (as any other ostomist) should be advised to explain the operation in simple terms, transposing some words to fit the patient's approach. For example, 'I was quite ill, with frequent diarrhoea and pain. My colon/rectum had to be removed and now I have to get rid of my body waste through an opening on my stomach. So now I have to wear a bag, but I'm feeling really fit again'. If an ostomist has a healthy body image, this confidence will spill over to his or her friends. Thus, their style of dress, leisure pursuits and so on, can reaffirm that they do not differ from their peer group.

## Adults

Young adults have the additional problem of deciding what to tell a partner when a relationship deepens. If the discovery causes the relationship to disintegrate, will they blame their stoma or accept that the relationship is over? One of the positive points of ulcerative colitis is that, once the colon and rectum are removed, the person is cured of the disease and, after a period of adjustment, can learn to live with the stoma. Their quality of life is usually enhanced and they feel well. Not so with Crohn's disease – this has different effects and a stoma will not cure all the problems. Many patients suffer persistent loss of weight and perianal abscesses, and thus to offer continuing support is paramount. So when should they tell new boyfriends or girlfriends about their stoma? And what if they are already married when they come to stoma surgery? How can we help their partners to accept it? What about their fear of odour; what do they do with their bag during lovemaking? Fear of damaging the stoma or displacing the appliance has its effect on body image, as does the confidence engendered by an ideal, secure appliance, and the interchangeable activity pouch available for sport or sexual intercourse.

It is difficult to make hard and fast rules about what or when a person with a stoma tells a boyfriend or girlfriend about their changed anatomy. By the third or fourth meeting, one usually knows if the friendship is going to deepen and this may well be a good time to explain. What should be avoided is continuing to delay coming out into the open about stoma surgery, for then it may be discovered by accident! A married partner can be helped to accept by encouraging discussion of the situation with the spouse as soon as it is known that stoma surgery is necessary. It can be explained (when discussing the implications of stoma surgery initially with the couple) that modern appliances are leakproof, odourproof, stay intact and can be concealed during close body contact. Male ostomists can wear a bag cover or a money belt to conceal their appliance and females can wear a pretty appliance cover to match their underwear, or alternatively, crotchless pants. Anxiety can be allayed by reasoning with the couple that the stoma is fairly durable and that no harm can be done when gentle pressure is applied. This gives both partners confidence in re-establishing their sexual relationship.

Advice about eating out at restaurants, or going for a 'pint', and the control of a full bag are all relevant to body image. Discussing the subject freely creates an understanding, which hopefully leads to acceptance. The person with a stoma may need to be reminded that it is better to eat first rather than to drink on an empty stomach, and that wine and beer may cause a more fluid stool. With a urostomy, a couple of pints of beer make it necessary for the bag to be emptied more frequently, and it may be appropriate to remind the ostomist that too much alcohol could cause them to forget to check their appliance.

There are 'tricks of the trade' a patient can learn to lessen or obviate the noise element of the stoma and it can be reassuring to be told that they will gradually become aware of and have a few seconds' warning beforehand of when they are about to pass flatus. This means that they can fold their arms or sit in such a position as to lessen the noise, or pretend to be adjusting their clothing and gently press a finger or palm of the hand over the stoma to eliminate the noise. The majority of colostomy bags now have an integral flatus filter, which reduces the expulsion rate of excess wind or flatus, thus causing less embarrassment.

Some ostomists may forego meals in the hope that their stoma will be less active a few hours later, but having regular meals is the rule to be adopted. If a patient finds that the stoma acts while he or she is lying down when previously it was inactive while sitting, it may be of help to wait for a few minutes or revert back to the former position. It may be suggested that sexual intercourse is not then spontaneous, but neither, in that case, is applying a sheath or cap. A supportive partner is usually willing to bide time while the stoma settles down, and a sense of humour works wonders!

To avoid postoperative catastrophies, preoperative counselling is of prime importance. The writer remembers a young married woman who expressed how she felt years ago: 'I think the blow of the hammer really fell when, 36 hours preoperatively the stoma site was marked and a "trial" appliance fixed. Then I realised I would never be the same again. I thought I had cried enough, but now began with a new fervour. The registrar, sensing my problem, gave me back my ego and asked me to look on myself as an ordinary young wife and mother who just happened to need a stoma. He gave me my first session in psychosexual counselling. I had a tremendously long way to go, but that helped so much, for not only did someone understand, but he was willing to spend time and talk to me about it. I shall never forget the care and kindness of that man, for he understood the physical mutilation and psychological trauma' (Salter, 1982).

Beware of the patient who wants no one to know of his or her stoma. Such people live on a knife edge that people will find out and are not really accepting the stoma themselves. Some people like to give their stoma a name, but it is felt that this should not be encouraged. After all, not many people name other parts of their anatomy with 'Rose' or 'Tom', for instance. Some parents simply need to know what to tell their children or relations in an honest and matter of fact way. This is particularly so for a parent with Crohn's disease who may well be in and out of hospital frequently. It is important to find out if children have any particular fears about their parent's frequent disappearance into hospital. Supporting the family is again paramount, and both hospital and community staff can work together in providing continuing care.

**The middle-aged patient**

Another example is that of a middle-aged married man who has a steady job but suddenly finds he needs stoma surgery for cancer of the rectum. This may have proceeded fairly rapidly. He could have had a change in bowel habit for 2 or 3 months before deciding he needed to do something about it. After a visit to his general practitioner (GP) he is given an outpatient appointment and is diagnosed as requiring an abdomino-perineal excision of the rectum for his carcinoma. He is usually in hospital within a week or so of diagnosis. If he has not been given any advice or counselling concerning his forthcoming surgery at an outpatient appointment prior to admission, he could well go home and make his own plans concerning his future. This is a good time for the primary health care team to become involved. At the same time as losing his control of continence in having a stoma, he may also, even if only temporarily, lose his bladder control and his position as chief bread winner. Added to this, owing to his weak physical condition, he may be forced to abdicate his role as the strong family member, and may be reduced to seeing his wife tackle the jobs he has always done until now.

Owing to the proximity of pelvic nerves involved when undertaking surgery of this nature, he may also suffer impotence. By now he may be a completely changed character: he may be embarrassed when his wife sees him undressed, or locking the bathroom door behind him, and the children may no longer see him in his underwear. This once-competent businessman may now become completely incompetent, and all fingers and thumbs when changing his appliance. It may be necessary to work towards solving one problem at a time, for example, once he is eating normally again it may be possible to suggest that he learns to irrigate his stoma (bowel wash out), thus giving him a degree of control over his colostomy. As he begins to feel stronger, he could begin to do a few odd jobs around the house and discuss his return to work. His bladder and sexual problems may need following up, and it is important that these are discussed freely with him. Involvement with his partner is crucial for, as one wife stated: 'You have cancer? Why you? We've had so much of happiness, of love, of fun and laughter and I'm greedy, I want more, years and years of tomorrows, but not alone, *never* alone . . . The intruder had come and would not leave us' (Randall, 1972).

**The elderly patient**

Elderly stoma patients will have grown up in an era when it was not considered nice to talk about body waste. They are likely to have greater physical problems of dexterity, co-ordination and eyesight than the able bodied. A leaking bag will not help their self-esteem, especially if it requires a relative to help clear up the mess. Thus, they may feel that they have regressed to childhood. Do the caring team stop to think how it feels for a mentally alert, but physically incapable man of 80 or 90 to have his daughter care for his stoma? If the patient and his or her relatives are happy with the arrangement, and if it means the difference between going home or staying in an institution, a patient may well choose the former. To help them accept the situation, nurses should seek ways of enabling such patients to think positively of the things they can still do for themselves and thus boost their self-esteem.

## The stoma patient with cancer

It is also important to mention the further onslaughts on a patient's body brought about by radiotherapy or chemotherapy. Cervical cancer, if not diagnosed early enough can, for example, result in a vesico-vaginal fistula from radiation damage or the disease process, necessitating stoma surgery. Emergency surgery to relieve obstruction from an ovarian tumour means that preoperative help is limited. Thus, more time and great patience will be needed afterwards, as the patient emerges from the shock of this further onslaught on her changed body.

Breckman (1980) states that for some patients the stoma is a constant reminder that they still have cancer; for others, who have also to contend with a vaginal or rectal discharge, it is an added insult to an already labouring body. To those whose stoma brings relief from pain it can bring a return of dignity for whatever time is left. Treatment for rectal cancer involves the majority of cases in radical mutilating surgery, life with a colostomy and low expectation of survival (Macdonald and Anderson, 1984). Results of Watson's (1983) study indicated that subjects who received counselling intervention demonstrated positive alterations in self-concept/self-esteem as compared with subjects who were not counselled. Age, sex and type of ostomy were not found to be significantly related to self-concept/self-esteem changes. However, within a year of surgery, the majority of patients, including those with colostomies, have recovered from surgery and if they survive for 5 years, are considered by their surgeons to be cured (Goligher, 1983). It can be said that rectal cancer patients are expected to take up their lives after a period of convalescence, but in an ambiguous and impaired social position – that of the chronic patient with the invisible but ever present threat of cancer (Zahn, 1973). Devlin *et al.* (1971) suggest that patients who undergo surgery for rectal cancer are different from other patients. They have a permanent colostomy and no control over the passage of flatus or stool from their body. They have altered their image and may feel acutely aware of the change.

## Case study

*Sue was a patient who had a recurrence of her cervical cancer and required an anterior pelvic exenteration (pelvic clearance) and the raising of an ileal conduit. She was a 'young', attractive 44-year-old, who flatly refused to allow her caring husband to look at her stoma, or for him to become involved in her stoma care. Whilst she was still an inpatient, her primary nurse had tried to establish some rapport with her – tried holding her hand when she was distressed, but she withdrew. Did she feel untouchable now she had a stoma? When she went home, there was concern about how she would manage for it seemed that she had not come to terms with her surgery at all. Contact was made with Sue at regular intervals. Her husband remained supportive and she eventually agreed to see a visitor from the Urostomy Association at home. She was attending an outpatient clinic every 3 weeks for chemotherapy. As time went by, she gradually came to terms with her stoma. Sue appeared much more cheerful, and staff and fellow patients she met on her hospital visits remarked on her changed and positive attitude as she encouraged those who had just had their surgery, urging them on by saying (in her tight slacks and trendy clothes), 'Look at me, you wouldn't know I'd got one unless I told you'. How was it that we knew that this was a real change and not just a facade? Because one day, about six months after surgery, she said 'You know I no longer wake up in the morning and think "Ugh, this dreadful thing to cope with again". It's taken its proper place in my life – it no longer looms large but represents a small factor in life'.*

*Rheaume and Gooding (1991) state that adaptation to ostomy has occurred when the person has become comfortable with his or her changed body image and is able to resume their previous lifestyle patterns. The results of this study suggest that support is at least partly responsible for a person's adjustment to a stoma. Subjects in the group with a high level of support had significantly higher quality of life scores than subjects in the group with low support.*

**Sexuality and stoma care**

Golis (1996) states that the person with a stoma faces many adjustments that affect sexuality. He or she must adjust to changes in body image and sexual self-image, all while learning new techniques of self-care and this, therefore, suggests that communication, education and experimentation are the key elements to sexual rehabilitation.

Sexuality is one part of an individual's personality that has biological, psychological and social aspects. Genetics, socialization, fashion, culture, race, education and the mass media all influence sexuality. The adaptation to the stoma is affected by gender, age, disease severity, pre- and postoperative teaching, beliefs or values, experiences, coping mechanisms and the nature of the stoma (Smith, 1992), Penninger (1989) states that any type of radical perineal or rectal surgery affects sexual function.

The creation of a stoma presents a physical alteration. This alteration may result in the ostomist having a poor self-concept and reduced self-esteem. In Nordstrom's (1988) study, patients very often perceived themselves to be less sexually attractive to their partner. A survey of ileostomists (Burnham *et al.*, 1977) suggests that this is the case in about 50% of ileostomists.

In considering physical factors further, stoma surgery can lead to the disruption of sexual functioning through damage to organs, nerves and blood vessels. The extent to which sexual problems arise depends largely on the extent of the surgery. This explains why people with a colostomy encounter more problems than people with an ileostomy. In the case of a colostomy, the operation is usually performed shortly after the diagnosis of cancer has been made and the operation performed is more radical than in patients with non-malignant disease. In the case of ileostomy, chronic intestinal inflammation often forms the reason why, after a long period of conservative treatment, the ultimate choice is to perform a stoma. The operation then brings an end to many years of physical suffering (Weil *et al.*, 1991).

In considering psychological factors, disruption of sexual functioning can also be caused by psychological mechanisms. Research into the field of sexuality in relation to illness and handicap has shown that the subjective experience of sexual arousal and/or orgasm are not determined solely by physiological factors, but that social factors also play a part (van San-Schoones, 1987; Schultz *et al.*, 1990). People tend to feel worthless after stoma surgery because they can no longer satisfy the demands which are implicitly or explicitly laid down for 'normal' men and women (Weil *et al.*, 1991).

**Caring for the homosexual person with a stoma**

Etnyre (1990, cited in Salter, 1996) states that the experiences, concerns and needs of gay and lesbian ostomates parallel those of anyone who has had ostomy or related surgery. However, many gay and lesbian patients are reluctant to bring up issues and concerns which in any way reveal their sexual orientation, thus making it difficult for them to receive the help they need. The stoma-care nurse is ideally placed to demonstrate sensitivity and receptiveness to persons who are same-sex orientated, thus paving the way for the patient to reveal significant personal concerns.

When caring for a homosexual patient, it is helpful to identify if he is the recipient or not in the relationship. The patient should be warned against using the stoma for penetration and, therefore, great sensitivity is needed in the care of the homosexual patient who has had his rectum removed. For homosexual men who participate in anal intercourse, the loss of the anus or rectum removes a major source of pleasure and possible sexual identity (Savage, 1987).

Etnyre (1990) states that the implications of receptive anal sex for the person who has had ileal pull-through surgery or rectal excision may not necessarily be addressed, particularly if the patient or helping persons are hesitant to broach the subject. Therefore, great sensitivity needs to be shown in this area of care.

## Care of the patient undergoing stoma surgery

Canese (1995) states that over and above the embarrassment and the negative influence which can be caused by the stoma during sexual activity, amputation of the rectum may involve loss of the sympathetic and parasympathetic nerve fibres (hypogastric plexuses) governing control of sexual function. Impotence in men, which may result, represents a severe and sometimes irreversible disability, which in the long-term causes traumas often greater than those of the stoma itself. Although impotence may be partial or total, potency can return even as long as 2 or 3 years after surgery. Various authors have demonstrated that the reduction of sexual function is related to the age of the patient at the time of surgery.

Gloeckner (1991) illustrates that men with stomas are often more disturbed by their new self-image than are their female counterparts. The man with a stoma often perceives himself as unattractive and sexually unappealing. Among men, organic sexual dysfunction is observed as impotence, the inability to achieve or maintain an erection that is sufficient for sexual performance. Sexual dysfunction may also take the form of retrograde ejaculation or 'dry' orgasm. In this condition, the bladder neck fails to close properly during orgasm, and semen enters the bladder, rather than being forced out through the urethra (Smith, 1992). Orgasm is a total body response and it is possible to reach orgasm without an erection, penetration or the antegrade expulsion of semen.

In Weil *et al.*'s (1991) study, the results confirm the hypothesis that stoma surgery can lead to serious disruption of sexual functioning. This is particularly valid for men, with males with a urostomy complaining of most sexual dysfunction. In the case of urostomy, the bladder is often removed as well, which directly damages the organs involved in the sexual response. Therefore, the rate of sexual dysfunction is highest in this group. Golis (1996) states that the most common organic sexual dysfunction among women is dyspareunia or painful intercourse (Bell, 1989). Scar tissue from pelvic operations may create bands round the vagina. Construction and lack of lubrication also create pain from friction during intercourse (Gloeckener, 1991). Lubrication insufficiency may be exacerbated by age-related decrease in oestrogen production or by surgical removal of the ovaries.

Canese (1995) suggests that women may complain of loss of libido owing to reduced perineal sensation. Dyspareunia may be caused by perineal scarring or by ligature of the posterior vaginal wall after rectal amputation. Some women complain of the impossibility of reaching orgasm as a result of decreased sensitivity of the clitoris.

## The patient with a continent bowel pouch

Dudley (1978) suggests that, however managed, however we delude ourselves, a permanent, potentially incontinent stoma is an affront and difficult to bear, so that he marvels that we and our patients have put up with it for so long. It says much for the social indifference of the one and the social fortitude of the other.

To this end, investigations into alternatives to conventional stomas have been under way for many years. There are now a variety of procedures being performed for bowel or bladder disease or dysfunction where the purpose is to eliminate the need to use an appliance whenever possible (Church, 1986).

Although the pouch procedure (also known as restorative proctocolectomy or ileo–anal reservoir) is not appropriate for patients with Crohn's disease, it is the operation of choice for patients with ulcerative colitis and familial polyposis coli, wishing to avoid permanent ileostomy (Nicholls and Harocopas, 1990). (An ileo-rectal anastomosis is also suitable for people with familial polyposis coli (Neal and Phillips, undated; Salter, 1993, 1995)). This eradicates all disease but preserves the anal sphincter so that patients can void normally. The pouch procedure is undertaken as a one-, two- or three-stage operation, but usually the pouch is made with a covering ileostomy to protect the anastomosis. The final stage involves closure of the temporary ileostomy so that the patient can void per anus, via the pouch.

Most of the literature indicates that patients with a continent pouch felt that such a procedure enhanced their lives over that of an ileostomy (Everett, 1989; Nicholls and Pezim, 1985; Pemberton *et al.*, 1988). For example, Pemberton *et al.* (1988), in an examination of seven areas of daily activities, revealed that a continent procedure was associated with improved performance in each category. However, a prospective study of quality of life after pelvic pouch operation found that the restoration of normal defaecation did not lead to much further improvement of quality of life after the disease was cured (Weinryb, 1995).

The pouch procedure does have complications, the major one being pouchitis (inflammation of the pouch) and Hanson (1989) sounds a note of caution, by advising that the procedure is not going to 'make you normal'. Too many people go into this procedure thinking that they are not going to have a stoma, can eat whatever they want and are going to be just like they were before they had ulcerative colitis. Whilst it helps to be positive about the surgery, one also has to be realistic as complications to the pouch can develop; ease and frequency of emptying can depend on the type of food eaten. Hanson suggests that patients need a great deal of education, because it is the patient who ultimately makes this procedure successful.

The most vocal advocates of continent procedures are the patients themselves, states Nicholls (1983). In his study, all but one of 54 patients were unequivocal in preferring their quality of life after restorative proctocolectomy to their previous experience with an ileostomy. The advantages of the reservoir most often cited included greater confidence, ease of management and the feeling of being more normal. The minimal interference of the reservoir operation with the activities of daily life restored a feeling of freedom to many patients.

Bragg's (1989) study shows that the continent ileostomy (for example, Kock ileostomy) makes no restrictions with regard to clothing or physical activity. Social, sexual and psychological anxieties are significantly diminished when compared with patients who have a conventional stoma. Therefore, it would appear, on the evidence presented on this and similar studies, that there are differences in the perceptions of body image in comparing those patients who have an ileostomy with those who have a reservoir.

Pemberton *et al.*'s (1988) study using questionnaires compared patients with conventional stomas with those who had a continent pouch. The authors were concerned that patients' feelings regarding the positive effects of the reservoir after pouch procedure had not been documented. Included in the study were 298 pouch patients and 406 conventional stoma patients. In order to determine the impact of the ileostomy or of the pouch on the daily lives of the patients, each patient was asked to enumerate in what manner their operation had affected seven activity categories. These categories were sports, sexual life, social activities, recreation, home, family relationships and travel. Respondents with a pouch were more satisfied.

**Patients with continent urinary pouches**

Although the ileal conduit has been the surgical preference for over 40 years, because the procedure is relatively simple to perform and has minimal postoperative complications, it does significantly alter the person's body image and, therefore, many different procedures have been devised in the lower urinary tract to provide continence. These procedures use various bowel segments for the collection and storage of urine, protection of the upper urinary tract, continence and the ability to empty on demand. The strongest indicators for a positive outcome of those patients undergoing a continent urinary reservoir are motivation, a positive self-image and a desire to be without an external appliance which makes them continent (Razor, 1993).

**Fistula care**

Inflammatory bowel disease (particularly Crohn's disease), pelvic cancer and radiation damage can cause fistula formation. Although a fistula is not surgically created, the output of intestinal fluid is often large and an appliance is, therefore, required. Such patients may suffer from the demoralizing effects of a leaking appliance over which they have no control. Body image is thus radically altered by the escape of intestinal contents, the appearance of the fistula and the need to wear a bag.

**The nurse's role**

The psychological preparation and counselling of patients in the preoperative period is of great importance. By preparing the patient for the outcomes of surgery, the patient is better able to accept a change in body image (Keighley *et al.*, 1987).

When a person first sees his stoma, the natural reaction may be one of horror and disgust. It is not helpful for the nurse to give false reassurance by commenting on what a nice stoma it is, or how much it resembles a 'rose bud'! It is appropriate for the patient to be allowed to voice their feelings of rejection and repulsion of the stoma, and to grieve the loss of their once-intact body.

Knowledge about actual and potential problems associated with sexuality and an alteration in body image enables the nurse to assess the meaning of this for the individual patient and family, to provide counselling before and after the surgery, and to intervene so that the individual will be able to adapt to an alteration in body image and return to one's previous activities of daily living and lifestyle (Cohen, 1991). This is of prime importance in caring for the person with a stoma.

Canese (1995) states that some problems fall outside the nurse's area of experience and expertise, and only a specially qualified adviser will then have the ability to provide appropriate therapy. As nurses, our aim is to allow the patient to reveal problems and to provide information within the limits of our expertise. When such problems exceed these limits, we must ask our patients to allow us to refer them to another professional adviser on sexual matters.

However, most patients and their partners can be helped, for instance, to accept the stoma by encouraging early discussion as soon as it is known that stoma surgery is necessary. Allaying anxiety by reasoning with the couple that the stoma is fairly durable and that no harm can be done by gentle pressure on it, gives both partners confidence in re-establishing their sexual relationship (Salter, 1995). It can be explained (when discussing the implications of the operation initially with the couple) that modern appliances are leakproof, odourproof, stay intact and can be concealed during close body contact.

Golis (1996) suggests that the nurse should advise the patient that the appliance should be emptied before sexual activity. Some people find that taping the bag to the abdomen, which prevents excessive movement during sexual activity, is helpful. Irrigating the stoma before sexual activity may prove helpful for patients who irrigate as a part of routine stoma care (Cohen, 1991). The patient is encouraged to eat at regular times to diminish gas during sexual activity and to avoid foods that are likely to cause flatus. The patient may wish to use deodorants or perfumes before sexual activity to enhance perceptions of desirability. Clothing may be used to cover and stabilize the stoma during sexual activity. Crotchless, backless garments are made specifically to cover the stoma during sexual activity. As an alternative, a T-shirt, or a silk or lace pouch cover may also be used (Golis, 1996). Some stomas allow short-term capping (e.g. Conseal plug) for use during sexual activity or rigorous physical exercise (Simmons, 1983). Penninger (1989) counsels men to buy moneybelt-style waistbands to cover the stoma to promote stability. The patient is encouraged to experiment with the many devices available to determine individual preference.

Golis (1996) states that medications that may complicate sexual activity and sexuality should be reviewed and adjusted as feasible. These agents may decrease libido, exacerbate depression and erectile failure and decrease lubrication for women. Patients should also be counselled regarding the use of alcohol. Although it decreases inhibitions, excessive intake of alcohol also diminishes libido and produces temporary impotence. Hormone replacement therapy may help increase lubrication for women. In addition, over-the-counter products are available for lubrication during sexual intercourse.

**Rehabilitation**      The goal of sexual rehabilitation is to restore the capacity for loving and receiving love (Carroll, 1988). Adaptive resolution and recovery are achieved when the couple learn to cope effectively with changes in sexuality that occur after creation of the stoma. The role of the nurse is enabling the patient to realize altered sexual function does not destroy sexuality. He or she offers specific suggestions to manage changes in sexual function that encourage exploration and rediscovery of sexuality. Golis (1996) states that, according to Gloeckner's (1991) research, the process of adjustment is typically completed within 1 year. If, at the end of that year, specific problems emerge or persist, more aggressive treatment options, including psychotherapy sessions or surgical management, may be indicated.

Whilst in hospital, the ostomist is sheltered from the normal environment, but on returning home may wait to see how those around him or her react – family, friends and the community staff/primary health care team. The trend today is for a shorter stay in hospital with the patient returning home as soon as possible, thus community staff are having to deal increasingly with the

**Table 10.1** Suggested guidelines in planning care for a stoma patient (e.g. colostomy)

| Patient's problems/needs | Aim | Implementation | Date solved/changed | Evaluation |
|---|---|---|---|---|
| 1 Need for preoperative counselling, incorporating partner/relative if possible, stressing return to normal lifestyle and continuance of social life, etc. | To ensure patient is physically and emotionally able to cope with stoma. (a) How does he or she feel about having stoma? (b) Does he or she foresee any problems? | Discussion with staff and S/C nurse; use of stoma care booklet. Patient invited to ask questions. Referral to stoma booklet and diagrams to show altered anatomy | Review daily and on discharge | Feeling able to cope; is happy to proceed with stoma surgery (confirmed by positive and optimistic attitudes) |
| 2 Postoperatively, the need for patient to look at his stoma and appliance | To be willing to view colostomy and appliance | Encourage patient to look at abdomen and as he or she does so, remind him or her of what he or she was told stoma would be like, e.g. red, swollen, etc. | When fully recovered from anaesthetic | Is happy to view stoma and bag |
| 3 Requires help in learning stoma management | To enable patient to manage own stoma, so that he or she is looking forward confidently to the future and in preparation for discharge | Use of equipment and explanation of principles involved | Ongoing | Can manage appliance adequately in readiness for discharge home |
| 4 Preparation for discharge: How does patient feel he or she is managing? | To enable patients to feel confident in all aspects of managing at home | Go over points mentioned previously, ensuring patient understands and has all necessary instructions written down | Prior to discharge | Feels confident and is looking forward to going home |
| 5 Need for partner to learn stoma care | So he or she feels confident with care of stoma | To incorporate partner/relative into stoma care management, with patient's approval | Prior to or after discharge home | Partner is happy to participate in stoma care |

physical and psychological effects of surgery. Caring and involved partners play an important role in their spouse's rehabilitation and the nurse can help here by explaining from the outset that there is no need for their sleeping arrangements to change because of the stoma.

The nurse needs to ensure ongoing support, where appropriate, in the important realm of coming to terms with changes in body image and how this affects activities of daily living, including sexuality. However, it has to be acknowledged that some patients will not want intervention in such a personal area of life and such views must be respected. But if health promotion is part of the nurses' role, then this area of care can be offered, even if it is not accepted. It is also important to give patients and their partners information on alternative ways of expressing love if sexual intercourse is not possible or desirable (Salter, 1996).

Therefore, whilst it is recognized that the patient needs to come to terms with the loss of a body part, the emphasis is on normality. The patient's grief at their loss of a body part and the acquisition of an artificial anus needs to be mourned, and the patient given adequate time to come to terms with their change in body image. Thus, there appears to be a balance between encouraging a return to normality and allowing an acceptable grieving period where the patient can mourn the loss of their altered body. This means allowing the patient to move forwards at their own pace as they perceive the situation, without the pressure of health care professionals putting their time limit on this period.

The ideal person to co-ordinate rehabilitation in this group of patients is the stoma-care nurse in conjunction with the patient, their partner/significant others and health care professionals, towards enabling the patient to come to terms with their body image change (Salter, 1995). Nurses have an important role in the rehabilitative process, which includes identifying and planning interventions for frequently occurring problems after stoma surgery. Their active involvement in comprehensive education and supportive counselling is fundamental in minimizing complications and facilitating adaptation (Rolstad et al., 1985). Often someone of the same sex and age group who has readjusted to his or her stoma surgery is a great boon, and beginning counselling as soon as possible encourages a quicker recovery. The voluntary associations, for example, the British Colostomy Association, train visitors for this who are a great help to potential patients, and they will often visit postoperatively and during the rehabilitation period. It is still of the utmost importance for the nurse, however, to discuss all aspects of stoma care. The clinical nurse specialist (stoma care) can offer patients this continuity of care both at home and in the hospital, as well as acting as a liaison and resource person within the multidisciplinary team.

Part of the rehabilitative process includes encouraging patients to view themselves as 'normal' after surgery. Nurses should encourage the patient to view the stoma as an inconvenience rather than a disability or handicap.

## Summary

This chapter has attempted to discuss the issues concerning altered body image and sexuality in people undergoing stoma surgery. Stoma surgery affects all ages and adjustment to surgery must be made accordingly. Some stoma patients will return to a normal life with few problems and one of the best ways to achieve this is to help them to see that, essentially, they are no different now from how they were before their operation. Others may need initial help and thereafter only specific help at particular milestones in their life. It is important that this help should be available when it is needed. This can be achieved by hospital and community staff working together in caring for the patient. If a normal lifestyle is not possible, perhaps the story of a young mother, standing before a group of nurses, sums it all up: 'I have a colostomy because by having it I will have a few more months to live and, if I can have a few more months to be with my husband and children, who cares if I have a hole in my side?' (Wilson, 1977).

## References

Bell, N. (1989) Sex and the ostomist. *Nursing Times* **85**, 5.

Bragg, V. (1989) Continent intestinal reservoir. *Ostomy/Wound Management* Summer, 32–41.

Breckman, B. (1980) The stoma and the patient. *Nursing Mirror* **150** (January 24), Suppl. i–iii.

Burnham, W., Lennard-Jones, J. and Brooke, B. (1977) Sexual problems amongst married ileostomists. *Gut* **18**, 673–677.

Cahoon, M. (1973) *The Needs of 343 Cancer Patients Living at Home in 3 Areas of Ontario*. Ontario Cancer Treatment and Research Fund.

Canese, G. (1995) Stoma nurses should know their limits when counselling on sexual matters. *Eurostoma*, Autumn (no. 12), 8–9.

Carolan, C. (1984) Sex and disability. *Nursing Times* September, 26–34.

Carroll, G. (1988) A study of ostomates and sexuality. *Australian Nursing Journal* **19**(2), 11.

Church, J. (1986) The current status of the Kock continent ileostomy. *Ostomy/Wound Management* Spring, 32–35.

Coe, M. and Kluka, S. (1988) Concerns of clients and spouses regarding ostomy surgery for cancer. *Journal of Enterostomal Therapy* **15**, 232–239.

Cohen, A. (1991) Body image in the person with a stoma. *Journal of Enterostomal Therapy* **18**(2), 68–71.

Devlin, H., Plant, J. and Griffin, M. (1971) Aftermath of surgery for ano-rectal cancer. *British Medical Journal* **14**, 413–418.

Druss, R., O'Connor, J., Prudden, J. and Stern, L. (1968) Psychologic response to colectomy. *Archives of General Psychiatry* **18**, 53–59.

Dudley, H.A.F. (1978) If I had carcinoma of the middle third of the rectum. *British Medical Journal* **1**, 1035–1067.

Dyk, R. and Sutherland, A. (1956) Adaptation of the spouse and other family to the colostomy patient. *Cancer* **9**, 123–138.

Eardley, A., George, W., Davis, F., Scholfield, P., Wilson, M., Wakefield, J. and Sellwood, R. (1976) Colostomy – the consequences of surgery. *Clinical Oncology* **2**, 277–283.

Etnyre, W. (1990) Meeting the needs of gay and lesbian ostomates. *Proceedings of 8th Biennial Congress, World Council of Enterostomal Nurses*, Hollister, Canada.

Everett, W. (1989) Experience of restorative proctocolectomy with ileal reservoir. *British Journal of Surgery* **76** (January), 77–81.

Gloeckner, M. (1991) Perceptions of sexual attractiveness following ostomy surgery. *Journal of Enterostomal Therapy* **18**, 36–38.

Goligher, J. (1983) Alternatives to conventional ileostomy in the surgical treatment of ulcerative colitis. *Journal of Enterostomal Therapy* **10**, 79–83.

Golis, A. (1996) Sexual issues for the person with an ostomy. *Journal of Wound, Continence and Ostomy Nursing* **23**(1), 33–37.

Hanson, P. (1989) Ileo anal reservoir. *Ostomy Quarterly* **2**(2), 87–89.

Keighley, M., Winsler, M., Pringle, W. and Allan, R. (1987) The pouch as an alternative to an ileostomy. *British Journal of Hospital Medicine* **12**, 1008–1011.

Kelman, G. and Minkler, P. (1989) An investigation of quality of life and self esteem among individuals with ostomies. *Journal of Enterostomal Therapy* **16**, 4–11.

Kelticangus-Jarvinen, L., Loven, E. and Maller, C. (1984) Psychological factors determining the long-term adaptation of colostomy and ileostomy patients. *Psychotherapeutics and Psychosomatics* **14**, 153–159.

Klopp, A. (1990) Body image and self esteem concept among individuals with stomas. *Journal of Enterostomal Therapy* **17**, 98–105.

Macdonald, L. and Anderson, H. (1984) Stigma in patients with rectal cancer – a community study. *Journal of Epidemiology and Community Health* **38**, 284–290.

Neal, K. and Phillips, R. (undated) *Familial Adenomatous Polyposis, A Guide for Nurses*. St Mark's Polyposis Registry and Clinimed.

Nicholls, R. (1983) Proctocolectomy: 1, Avoiding an ileostomy. *Nursing Mirror* February **16**, 46–47.

Nicholls, R. and Harocopas, C. (1990) *Ulcerative Colitis – A Guide for Patients*. Uxbridge, Convatec.

Nicholls, R. and Pezim, M. (1985) Restorative proctocolectomy with ileal reservoir for ulcerative colitis and familial polyposis coli. *British Journal of Surgery* **72**(June), 470–474.

Nordstrom, G. (1988) Urostomy patients – a strategy for care. *Nursing Times* **85**(18), 32–34.

Orbach, C. and Talent, H. (1965) Modification of perceived body and of body concepts. *Archives of General Psychiatry* **12**(February), 126–135.

Orbach, C. and Talent, H. (1974) Ideas of contamination in post-operative colostomy patients. *Psychoanalytical Review* **61**, 269–282.

Padilla, G. and Grant, M. (1985) Quality of life as a cancer nursing outcome variable. *Advances in Nursing Science* **8**, 45–60.

Pemberton, J., Phillips, S., Ready, R., Zinsmeister, A. and Beahrs, O. (1988) Quality of life after Brooke ileostomy and ileal pouch–anal anastomosis: comparison of performance status. *Annals of Surgery* **209**(5), 1620–1628.

Penninger, J. (1989) After the ostomy: helping the patient retain his sexuality. *Registered Nurse* **48**(4), 46–50.

Randall, N. (1972) *This Road can be Travelled*. London, Readers Digest Association, i–iv.

Razor, B. (1993) Continent urinary reservoirs. *Seminars in Oncology Nursing* **9**(4), 272–295.

Rheaume, A. and Gooding, B. (1991) Social support, coping strategies and long term adaptation to ostomy among self-help group members. *Journal of Enterostomal Therapy* **18**, 11–15.

Rolstad, B., Wilson, G. and Volk-Tebbitt, B. (1985) Long term sexual status concerns in the client with ileostomy. *Journal of Enterostomal Therapy* **9**(4), 10–12.

Rosenberg, M. (1965) *Society and the Adolescent Self-Image*. Princeton, J.J. University Press.

Salter, M. (1980) A cross to bear. *Community View* **4** (March), iii–iv.

Salter, M. (1982) Towards a healthy body image. *Nursing Mirror* **157** (September 14), iv–vi.

Salter, M. (1992a) Aspects of sexuality for patients with stomas and continent pouches. *Journal of Enterostomal Therapy* **19**, 126–130.

Salter, M. (1992b) What are the differences in body image between patients with a conventional stoma compared with those who have had a conventional stoma followed by a continent pouch? *Journal of Advanced Nursing* **17**, 841–848.

Salter, M. (1993) Advances in ileostomy care. *Nursing Standard* **7**(38), 31–34. (Reprint, August, 1995.)

Salter, M. (1995) Sexuality and the stoma patient. In: Myers, C. (ed.) *Stoma Care Nursing – A Patient Centred Approach*. London, Arnold, pp. 203–219.

Salter, M. (1996) Body image study shows most patients need support. *Eurostoma* Autumn, 10–11.

San-Schoones, Van P. (1987) Contribution of physical and psychological determinants to the sexual experience of spinal cord injured inpatients. In: Kockott, G. and Herms, V. (eds) *8th World Congress of Sexology*. Heidelburg, p. 140 (abstract).

Savage, J. (1987) *Nurses, Gender and Sexuality*. London, Heinemann.

Schultz, W., van de Weil, H., Hahn, D. and Bouma, J. (1990) Psychosexual functioning after treatment of cancer of vulva: a longitudinal study, *Cancer* **66**, 402–407.

Simmons, K. (1983) Sexuality and the female ostomate. *American Journal of Nursing* **83**, 409–411.

Smith, D.B. (1992) Psychosocial adaptation. In : Hampton, B.G., Bryant, R.A. (eds) *Ostomy and Continent Diversions: Nursing Management*. St Louis, Mosby-Yearbook, pp. 15–18.

Wade, B. (1990) *A Stoma is for Life*. London, Scutari Press.

Walsh, B., Grunert, B., Telford, G. and Otterson, M. (1995) Multidisciplinary management of altered body image in the patient with an ostomy. *Journal of Wound, Continence and Ostomy Nursing* **22**(5), 227–235.

Watson, P. (1983) The effects of short term post operative counselling on cancer/ostomy patients. *Cancer Nursing* February, 21–29.

Weil, van de H., Schultz, W., Hengevelam M. and Staneke, A. (1991) Sexual functioning after ostomy surgery. *Sexual and Marital Therapy* **6**, 195–209.

Weinryb, R., Gustavsson, J., Liljeqvist, L., Poppen, B. and Rossel, R. (1995) A prospective study of the quality of life after pelvic pouch operation. *Journal of the American College of Surgeons* **180**(May), 589–595.

Whitethread, M. (1981) Ostomists: a world of difference. *Journal of Community Nursing* August 5, 4–6/10.

Wilson, C. (1977) I am an Ostomate. *Chicago International Ostomy Association Bulletin.*

Zahn, M. (1973) Incapacity, impotence and invisible impairment: their effects upon interpersonal relations. *Journal of Health and Social Behaviour* **14**, 115–123.

## CHAPTER 11

# Body image and HIV/AIDS

*Sarah Hart*

**Introduction**

The aim of this chapter is to discuss the altered body image experienced by people who are human immunodeficiency virus (HIV) antibody positive or who have acquired immunodeficiency syndrome (AIDS) in an attempt to increase the nurse's understanding of the complex and diverse nature of HIV disease. It is hoped, therefore, that it will help the nurse to be more aware of the profound psychological and physical nature of HIV disease, which may affect a person's subjective concept of themselves.

The diagnosis of HIV/AIDS represents a major change to the lives of persons infected with HIV and of their significant others. A range of reactions may occur which have a direct relationship to body image. These include shock, fear of illness and death, fear of telling and the reaction of others, sadness, depression, anger, guilt, decreased self-esteem, loss of identity, loss of control, loss of future hopes and plans, and isolation from family, friends and/or work colleagues. King (1989) suggests a quarter of all HIV-positive people experience rejection by the people they tell that they are HIV antibody positive. Schag *et al.* (1992) supports this view, reporting that 70% of 106 HIV antibody-positive persons had problems including body-image stigma. MacGinley (1994) reiterates that a person's body image is influenced by the environment and the people around them.

These reactions can occur for many reasons, which may be directly related to how people respond to life-threatening illness. However, for HIV antibody-positive persons, there is the added burden of the issues directly related to HIV, which can include the issues of infection, infectiousness, death, dying, dependency, disability, disfigurement, sex, drug abuse and minority groups, which led Carlisle (1994) to state that HIV-positive people may face

'Stigmatisation, avoidance, isolation, criticism, rejection and discrimination'.

Perry *et al.* (1990) reported high levels of anxiety, depression and psychiatric symptomatology in people discovering their HIV anti-body-positive diagnosis, and Wright (1992) states that depression and anxiety reactions were frequently triggered by the loss and uncertainties associated by HIV. Firn and Norman's (1995) small study into the psychological and emotional needs of people with HIV indicated that one theme was changes in body image.

The following text will highlight some of the factors implicated with HIV and AIDS that are relevant to body image. Some of these factors will be due to change in appearance, which may make a person feel physically unattractive, whilst other factors will have psychological implications which may make a person feel different within themselves.

AIDS was first described in 1981 [*Mortality and Morbidity Weekly Report* (MMWR), 1981a, 1981b]. Within 2 years it was shown to be the result of infection with a virus (Levy, 1984), now known internationally as HIV. This disease is the most serious worldwide threat to public health today (Stine, 1993).

The World Health Organization (1993) suggests that there are more than 14 million people in the world who are infected with HIV, with at least 600 000 of these people having already developed AIDS. Current evidence suggests that ultimately almost all HIV infected people will eventually die of AIDS (Stine, 1993).

AIDS is the end point in a wide spectrum of diseases characterized by the presence of antibody to HIV and by the presence of certain opportunistic infections and cancers that affect both the body and the brain, or by the loss of more than 10% body weight (MMWR, 1992).

**Effects on appearance**

HIV infects the body's immune system cells, in particular, the T-helper cells which co-ordinate the immune system's fight against infection and cancer. Initially, asymptomatic infection can persist for many years, although some people will develop a persistent, generalized lymphadenopathy (PGL), which is palpable lymph-node enlargement at two or more extrainguinal sites for more than 3 months in the absence of causes other than HIV. PGL of internal nodes can produce painful debilitating ill health, whilst PGL of nodes that are visible cause altered body image and provide a constant reminder of the person's diagnosis.

Because HIV weakens the immune system, viruses, bacteria, fungi and protozoa that commonly are not pathogenic cause infection in HIV-positive patients, and latent organisms reactivate causing reinfection. Many of these infections produce signs and symptoms that are directly related to body image. Table 11.1 indicates just a few of the more common signs and symptoms associated with HIV disease and the causative organisms.

*Table 11.1*    Common symptoms associated with HIV and causative organisms.

| Symptoms | Causative organisms |
| --- | --- |
| General | |
| Fever, weight loss, malaise | *Pneumocystis carinii* |
| | Cytomegalovirus |
| | *Mycobacterium avium intracellulare* |
| Chest | |
| Dyspnoea, pneumonia, chest pain | *Pneumocystis carinii* |
| | Cytomegalovirus |
| | *Mycobacterium avium intercellulare* |
| Gastrointestinal | |
| Sore throat, dysphagia, diarrhoea, pain, weight loss, hairy leukoplakia | *Candida* |
| | Herpes simplex |
| | Cytomegalovirus |
| | *Shigella* |
| | *Salmonella* |
| Neurological | |
| Meningitis, dementia, convulsions | Cytomegalovirus |
| | Herpes |
| | *Toxoplasma* |
| Eyesight | |
| Diminished vision | Cytomegalovirus |
| Skin | |
| Seborrhoeic dermatitis, folliculitis, shingles, cold sores, genital warts | *Tinea cruris* |
| | *Herpes simplex/zoster* |

**Treatment and care of people with HIV/AIDS**

Prophylaxis to prevent infections occurring or reoccurring has been seen to improve the quality and length of life of HIV-positive persons (Masur, 1992). Although this does mean regular administration of oral, intravenous or aerosol drugs, which, besides being intrusive, can be a constant reminder of the person's HIV-positive status, for some patients this can entail a permanent intravenous device, for example, a skin tunnel catheter or implantable ports. Clinical interventions will also include extensive tests and physical examinations, which may cause a perceived loss of dignity by the patient. Such dignity and privacy are very important and play a major part in our feelings about ourselves. Nurses can help to prevent such feelings by being sensitive to the patient's needs for dignity and privacy. Such interventions can include patient education to ensure the patient fully understands what is proposed.

HIV has affected a group of people who would normally be at the peak of their physical fitness. As people with HIV and AIDS are generally young (when physical fitness and appearance is particularly important), any alteration to this status may cause significant distress.

The natural history of HIV indicates a long duration of 15–20 years, having an insidious onset, characterized by recurrent episodic complications which ultimately lead to death (Clarke, 1994). McCarthy and Mercey (1994) discuss the problem of providing treatment and care for patients with late-stage disease, with George and Jennings (1993) suggesting that many of the conditions that AIDS patients are developing have no specific curative treatment and palliation remains the physician's goal. Wells (1993) explains that 'AIDS must be viewed as a chronic disease rather than as a acute illness' suggesting that this will allow nurses to understand the implications of living with HIV, so preventing the idea that everyone with AIDS will succumb to a rapid and painful death, making it unnecessary to offer rehabilitation to patients with AIDS.

HIV is associated with the fear of contagion. Brendon's (1988) study indicated that 25% of people surveyed believed that HIV can be transmitted by coughing, spitting and sneezing, with 10% of this study's respondents believing that touching an HIV-positive person was dangerous. Such attitudes can cause people to avoid social and physical contact with HIV antibody-positive people, whilst conversely HIV antibody-positive people may avoid contact with others because of their fear of being rejected.

Such attitudes are not restricted to the general public. Two British studies which assessed nurses' attitudes and knowledge towards patients who were HIV antibody positive, revealed poor attitudes (Bond et al., 1990; Akinsanya and Rouse, 1991). Danziger (1994) suggests education is the most effective tool available for reducing HIV/AIDS discrimination, as education can help people to understand such bias is unjustified.

Unfortunately, they may nevertheless continue to undertake discriminatory action. Flaskerud (1991) supports this view, suggesting that educational programmes to improve attitudes is essential, as the quality of nursing care can be seriously impaired through negative attitudes towards HIV/AIDS patients.

Health care workers' poor attitudes towards HIV antibody-positive patients may be due to homophobia (Stables, 1990) and intravenous drug use (Forrester and Murphy, 1992), with the belief that the patient is responsible for their illness (Boland, 1990) and education is associated with increased empathy and lower fear (Royce *et al.*, 1987). However, Taylor and Robertson (1994a) question whether the nursing profession is ready and willing to meet these needs.

It is inevitable that the occupational risk of HIV infection will be a major issue for health care workers. Up to September 1993 there had been 64 definite and 118 possible occupationally acquired HIV infections globally (Heptonstall *et al.*, 1993). This steadily increasing trend is bound to cause increased concerns.

The adoption of universal precautions whilst providing care for all patients (Wilson and Breedon, 1990) is intended to prevent skin exposure to blood and body fluids (Hart, 1991). Yet Melby *et al.*'s (1992) study established that nurses employed increasingly restrictive infection control measures when caring for HIV-positive patients compared with HIV-negative patients. Gelbert *et al.* (1991) warns that, if fears are high, practice may suffer, whilst Burgess *et al.* (1992) considers some fears are justified when they stimulate attention to the positive adoption of appropriate precautions. Such diverse opinions related to this issue can only cause variation in bedside care, which adds to the patient's feelings of being different.

Pinching (1989) stated it is crucial to introduce consistency into nursing procedures, warning that variation in infection-control policies can be divisive and confusing for the patients. Yet nurses have been blamed by patients for mistakes and errors of judgement when planning care. Such errors can lead to the patient feeling stigmatized and lonely (Knowles, 1993). Whether this is due to covert discrimination or from fear of infection is unclear.

Conversely, nurses have been seen to set good standards of care for persons with AIDS. In 1993 the first recorded person with Kaposi's sarcoma to announce publicly that he had AIDS was a nurse in the USA, in an attempt to heighten awareness of the needs of persons with AIDS (Shilts, 1987). This was at a time when health care professionals felt they should not be required to work with AIDS patients (Scherer *et al.*, 1989).

In the 15 years since AIDS has been identified as a distinct clinical disease, much has been learnt about the biological and epidemiology of HIV. It is clear that the virus is not casually nor easily spread (Stine, 1993). It is also clear that a vaccine and cure for HIV will not be readily found (McCarthy and Mercey, 1994), and that education remains the most important instrument to prevent further spread of the virus and to promote social under-standing regarding the disease (World Health Organization, 1992). A third and equally important goal of education is to ensure carers of people already infected provide optimum care and attention to allow infected people to remain healthy for as long as possible.

For many patients, discovering they are HIV antibody positive may not immediately cause them to experience body image prob-lems; however, treatment may. Currently, there are several antiviral therapies for HIV infection, which may be used as monotherapy or in combination chemotherapy treatment programmes. These have been seen to prolong survival in patients with AIDS as well as improve clinical well-being and performance (Lee *et al.*, 1991). Unfortunately, such treatments are not completely specific to HIV and healthy body cells can be affected.

Three of the main therapies for HIV infection are zidovudine (AZT), didanosine (ddC) and zalcitabine (ddC). All act as reverse transcriptase inhibitors, blocking viral replication. Unfortunately, all three drugs are associated with toxicity, in particular, peripheral neuropathy can develop, resulting in loss of sensation in the patient's extremities, which may severely affect daily activities. Switching to other antiviral agents or combining agents is gener-ally attempted. Combination therapy has the added possible advantage of increasing antiviral effectiveness whilst reducing the risk of developing resistance to treatment, as well as allowing for lower doses of each drug, so lessening the risk of side effects.

In practice, because HIV is a relatively new disease with little established medicine, a person with HIV disease has to weigh up the benefits against possible harms of the proposed treatment pro-grammes. For some this decision about their health care causes considerable stress. This has been increased in the past by major debates about HIV therapies, in particular AZT, where prelimi-nary research studies indicate that AZT improves survival. Yet in April 1993 a major Anglo-French Concorde study suggested that

AZT was not the treatment of choice for early intervention therapy (Concorde Coordinating Committee, 1994).

This has caused major dilemmas within the medical profession, and caused great anxiety and uncertainty within the patient population. Ross et al.'s (1994) study highlighted the feelings of helplessness and hopelessness amongst patients with HIV. Such feelings can lead to a sense of loss of security and control, with the virus appearing to have taken over control of the patient's life. With no one able to offer the ideal therapy to control this disease, it is essential that the patient is allowed to be included in decisions related to their care in an attempt to reduce these negative feelings. Patients have to try to strike a balance between freedom from illness and freedom from drugs and medical intervention. Ross et al.'s (1994) study indicated that HIV antibody-positive patients can have a fighting spirit, which suggests these patients can influence the course of their illness personally. These feelings need to be encouraged.

Besides the opportunistic infections that people with AIDS develop, the weakened immune system also allows for the development of certain types of cancer. The HIV/AIDS-associated Kaposi's sarcoma has been seen to be especially virulent, marked by flat to raised pink to purplish skin and mucosal membrane lesions which may spread to lung, liver, spleen, gut. This sarcoma is 20 000 times more common in men with HIV than in the general population (Beral et al., 1990). Whilst deaths in AIDS patients are generally due to opportunistic infections, Kaposi's sarcoma can cause a painful disfiguring and debilitating disease.

The consequence of being HIV antibody positive has resulted in these patients demanding reliable and up-to-date medical information, which, in turn, has resulted in the medical and nursing profession becoming closely linked with their patients. Action groups comprising people with HIV and patient advocates, who argue for the interests of people with HIV, have also developed behind the scenes. This has led to public debates regarding priorities and ethics of scientific research, in particular, how some drugs are only available in clinical trials and that it is unethical that people have to enter placebo-based trials in order to receive treatment. While on such trials, these patients are not able to use other drugs which might be beneficial to them because this would undermine the validity of the trial results.

Harvey (1991) suggests anxiety and uncertainty is generated by the many known and unknown factors related to HIV/AIDS.

McCarthy and Mercey (1994) state that, whilst the natural history of HIV remains unchanged, early detection and effective prophylaxis for opportunistic infections can lead to prolonged survival. However, this, in turn, has allowed for the emergence of rarer infections and cancers, which are more difficult to treat.

**Homosexual men**

As the first patients with AIDS were homosexual men, AIDS was seen as a 'gay disease' or 'gay plague'. Dowell *et al.* (1991) discusses how homophobia negatively affects people's view of AIDS patients. Burt (1995) stresses how body image and sexuality are intricately linked, and James *et al.* (1994) point out how gay men fear such attitudes. Taylor and Robertson (1994b) support this view, explaining how homophobia causes emotional distress in gay men and that nurses need appropriate training about gay issues to be able to deal with such issues.

**Cultural issues**

As gay men continue to make up the largest group with HIV and AIDS, this can lead to certain people being completely out of place and isolated in clinics, and wards catering predominantly for gay men. In particular, the black voluntary organization BHAN (1991) state that black people living with HIV infection and AIDS face prejudice, hostility and isolation. This is increased by the acceptance by many that HIV originated from Africa, which led to the practice of categorizing Africans as a 'high-risk group', producing a problem in provision of non-discriminatory health care. It is essential that HIV/AIDS issues are dissociated from accusations of blame, to allow people with HIV and AIDS to come to terms with their infection.

The cultural and language barriers can cause problems in hospital, necessitating health care workers addressing such issues as provision of foods and interpreters to ensure ethnic needs are met. Culture, religious and traditional customs must be handled with sensitivity and skill which can aid self-affirmation and emotional well-being. Primary care and support services must be non-judgemental, which generally requires racism awareness and antiracist training, thus addressing specific social, cultural and political issues raised by HIV/AIDS within the black community. This should produce a positive approach to empower people living with HIV/AIDS to allow them to live without guilt and fear, but with dignity and determination.

**Women**

Women do not fit the perceived HIV image and continue to be misdiagnosed because they are not seen as at risk (Schneider, 1992). Yet HIV and AIDS has a profound impact on women with the stigma attached to HIV subjecting women to discrimination, social rejection and other violations of their rights (Stine, 1993). This problem is increased as many women affected by HIV will already be in a vulnerable position (Barlow, 1992). If the woman has children, this will bring additional difficulties in coping with personal issues (Sherr, 1991). Orgnero and Rodway (1991) recommend social work intervention, which facilitates self-awareness leading to self-help, which provides a sense of control over one's life. The voluntary organization 'Positively Women', which was developed in response to this need, can offer practical and emotional support to women with HIV.

**Nursing research**

Three components may improve attitudes and care of HIV antibody-positive persons, which in turn may improve body image for the affected person. These are education, counselling and research. Yet, when Larson (1988) reviewed 169 nursing articles related to HIV/AIDS, it was found that none were based on nursing research. Abdellar et al. (1985) suggest no single hypothesis has greater significance for nursing research than that which appreciates that all patients are persons. Nursing research, therefore, plays a major contribution in furthering the scope of nursing by addressing the problems of HIV antibody-positive persons, so that, ultimately, the promotion of effective research programmes will encourage the utilization of research findings to improve nursing practice. Such research will allow nursing to keep pace with the changing needs of the person with HIV as new medical treatments mean that patients are living longer but develop conditions that are increasingly more difficult to treat, which are producing new challenges for nurses. It is also essential to measure the effects of nurses' action on the physical and emotional health of these patients, which will help to provide an understanding of problems, so leading to the revision and development of good nursing care.

**Education**

Psychoneuroimmunological research suggest that support and favourable attitudes contribute to the well-being of patients with terminal diseases and may improve prognosis (Coates et al. 1984;

Kiecolt-Glaer and Glaser, 1988). Danziger (1994) suggests education is regarded as the major effective tool available for reducing HIV/AIDS discrimination with education helping people to understand such bias is unjustified.

The goal of educating people about HIV/AIDS is related to the promotion, maintenance and restoration of health by influencing knowledge, beliefs, attitudes and behaviour, and through empowering people to acquire greater health-related skills (Lovejoy et al., 1992).

**Counselling**

Green and McCreaner (1989) suggest counselling of those infected with HIV can promote and maintain their physical and mental well-being by helping them to adjust to their difficulties by asserting control over their lives in an attempt to maintain their quality of life. This can be achieved by the counsellor having good interpersonal skills and a wide knowledge of the social, moral and ethical issues related to HIV. Wright (1992) warns such support must be proactive and not simply reactive, thus ensuring that the patient's personal resources can be examined and promoted. Bor et al. (1992) emphasize the need for empathy in counselling relationships.

Green and Hedges (1991) suggest there are two main aims in counselling related to HIV/AIDS. Firstly, issues related to prevention of transmission of HIV and secondly to 'maximize quality of life for infected persons'. Counselling needs to be available as problems occur, thus helping with the psychological consequences of HIV. Yeilding (1990) supports this view, suggesting that counsellors can help a patient come to terms with their problems. This can be important as long-term survivors of AIDS have associated their well-being with their ability to cope with HIV (Carson et al., 1990).

Other factors which may increase an HIV antibody-positive person's feelings of well-being, which in turn may improve body image, are for people to provide encouragement and companionship (Hays et al., 1994). Supportive therapies which may improve quality of life should be made available (Wells, 1993). Support groups for HIV antibody-positive persons are also important and have been seen to provide help and support (Hart et al., 1990).

Hays et al. (1994) identified breaking confidentiality as an unhelpful behaviour from the perspective of the person with

AIDS. Allmark (1995) stresses how confidentiality is an acknowledged duty of the nurse, yet when this information spreads to non-involved professionals, it is a cause for concern.

**Summary**

This chapter has indicated how body image and HIV/AIDS affects the psychological and emotional well-being of HIV antibody-positive persons. The nurse's role is important for, if the nurse adopts a negative attitude, this can result in a negative body image in the patient. Both Cronan (1993) and Price (1990) suggest nurses are well placed to help patients come to terms with altered body image. The nurse must promote feelings of normality, which will improve body image. This can be achieved by building up a good relationship with the patient, which will require sensitivity, tolerance and knowledge.

**References**

Abdellah, F.G., Levine, E. and Levine, B. (1985) *Better Patient Care through Nursing Research*, 3rd edn. New York, Macmillan Publishing Company.

Akinsanya, J.A. and Rouse, P. (1991) Who will care? *Journal of Advanced Nursing* **16**, 262–269.

Allmark, P. (1995) HIV and the boundaries of confidentiality. *Journal of Advanced Nursing* **21**, 158–163.

Barlow, J. (1992) Social issues: An overview. In: *Working with Women and AIDS*. Bury, J.K., Morrison, V. and McLachlan, D. (eds). London, Tavistock Routledge.

Beral, V., Peterman, T.A., Berkelman, R.L. *et al.* (1990) Kaposi's sarcoma among patients with AIDS. A sexually transmitted infection. *Lancet* **335**, 123–138.

Black HIV/AIDS Network (BHAN) (1991) *AIDS and the Black Communities*. London, Black HIV/AIDS Network BCM BHAN.

Boland, P. (1990) Fear of AIDS in nursing staff. *Nursing Management* **21**(6), 40–44.

Bond, S., Rhodes, T., Phillips, P. *et al.* (1990) HIV infection and AIDS in England: The experience, knowledge and intention of community nursing staff. *Journal of Advanced Nursing* **15**, 249–255.

Bor, R., Miller, R. and Goldman, E. (1992) *Theory and Practice of HIV Counselling: a Systemic Approach*. London, Cassell.

Brendon, R.J. (1988) Discrimination against people with AIDS: The public perspective. *New England Journal of Medicine* **319**, 1022–1026.

Burgess, A.W., Jacobson, B.S., Buker, T. *et al.* (1992) Workplace fears of AIDS. *Journal of Emergency Nursing* **18**(3), 233–238.

Burt, K. (1995) The effects of cancer on body image and sexuality. *Nursing Times* **91**(7), 36–37.

Carlisle, C. (1994) Psychosocial care of HIV positive people. *Nursing Standard* **26**(8), 37–40.

Carson, V., Soeken, K.L., Shanty, J. and Terry, L. (1990) Hope and spiritual well being essential for living with AIDS. *Perspectives in Psychiatric Care* **26**(2), 28–34.

Clarke, A. (1994) What is a chronic disease? The effects of a re-definition in HIV and AIDS. *Social Science Medicine* **34**(4), 591–597.

Coates, T., Temoshok, L. and Mindel, J. (1984) Psychosocial research essential to understanding and treating AIDS. *American Psychologist* **39**, 1309–1314.

Concorde Coordinating Committee (1994) Concorde MRC/ANRS randomised double blind controlled trial of immediate and deferred zidovudine in symptom free HIV infection. *Lancet* **343**, 871–818.

Cronan, L. (1993) Management of the patient with altered body image. *British Journal of Nursing* **2**(5), 257–261.

Danziger, R. (1994) The social impact of HIV/AIDS in developing countries. *Social Science Medicine* **39**(7), 905–917.

Dowell, K.A., Lo Presto, C.T. and Sherman, M.F. (1991) When are AIDS patients to blame for their disease? Sexual orientation and mode of transmission. *Psychological Report* **69**, 211–219.

Flaskerud, J.H. (1991) A psychoeducational model for changing nurses' AIDS knowledge, attitudes and practice. *Journal of Continuing Education in Nursing* **22**(6), 237–244.

Firn, S. and Norman, I.J. (1995) Psychological and emotional impact of an HIV diagnosis. *Nursing Times* **91**(8), 37–39.

Forrester, D.A. and Murphy, P.A. (1992) Nurses' attitudes towards patients with AIDS and AIDS related risk factors. *Journal of Advanced Nursing* **17**, 1260–1266.

Gelbert, B.C., Maquire, B.T., Coates, T.J. *et al.* (1991) Primary care physicians and AIDS. Attitudes and structural barriers to care. *Journal of American Medical Association* **266**, 2837–2842.

George, R.D. and Jenning, A.L. (1993) Palliative medicine. *Postgraduate Medical Journal* **69**, 429–440.

Green, J. and Hedges, B. (1991) Counselling and stress in HIV infection and AIDS. In: *Cancer and Stress: Psychological, Biological and Coping Studies.* Cooper, C.L. and Watson, M. (eds) Chichester, John Wiley and Sons, pp. 237–255.

Green, J. and McCreaner, A. (1989) *Counselling in HIV Infection and AIDS.* London, Blackwell Scientific Publications.

Hart, S.M. (1991) Blood and body precautions. *Nursing Standard* 5(25), 25–27.

Hart, G., Fitzpatrick, R., McLean, J., Dawson, J. and Boulton, M. (1990) Gay men social support and HIV disease, a study of social integration in the gay community. *AIDS Care* 2, 163–170.

Harvey, N. (1991) The psychosocial context of HIV/AIDS. *Nursing Standard* 5(27), 50–51.

Hays, R.B., Magee, R.H. and Chauncey, S. (1994) Identifying helpful and unhelpful behaviours of loved ones, the PWA's perspective. *AIDS Care* 6(4), 379–392.

Heptonstall, J., Gill, O.N., Porter, K., Black, M.B. and Gilbart, V.L. (1993) Health care workers and HIV: surveillance of occupationally acquired infection in the United Kingdom. *Communicable Disease Report* 3(11), 147–154.

James, T., Harding, I. and Corbett, K. (1994) Biased care. *Nursing Times* 90(51), 28–30.

Kiecolt-Glaer, J. and Glaser, R. (1988) *HIV Prevention for Gay Men. A Survey of Initiatives in the UK.* London, North West Thames Regional Health Authority.

King, M.B. (1989) Prejudice and AIDS, the views and experiences of people with HIV infection. *AIDS Care* 1, 137–152.

Knowles, H.E. (1993) The experience of infectious patients in isolation. *Nursing Times* 89(30), 53–56.

Larson, E. (1988) Nursing research and AIDS. *Nursing Research* 37(1), 60–62.

Lee, C.A., Phillips, A.N., Elford, J., Janossy, G., Griffiths, P. and Lerroff, P. (1991) Progression of HIV disease in a haemophiliac cohort followed for 11 years and the effect of treatment. *British Medical Journal* 303, 1093–1096.

Levy, J.A. (1984) Isolation of lymphocytopathic retrovirus from San Francisco patients with AIDS. *Science* 225, 840–842.

Lovejoy, N.C., Morgenroth, B.N., Paul, S. and Christianson, B. (1992) The potential predictors of information seeking behaviour by homosexual/bisexual men with a HIV sero positive health status. *Cancer Nursing* 15(2), 116–124.

MacGinley, K.J. (1994) Nursing care of the patient with altered body image. *British Journal of Nursing* **2**(22), 1099–1102.

Masur, H. (1992) Drug therapy, prevention and treatment of pneumocystis pneumonia. *New England Journal of Medicine* **327**, 1853–1860.2

McCarthy, G.A. and Mercey, D. (1994) The changing clinical features of HIV-1 infection in the United Kingdom. *Communicable Disease Report Review* **4**(5), R53–58.

Melby, V., Boore, J.R.P. and Murrey, M. (1992) AIDS: knowledge and attitudes of nurses in Northern Ireland. *Journal of Advanced Nursing* **17**, 1068–1077.

Morbidity and Mortality Weekly Report (MMWR) (1992) Revised classification system for HIV infection and expanded surveillance case definition for AIDS among adolescents and adults. *Centers of Disease Control (CDC)* **41**, RR17.

MMWR (1981a) Pneumocystis pneumonia. Los Angeles. *CDC* **30**, 250–252.

MMWR (1981b) Kaposi's sarcoma and pneumocystis pneumonia among homosexual men. New York and California. *CDC* **10**, 305–308.

Orgnero, M.I. and Rodway, M.R. (1991) AIDS and social work treatment: a single system analysis. *Health Social Work* **16**(2), 123–124.

Perry, S.W. Jacobsberg, L.B., Fishman, B. *et al.* (1990) Psychological response to serological testing for HIV. *AIDS* **4**, 145–152.

Pinching, A.J. (1989) Models of clinical care. *AIDS* **3**(Suppl. 1), S209–S231.

Price, B. (1990) A model for body image care. *Journal of Advanced Nursing* **15**(5), 585–593.

Ross, M.W., Hunter, C.E., Condon, J., Collins, P. and Begley, K. (1994) The mental adjustment to HIV scale measurement and dimensions of response to HIV/AIDS disease. *AIDS Care* **6**(4), 407–411.

Royce, D., Dhooper, S.S. and Hatch, L.R. (1987) Undergraduate students' attitudes towards AIDS. *Psychological Reports* **60**, 1185–1186.

Schag, C.A., Ganz, P.A., Kahn, B. and Petersen, L. (1992) Hopes: a quality of life tool for HIV. *Annual Meeting of the American Society of Clinical Oncology* **11**, A11.

Scherer, Y.K., Haughey, B.P. and Wu, Y.W. (1989) AIDS: What are nurses' concerns. *Clinical Nurses Specialist* **3**, 48–54.

Schneider, B.E. (1992) *The Social Context of AIDS*. London, Sage Publications.

Sherr, L. (1991) *HIV and AIDS in Mothers and Babies. A Guide to Counselling*. London, Blackwell Scientific Publications.

Shilts, R. (1987) *And the Band Played On. Politics, People and the AIDS Epidemic*. Harmondsworth, Penguin.

Stables, T. (1990) AIDS and gay men. *Journal of District Nursing* **8**(10), 20–26.

Stine, G.J. (1993) *AIDS Update*. London, Prentice-Hall International.

Taylor, I. and Robertson, A. (1994a) A sensitive question. *Nursing Times* **90**(51), 31–33.

Taylor, I. and Robertson, A. (1994b) The health needs of gay men: a discussion of the literature and implications for nursing. *Journal of Advanced Nursing* **20**, 550–566.

Wells, R (1993) The rehabilitation of people with AIDS. *Nursing Standard* **7**(25), 51–53.

Wilson, J. and Breedon, P. (1990) Universal precautions. *Nursing Times* **186**(37), 67–70.

World Health Organization (1992) *Effective Approaches to AIDS Prevention. Report of a Meeting in Geneva*. Geneva, World Health Organization.

World Health Organization (1993) *Press Release* 38. Geneva, World Health Organization.

Wright, J. (1992) Developing a supportive role. *Nursing Times* **88**(37), 63–65.

Yeilding, D. (1990) *Caring for Someone with AIDS*. London, Hodder and Stoughton.

## CHAPTER 12

# Sensory impairment and body image

*Margot Lindsay*

## Introduction

When studying sensory behaviour in relation to sensory depriva-tion, it is helpful to classify the five senses into distance and close senses. Hearing and vision are the distance senses, while olfaction (smell), gustation (taste) and taction (touch) are the close senses.

Hearing provides what Myklehurst (1964) describes as an 'antennae-type of contact, constantly warning the organism regarding the stability and friendliness of the total environment'. In some respects and at some levels, hearing persists unceasingly, even during sleep. This distance sense functions uninterruptedly, keeping the person in contact with the environment at all times. Vision is discontinued during sleep and can be suspended any time by closing the eyes. When using sight, a person has to focus on a specific area, but in contrast to the directional nature of vision, the stimulus of hearing can come from all directions and be received by the listener.

Hearing can be described as a background sense while vision is a foreground sense, focused on an experience after it has been identified by hearing. Although hearing is more often the back-ground sense and vision the foreground sense, these distance senses are so highly developed in human beings that either of them can take the leading role in human experience. There are occasions when we listen so intently to what is being said or to a piece of music that vision becomes the background sense.

The close senses – touch, smell and taste – are more primitive and immature when compared with distance senses. Primitive humans were more dependent on the close senses than modern people. Psychologists have shown that infants in early life are dependent essentially on the close senses, gradually developing maximum use of their hearing and vision. In the immature organism, touch, taste and smell are used more than hearing or vision for exploring the environment and meeting needs. When a distance sense is deprived, the individual naturally is forced into greater dependence on the close senses.

The skin, which covers the whole body, is a multiple sense organ used for sampling and exploring the environment. We can immediately perceive by touch that an object is hot or cold, rough or smooth, sticking or slippery, wet, damp or dry, heavy or light, hard or soft, that it is exerting or not exerting pressure, and that it has a certain size, shape, position and state of motion. Much evidence suggests that the desire for physical contact stems from deeply rooted, perhaps physical, need. The importance of physical contact to infant development has often been demonstrated, and there is evidence that this need continues through adult life.

The process of smell (olfaction) is the earliest and the most primitive of the methods which test the nature and the safety of the environment from a distance. The primitive organism constantly both scans and samples the environment in the interest of individual survival by promptly distinguishing the scent of safety from the scent of danger. Infants appear to 'like' all classes of odorous materials. Children under five rated sweat and faeces odours as pleasant, but those above five years of age rated them as unpleasant. The sense of smell declines in elderly persons.

The human sense of taste perceives four distinctive tastes: sweet, sour, salt and bitter. The perception of sweet and salt is most acute at the tip of the tongue, sour is best at the sides and bitter is best tasted posteriorly. The mid-dorsum of the tongue is insensitive to taste. Perception of a bitter taste requires a lower concentration of test substance than that of a sweet taste.

Folklore has it that human infants spontaneously select foods which are nutritionally satisfactory, if they are given a full choice. Apparently flavour or taste is the dominant factor in this selection. Some support for this belief may be derived from the studied case of a boy with adrenal deficiency, who compensated for this deficiency by ingesting large quantities of table salt. Also, human subjects in whom hypoglycemia has been therapeutically induced for the treatment of severe anxiety report that strong sugar solutions then become palatable. When their blood sugar later returned to normal, they rejected these syrupy solutions as unpalatable. But experience with obesity and other forms of malnutrition suggests that people do not spontaneously choose the 'proper' diet, and the widespread use of tobacco and alcohol shows that, if people are left to their own devices, they will put all manner of things into their mouths.

**Leading and supplementary roles of the senses**

When a distance sense is impaired, the remaining distance sense and the close senses take on different roles. When deafness is present, the other distance sense, vision, must serve a dual leading role of both foreground and background alertness to the environment. Even the hard of hearing, with a moderate impairment, must use vision as the principal contact and exploratory sense, with hearing serving a supplementary place. Likewise, someone who has a visual impairment uses hearing as the lead sense, with vision as the basic supplementary sense.

**Attitudes towards the blind person**

There is a widely held belief that blind people have unusual perceptual skills. It is not uncommon for the sighted to assume extraordinary auditory and tactile powers in the blind. It is generally accepted that vision is the most efficient means of acquiring and processing information, and that when sight is absent, there is a necessary reliance on the other senses – touch, hearing and smell. The newly blind have lost their primary mode of providing confirmation for what is heard, felt, smelled or tasted. They have to develop trust in the information provided by the remaining avenues of information.

Nature does not compensate for loss of vision by providing extraordinary power, nor are the blind any more accurate than the sighted in their ability to make distinctions using auditory and tactile cues. A blind person has no more ability than a sighted person in identifying new objects or sounds not previously experienced. People with intact sight and hearing rarely develop to the fullest extent the sensitivity possible from touch, taste or smell, nor do they develop kinesthetic awareness or muscle sense to the maximum degree that is possible.

**Self-image of the partially sighted and the blind**

Professionals working with the blind have observed differences between partially sighted and totally blind individual. A person with residual vision often suffers an identity problem – 'Am I sighted or am I blind?' In some situations, the person can see well enough to function, and residual vision provides access to information and the ability to be independently mobile in situations where a totally blind person could not function. However, if one 'passes for sighted', there is pressure to behave as others think a sighted person should. The partially sighted person does not look blind, since he moves more freely and obviously uses vision to a degree. This may confuse the sighted and cause them to question the reality of the partially sighted person's visual limitations. Little public information is available about the partially sighted which may contribute to their identity struggle.

**Self-image of the blind person**

A person who was born with partial but significantly limited sight, may be pressed to do things: 'He can still see, he is not totally helpless, he can still work and travel'. He will then either fight back with renewed effort or capitulate and surrender to dependency and defensive strategies to explain why he cannot accomplish things. In contrast, someone who acquires total or partial blindness later in life may be less pressed and be told 'You are blind, helpless, not expected to . . . ' which encourages that person to be dependent. People who are employed and mobile are more able to cope and less dependent on being defensive than those who are unemployed and less mobile. Those with a better employment record and better mobility are also more articulate, less distractable and more capable of making objective decisions than those who are unemployed and less mobile.

A blind person may accept popular notions of the limits and weaknesses in blindness, but he may also claim that being blind makes him in some indirect way a better human being. Those who lost their sight early in life have been found to be more socially independent. The higher the level of prior educational attainment, the greater the problem of readjustment and adaptation, indicating that the less one's life has become dependent on visual acuity prior to visual loss the less there is to overcome. How a person adapts to being blind depends on the degree of visual loss, the point of life in which it occurred, early training experiences, basic personality, and societal expectations and images.

**Attitudes to deafness**

Deafness is the cruellest form of sensory deprivation. Unlike blindness, it often provokes ridicule rather than sympathy: unable to hear what is said and unable to control their own voice, severely deaf people appear stupid. Isolated from family and friends, and greeted by unsympathetic attitudes, they are often depressed. The reaction of other people to deafness may make sufferers feel socially unacceptable; they may feel (sometimes justifiably) that to admit to being deaf is to be rejected, but rejection may be avoided by using guesswork or dominating the conversation. All types and degrees of deafness, at any age, bring about isolation and detachment from the environment, especially from easy, normal contact with other people. Even when an audiometric test shows only a mild loss, a disturbance of the person's contact with his or her environment, impairing the background function of hearing, requires a change in the individual's way of exploring and acquiring experiences.

## Self-image of the deaf person

Early communication minimizes the isolation that might accompany a severe hearing impairment from birth, and facilitates important interaction between the parents and the child at a critical stage of development. The linguistic limitations of the deaf child are detrimental both to social interaction and to the development of self-identity. The deaf child may fail to develop self-understanding and interpersonal relationships. Myklehurst (1964) argued that deafness imposes on experience by limiting interaction and linguistic feedback from the social environment, thus affecting the development of the self-concept. Hearing-impaired children tend to differ from children with normal hearing in terms of body image and self-perception.

To maintain feelings of well-being, each person requires constant assurance from his or her environment. They need a continuous indication that they are accepted, and that their needs will be met. It has been observed that deaf children born to deaf parents experience greater parental acceptance than those born to hearing parents. This greater acceptance probably encouraged the child to develop a more wholesome self-image. Deaf students with deaf parents had higher self-concepts, were more internally controlled and were better achievers than those with hearing parents (Koelle and Convey, 1982).

Adolescence for hearing-impaired children and their parents may be a particularly stressful time, as attempts are made to establish an independent identity and stable self-concept. Some studies found that deaf students rated themselves lower on self-esteem measures than hearing students, whereas other studies found hearing-impaired students to rate themselves more positively than hearing students. It has been found that deaf people had more negative attitudes to deafness than hearing people. Negative perceptions of self frequently were associated with beliefs that hearing persons perceive the deaf in terms of defects, real or imaginary (Furnham and Lane, 1984).

The overriding social effect of acquired deafness is loneliness: 24% of the hearing-impaired described themselves as lonely compared with 14% of the control group. Extreme loneliness (feeling lonely all the time, or very often) was found more often amongst the hearing-impaired of employment age than in populations of the retired and elderly. Of 209 people, 42% felt that their hearing problem was not understood by those nearest to them. Only 48% of all those who were married in the hearing-impaired group felt that their spouse understood what it was like to have impaired hearing. This research has shown that deaf individuals can be very lonely even at home. They are unhappy at work and appear to have a significantly depressed self-image (Thomas and Herbst, 1979).

## Personal experiences of people with sensory impairment

*Exclusion*

1. 'As I was the only deaf girl in school, it quickly dawned on me that I was "different" from the others. I saw my friends talking to each other and to adults in a quick, mumbling way, which was impossible to lipread. That made me feel younger, backward and very humble. I hopefully thought that I would catch up somehow and talk like the others.'

2. 'As a mother of two small children I can be excluded in subtle ways even by those who otherwise understand my needs. People will speak beautifully for me and then drop the signs and turn to talk "normally" to the children. Don't I exist any more? A child can be rushed from the room for a wee-wee or a drink and I am left wondering what calamity has occurred. Ears have heard what my eyes were not allowed to see. Doctors and school teachers address questions to the children which would otherwise be addressed to me.'

*Threatened self-image*

'I was to come to terms with a world viewed largely through a plate glass window where other people live, laugh and suffer and barely know of my existence. Deprived of much positive feedback on the woman I really was, my self-esteem took an insidious dive. I began to mistrust my own perception of the world and the people around me. How could I be sure of my impressions when I couldn't hear? When the views of others differed I quickly adjusted mine. They were right because they could hear and my experience seemed invalid. I felt I had little to offer anyone and rather than face rejection, I avoided people. Grieving over the lively, gregarious woman I had once been, I felt very isolated.'

*New self-image*

1. 'I seemed to be near breaking point when one evening something happened that proved to be the beginnings of my birth as a deaf woman. I was in an Indian restaurant with friends doing my little smiling and nodding act when I noticed the people opposite. They were deaf like me! They were laughing and talking and didn't give a damn that the whole place knew they were deaf. My years of pretence seemed suddenly absurd. I had been making things "normal" and easy for everyone except myself. It was time to give up my mourning and come out deaf' (Campling, 1981).

2. 'Adults have stared at him or commented on his appearance very little. Children express their reactions more freely. When this first happened he felt quite hurt and thought of giving up work and withdrawing completely. Gradually he became hardened to the comments and began to write them off as curiosity in children . . . his relationship with his wife and his family had, if anything, been made closer' (Andreasen *et al.*, 1971).

*Included*

'When I walk into the busy staff room at college or join a room full of friends and see them switch, as if by reflex action, to speaking and signing so that I can understand, I feel a glow of joy. This is how it should be because I am important and lovable enough to be included and when I am included I am no longer disabled' (Campling, 1981).

**References**

Andreasen, N.J.C., Norris, A.S. and Hartford, C.E. (1971) Incidence of long-term psychiatric complications in severely burned adults. *Annals of Surgery* **174**(5), 785–793.

Campling, J. (ed.) (1981) *Images of Ourselves*. London, Routledge and Kegan Paul.

Furnham, J. and Lane, S. (1984) Actual and perceived attitudes towards deafness. *Psychological Medicine* **14**(2), 417–423.

Koelle, W.H. and Convey, J.J. (1982) The prediction of the achievement of deaf adolescents from self-concept and locus of control measures. *American Annals of the Deaf* **127**, 769–779.

Myklehurst, H.R. (1964) *The Psychology of Deafness*. New York, Grune and Stratton.

Thomas, A. and Herbst, K.G. (1979) Social and psychological implications of acquired deafness for adults of employment age. *British Journal of Audiology* **14**, 76–85.

## CHAPTER 13

# Body image disturbance in burns

*Adele Atkinson*

**Introduction**

Each year more than 10 000 patients are treated in hospital for burns injuries (Department of Health, 1995). Many will suffer extensive, and often disfiguring, injuries, and will continue to need treatment in hospital and at home for years to come. This chapter will address the question of why some burns scar, the reasons for altered body image following a burns injury and the approaches that nurses can adopt to help patients adapt to their new body image.

Someone who has been burned will carry a disfigurement owing to the effect of scarring that marks them out from other people in a very obvious way. To understand the lasting effects of a thermal injury, it is helpful to look briefly at the different depths of injury that can be caused.

There are three depths of burn: superficial, partial thickness and full thickness. Superficial burns destroy the epidermal layer of the skin, but the hair follicles and sweat glands survive intact. This kind of burn heals quickly leaving skin that is elastic, supple and of good quality, with no scarring. A minor sunburn is one example of such an injury.

Partial-thickness burns can be divided into two types: superficial dermal and deep dermal. Superficial dermal burns destroy all of the epidermis and cause some damage to the dermis; deep dermal burns destroy varying levels of dermis, most of the sweat glands and hair follicles, and leave only the deepest epithelial elements to effect healing. Such healing will be slow, leaving a less elastic skin which may scar badly. The deeper the burn, the more likely it is that skin grafting will be required to aid healing.

Full-thickness burns destroy all layers of the skin and, some-times, deeper structures, such as muscle, bone, periosteum, nerves and tendons. Owing to the nature of the healing process, colla-gen is laid down and scar tissue is formed. Myofibroblasts involved in the healing process pull the remaining healthy tissue together by contracting, causing scarring in the process. Skin grafts will be used to heal full-thickness areas in an attempt to minimize scarring and to gain wound coverage. However, skin grafts themselves undergo shrinkage and can cause tightness owing to skin shortening. Burns caused by electricity are invari-ably full thickness.

Burns scars, like all other scars, go through a series of phases before they mature, an event which can take many years. They may be initially red or purplish in colour, but relatively flat. In the first 6 months they may thicken and harden; they may become raised and irritable – hypertrophic scars – and can be extremely disfiguring and disabling (Muir, 1990).

Over the following 12–18 months, they may soften, flatten and fade, although very few will become inconspicuous. The speed of this maturing process differs from individual to individual, how-ever, and, although such a timetable is typical, in some people the process may be slower (McNee, 1990).

Some of the measures that can be taken to minimize and cor-rect the scars which do form will be described later, but it can be seen from this brief description that any patient with a severe burn will suffer from some degree of scarring. This will depend partly on the size and extent of the injury, the patient's age and the loca-tion of the injury.

The change in appearance that a burn causes is something that the patient has to come to terms with, and requires adaptation to their altered body image. What happens to the individual whose whole appearance to the world is suddenly irrevocably altered? How does it affect their identity, interpersonal relationships and place in society as a whole? These are questions which the nurse, if he or she is to look at the patient as a whole, must consider, although the first priority is to meet physiological and then, later, social and psychological needs if he or she is to be successful in helping the individual on the way to rehabilitation in the full sense of the word.

A severe burn injury will require that the patient is treated in a specialized burns unit, where the combined skills and resources of the multidisciplinary team (e.g. surgeons, nurses, physiotherapist, occupational therapist, clinical psychologist, dietitian) are all available. Other specialist personnel may also be called upon.

A large burn is life threatening and may require hospitalization for many months. The patient will be anaesthetized on numerous occasions for grafting and dressing changes. They may suffer disheartening setbacks and, although there are some surgeons who believe the cosmetic results of treatment should be taken into consideration (Burns *et al.*, 1993), many other factors, such as the final coverage of the raw areas with good skin, will usually take precedence. The patient's appearance will be suddenly and shockingly altered from the outset, possibly owing to blackened charring or the red, raw appearance of partial thickness burns. Gross oedema occurs, especially on the face, although this is of a transient nature. The patient's body may be hidden under dressings and bandages for many months, and because some dressing changes may be performed under anaesthesia, it could be many weeks before they are able to see for themselves what has happened to the appearance of their body. Even then, the demands of physiotherapy and of meeting dietary requirements, or the simple desire to get well enough to go home, may take priority over concern for appearance.

Once the burns or grafts are healed, they may be tight and dry. Moisturizing lotion is recommended to the patient to be rubbed gently into these areas – although the main benefit from applying lotions comes from the massaging of the scar. Splints may be necessary to prevent contractures over joints. Pressure garments made of Lycra are shaped to cover the areas of scarring. These can be anything from a single glove to a full vest-top and leggings, and will have to be worn continuously by the patient until the scars mature. This means wearing them for at least 23 hours a day until the scars mature, with removal only for washing purposes. These garments help to flatten the scars and prevent many of the deformities due to contracture of scar tissue. Similarly, face masks made of a transparent soft plastic can be used to aid facial scars. Silicone gel may also be used to flatten hypertrophic scars (Quinn *et al.*, 1985).

Facial scars can cause the appearance to become mask-like, with facial expression being completely lost as the scar tissue is unable to respond to muscle movements. Scars around the mouth may distort it to one side, or make it difficult for the patient to eat or even to talk normally. Damage around the eyes may lead to distortion of the eyelids, or an inability to close the eyes during sleep or when blinking. Parts of the nose or ears may be missing, eyebrows may be lost, or partial baldness may result when a skin graft replaces part of the scalp. Large burns of the body may have been covered with meshed skin graft leaving a healed appearance often described as 'crocodile skin'. There may be altered sensation in the graft or scarred areas, which may react differently from normal skin to touch, or heat and cold.

Many patients face years of repeated corrective surgical procedures and inevitably some will opt out of treatment. More complicated surgery can be done at a later date, after the initial scars have settled, but this usually involves a wait. Reconstruction of areas may be necessary (e.g. parts burned away, contractures etc.). There are various ways that this can be done, for example, using flaps or tissue expanders.

Although much improvement can be made, patients will never lose the scarring that causes disfigurement. Patients will have areas of their body where the texture of the skin will both be and feel different, and for some, those with scarring of the face and hands, the defect will always be on show. As one burns survivor, Michelle McBride (1979), says in her book about her experiences: 'Being "a burn", is not a part-time hobby, it is an entire lifetime full of achievement. Being a burn is to be immensely lonely; it keeps loved ones at a distance and makes strangers curious enough to ask hurtful questions. Being burnt is never in the past tense, it is a chronic health problem'.

**Body-image disorders due to burns**

The concept of body image has already been discussed in an earlier chapter and from the description here of the injuries caused by burns it will be obvious how relevant this concept of body-image disorder is to the nursing of such patients. The injuries may involve disfigurement and/or loss of function, and in all cases the speed of the change is swift, and mostly unforeseen. The individual has no time to contemplate a 'new/different' body image.

Anyone who suffers scarring from a burn injury has to adjust to their new body image, whether the injuries are visible to others or not. The individual with a visible disfigurement has to learn to re-enter society as a person with a different appearance from others. If the defect is hidden under clothing, or by wearing a wig to cover baldness where the scalp has been burnt, there is always the fear of being found out. Others feel that they look so awful that it is not worth bothering about taking trouble about their appearance (Bradbury, 1991). Society places a great premium on what is considered 'normal'; the individual who deviates from this can be shunned and excluded (Goffman, 1963).

**The importance of appearance**

Permanent, visible disfigurement is one of the most prominent sequelae of major burns. Appearance is an extremely important concept – how we are valued by others and how we value ourselves. Vast sums of money are spent annually on advertising to encourage us to strive to achieve the appearance of youth, health and beauty. Western culture places considerable importance on an attractive, physical appearance (Berscheid and Gangestad, 1982). It is believed that the beautiful are more desirable to play with, nicer people, more desirable to date, more successful professionally, more intelligent, better mates, happier and more outgoing. The disfigured, therefore, have many cultural stereotypes to overcome.

Whether mild or severe, a facial disfigurement has been discovered to be a deterrent to normal living (Konigova, 1992). Among the 'normal' there is a hierarchy of disability with facial disfigurement coming at the bottom of the hierarchy (Richardson, 1962). For those who have been burned, the individual not only has to adjust to the physical consequences of impairment, but also has to cope with the social and psychological consequences resulting from what has been termed a 'spoiled identity' (Goffman, 1963). 'Any disfigurement is a source of embarrassment, but burn accidents are particularly traumatic and mutilating because they so often involve the unprotected face and hands. People stare, comment thoughtlessly, ask rude questions, are embarrassed into silence, or are unable to converse easily. Without intending to, strangers and friends in one way or another repeatedly make the disfigured person feel abnormal, out of place, unwelcome or unwanted' (Cape, 1976).

The problems facing such patients, then, are enormous. Rehabilitation will involve much more than physiotherapy and occupational therapy to make them fit enough to go home after surgery. What role can nurses play in helping these people re-enter society, faced with such a vast need. How can they begin to help these people, particularly those with visible scarring?

**The nurse's role**

Admission to a burns unit is unplanned and follows some kind of incident, often in the home or at work, sometimes as a result of a house fire or road traffic accident. Sometimes, such injuries are self-inflicted, as in a suicide attempt, or as a result of a schizo-phrenic episode when 'a voice told me to climb into the gas cooker'. Whatever the cause, the nursing principles involved remain the same.

A study by Morse and O'Brien (1995) showed that people who went through burns and other traumatic experiences went through four stages before coming to terms with their 'new selves'. These were vigilance (becoming engulfed), disruption (taking time out), enduring the self (confronting and regrouping) and striving to regain self (merging the old and new reality). Although the sample was small and one should be cautious about generaliz-ing to too great an extent, the headings serve to form a structure with which to explore the stages through which a patient pro-gresses and the corresponding nursing interventions.

**Stage 1 – vigilance**

This is the actual event. People who suffer burns injuries fre-quently recall being highly aware of what was happening to them and of what they should do. According to Morse and O'Brien (1995) such patients function on 'auto-pilot' in order to preserve their life.

Like any accident, a burn happens suddenly and events move fast. The patient is usually admitted within an hour or two of the incident, and often arrives at the burns unit via an accident and emergency department or by air ambulance. Even with very severe injuries, the patient is often conscious and able to respond; he or she is aware what has happened and will be able to tell the nursing staff what happened in great detail.

Medical and nursing staff inform relatives of the severity of the injuries and the patient's chances of survival. People tend to think that someone who is critically ill will be unconscious. The fact that a burns patient does not fit this picture makes it difficult for rela-tives to understand the severity of the situation. Even when told that there is a possibility that the person may not survive, relatives will still be concerned about the effects of scarring and skin graft-ing.

This stage usually ends soon after the person is admitted to the burns unit and he or she allows the burns staff to take over treat-ment. In some instances, however, the person may not trust the staff and will try to direct their own treatment (Morse and O'Brien, 1995). The value of telling the patient and their relatives not only *what* is happening but *why* is paramount to allay anxiety

(Wilson-Barnett, 1985) and to start to build a trusting relationship with both the patient and relatives.

**Stage 2 –
disruption:
taking time out**

This stage coincides with the most critical period for patients with large burns [over 15% for adults and 10% for children (Cason, 1981)] – the 'shock phase'.

With large burns, the efforts of the medical and nursing staff at this stage are directed at preventing the onset of hypovolaemic shock owing to the loss of plasma, and at making a full assessment of the injuries. It is often apparent on admission just how extensive the injuries are, how much surgery will be needed and how extensive the final disfigurement or disability will be. However, the first priority is adequate fluid, resuscitation and ensuring that the patient survives the injuries. In an extensive injury, the patient may become very ill and could die, often after a period of some weeks in hospital. Once again, it is essential that medical and nursing staff communicate effectively with the patient and his or her relatives.

Although the emphasis in this stage is on life-saving treatment, it is only when physiological stability has begun that the nurse's assessment can focus on issues related to body image (Di Maria, 1989). At this stage, the patient's perception of their body image may well have altered through an extension of their body image (Price, 1990) owing to intravenous infusions, nasogastric tubes, urinary catheters or even a ventilator, if this is required. The nurse must be aware of this and enforce the temporary nature of these interventions as well as the reason for them.

Often at this stage, the nurse will need to spend time with the family as well as with the patients, explaining the treatment to them and the extent of the injuries. The patients are caught up in what is happening to them. They know they need treatment, that they are badly injured and they are prepared to accept that what is going on is necessary. Their relatives may not be as aware.

Patients will experience intense pain. Price (1990) believes that this pain will also cause an alteration in body image, because they will not be able to 'trust' their body in the same way as before the burn. Analgesia or alternatives are extremely important, for the patient's perception of the eventual cosmetic result appears to affect their response to pain (Kinsella, 1991).

Initially analgesia is given through an intravenous infusion, this method being most appropriate for patients in shock. There is no reason why patients should not administer some pain relief themselves through a patient-controlled analgesia pump. This may be inappropriate if patients have injuries to their hands. Studies on adults and children (Kinsella *et al.*, 1988; Gaukroger *et al.*, 1991) show this to be an extremely effective method, which gives patients some control over their pain. Other techniques to lessen pain could involve the use of distraction (McCaffery and Bebe, 1989), for example, through using music during dressing changes, or by allowing patients to have some control during dressing changes by removing the dressings themselves.

Studies by Iafrati (1986) and McCaffery and Bebe (1989) have shown that nurses are not effective at assessing patients' pain and should, therefore, rely to a larger extent on what patients tell them. A pain assessment chart may be a useful tool to do this.

In the shock phase, a nurse will be with the patient at all times, but research by Morse and O'Brien (1995) found that the patients wanted someone they knew, a relative or friend, with them, possibly to help give a sense of security and reality. In light of this, the importance of both open visiting and of enabling relatives to stay overnight becomes apparent. Patients may also suffer from nightmares about the incident (Morse and O'Brien, 1995) and the reassurance of someone they know will help them tremendously.

This stage ends as the reality of the situation sets in and, at last, patients start to question. Initial questions may be about possible scarring and length of hospital stay.

**Stage 3 – enduring the self: confronting and regrouping**

It takes a great deal of personal courage to ask questions about scarring, and the majority of patients do not voice this fear in the first stages of treatment. However, just because the question is unasked, this does not mean that it is not in the forefront of the patient's mind. The nurse should always be aware of the likelihood that it is and of the distress that this will cause the patient. Whatever area of the body has been burned, there will be swelling. This is particularly the case with facial injuries. This swelling lasts for several days and then gradually subsides but, while it persists, it can be extremely distressing to the patient and their family. Constant reinforcement by the nurse that the swelling is a normal response to the injury and that it will subside is needed. With a facial injury, the patient will often be unable to see properly for several days which makes the experience all the more frightening. The nurse should be aware of just how frightening and disorientating this is, and should explain everything that is going on or is about to happen.

Bernstein (1976) comments: 'In spite of the most human efforts on the part of treatment, care is long and complex and relentlessly agonising to the patient'. The priorities for medical and nursing staff will be those of gaining wound coverage with skin grafts, preserving function through physiotherapy and splinting, nutrition and, possibly, nasogastric feeding, plus wound care. It will be the nurse who spends the most time with patients and their families: he or she will be involved in many procedures that cause the patients pain and discomfort, and will also have to carry out many intimate procedures, such as helping with toileting and catheter care.

The nurse can help to bring a sense of reality to the patient by talking to the patient about everyday activities (Morse and O'Brien, 1995), about what they have been doing, their interests and what has been happening in the news.

The severely burned patient can be very dependent for many weeks or months. During this long and difficult stage of treatment, nurses will get to know the patients and their families and close friends well. They will learn how these social networks function and how patients have coped with past crises, which will help them to support the patients in their present trauma. Bowden (1980) discovered that one of the important factors in burns patients' self-esteem was their social support system: there appeared to be a correlation between the amount of social support and a patient's positive self-esteem. This emphasizes the need to help patients further develop their social support system.

Belfer *et al.* (1982) found that both positive and negative body images were initially shaped by parents' attitudes to their children. Thus, because feedback from others who are valued (parents, friends, etc.) shapes people's body image, then it is important that not only nursing and medical staff, but also relatives are encouraged to be positive, but realistic, about how patients look and, more importantly, about how they will look when surgery is eventually finished.

A number of reactions are usually seen as patients come to terms with what has happened to their body and their life. After a severe burn, the body's appearance is changed and the new body image must be incorporated into the patient's self-concept. In order to adjust in a positive way, patients must develop/retain a sense of self-esteem despite the changes in their appearance. This phase may continue long after discharge from hospital, and it follows the path of the grief process described by Kubler-Ross (1969) (see Figure 13.1). She describes five phases, which may also be seen in the burned patient and their family, namely, denial, anger, bargaining, depression and acceptance. The first three phases are usually experienced while the patient is in hospital, but the individual can shift both backwards and forwards between the various phases, and a patient who is depressed may re-enter the phases of denial and anger. Bargaining is seen when the patient says things such as: 'Everything will be all right when I have my nose reconstructed', or 'Things will be OK when I stop wearing my pressure garments'. It may take many years to complete all five phases, and Kubler-Ross states that it is incomplete until acceptance is reached. Berstein (1976), by contrast, argues against this, saying that some patients never get over their grief, although they manage to adjust and to re-enter society.

Nurses needs to be aware that they will see many reactions from burns patients in hospital, including denial, which can be very pronounced. The most severely disfigured patients may never question their appearance and appear quite happy, as if they were totally unaware of what has happened to them. This may be welcomed by the family and staff at first, but it soon becomes increasingly obvious that the patients are just not acknowledging what has happened. It is important for patients to come to terms with this while still in hospital.

Gentle prompting can elicit whether the patients have any reservations about coping when they get home. For example, nurses may ask whether the patients wish to see themselves in a mirror, although this is not usually encouraged until after grafting

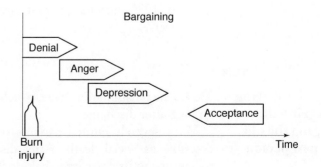

***Figure 13.1***   The five stages of the grieving process. Reproduced from Kubler-Ross (1969) with permission.

and the best possible initial result has been obtained. This prompting may go on for several days until, often in the presence of relatives, patients first look at their appearance. Nurses may find that the family would like to have moral support at this time, but they may prefer to be left alone to deal with their own reactions.

Anger is often seen as a natural reaction to the injury. It may be directed at the nursing staff by patients who are struggling with their own emotions or, in the case of a child, at parents who often have feelings of their own guilt with which they have to come to terms. Severe depression may also be seen, with apathy and lethargy, dulled senses and loss of appetite. This, again, is a natural reaction which nurses must understand and expect. However, any of these reactions may become exaggerated or difficult for the nursing staff to cope with, and in such cases the help of the clinical psychologist and the psychiatrist should be sought.

It appears that there is a tendency for nursing staff to overlook their role as a psychological support for the patients (Partridge, 1993). Therefore, nurses should find time to sit with the patients. Good communication skills, especially in the use of active listening, will help patients enormously.

At some time during this stage, the patients will be transferred out of single cubicles/wards and into a more general ward with other patients. They must be well prepared by nursing staff as they will be frightened. Because mirrors are not generally in use in such cubicles on burns units, it may well also be the first time that they and other people see their scars. Morse and O'Brien (1995) found that, once patients had become used to their new environment, the support that other patients gave them was very encouraging.

At this stage, use of short-term goals as described by Morse and O'Brien (1995) may help to motivate patients and reinforce positive aspects.

**Stage 4 – striving to regain self: merging the old and new person**

This is the rehabilitation stage, which starts in hospital and carries on long after discharge.

Many severely burned patients suffer what Bernstein (1976) describes as 'social death'. After discharge they are lost to any follow-up, and retreat into sheltered lives, never able to re-enter society fully. Several studies on the outcome of severe burns injuries have been undertaken, but many do not take into account the fact that a large proportion of discharged patients were untraceable. There is little agreement among the authors over the social and psychological effects of severe burns. White (1982) found that patients with serious injuries were twice as likely to have psychiatric problems after discharge. An increased incidence of depression was found by Chang and Herzog (1974) in those with hand and facial injuries. Some authors have found that young adults were the most likely to have problems (Andreason and Norris, 1972), while others have demonstrated that mid-life was the most vulnerable time.

Andreason and Norris (1972) showed that women were more likely to have problems than men but this is disputed by White (1982), who found no differences between the sexes. Kolman (1983) suggests that the underlying reason for the increased depression noted by some authors is probably the change in physical appearance, and the loss of social and work roles with a consequent lowering of self-esteem.

Helm and Walker (1992) have attempted to develop data which can predict when a patient is likely to be able to return to work post-burn, with positive results. They say that this information will help not only patients but employers. This type of prediction would help to alleviate anxiety caused by the uncertainty of future work prospects.

Although there is much evidence to suggest that burned patients suffer psychiatric problems after discharge, hospital nursing staff have been unable to address these problems in the past. With the advent of outreach/community liaison nurses in which the burns unit nurse visits the patient at home and liaises with district nurses, they may help not only to pick up these problems, but also provide continuity of care.

The outreach nurse can also help prepare schools for when children who have been burned eventually go back. This and other school reintegration programmes may prevent the negative reactions experienced from other children (Blakeney, 1995).

Reintegration into the community should begin in hospital. Nurses can encourage patients to go shopping, at first accompanied by a nurse or social worker, and home visits at weekends can be used to rebuild experience of home life. Close members of the family too may find this helpful and will often need support themselves. Advice can be given to the patient on suitable styles of clothing that will help to hide scars, or on wigs or a change of hairstyle to hide bald spots. Severe burns may cause mobility disadvantages, and clothes have been designed for wheelchair users and others to make dressing easier (Eggleston *et al.*, 1994).

Encouragement about the progression of scarring, or the effectiveness of the pressure garments, can be given. This is important. Johnson *et al.* (1994) found that many patients do not wear their pressure garments for the recommended time (at least 23 hours a day for at least 12 months). This appeared to be due to the area on which the garment was worn; patients felt that garments on the head and neck area looked unsightly. In the light of this, it is important that pressure garments for these areas are made of a transparent material, which looks less obvious and unsightly. To encourage compliance and to emphasize the importance of these garments, nurses could show patients photographs of hypertrophic scars before and after wearing garments. This may emphasize the more normal appearance that can be achieved.

It may be appropriate to refer the patient to the British Red Cross Society, which provides a camouflage make-up service. This is often effective in restoring confidence at a time when the patient is waiting for the scars to settle and surgery is not immediately possible. Men as well as women may find this service useful.

At this stage of rehabilitation nurses should be a source of advice and encouragement. They should be supportive of the patients' efforts to re-establish their lives, and understanding about the problems that they are encountering. Some burns units have patient self-help groups, often run by burns patients themselves, but with members of the treatment team being available to give advice and support. Support groups for burns patients are few, but one support group that helps patients develop coping strategies through social skills training is Changing Faces, which was started by a burned patient as a direct result of the lack of support available (Partridge, 1993).

Let's Face It is another such group which holds meetings at a number of venues and distributes a newsletter. Its founder, Christine Piff (1985) wrote: 'However the face is damaged, the pain and distress caused to the unfortunate person is immeasurable. In many cases it has disturbing effects upon the close family circle and friends. Not being able to communicate their feelings to others can cause great distress. This, and not being able to understand why they feel the way they do can cause deep psychological problems. The sensation of isolation and rejection makes one feel completely cut off and alone'.

Although a great deal of the emphasis in work on burns disfigurement is about facial injuries, for some people – women in particular – scarring on the legs or other visible parts of the body may also be a problem. Strategies employed by self-help groups will also be relevant for these patients.

Collyer (1984) produced guidelines for staff involved in the treatment of disfigured patients, to aid successful rehabilitation, and they bear repetition here:

1.  Realization that the patient's confidence is created or destroyed in many ways, and that *every* contact is significant.
2.  Making time to communicate with the patient and family.
3.  Making time to listen.
4.  Recognizing that what is said to the patient and what is heard by the patient are two different things.
5.  At the right time giving a realistic prognosis, supportively.
6.  Ensuring that patients and families acquire the necessary daily living skills for their disfigurement, and regard those skills with pride.
7.  Through experienced patients, further securing that new patients have a realistic awareness of the limits and of the benefits that medical and related skills may bring.

Gilboa *et al.* (1994) lists 'dos' and 'don'ts' which in many respects coincide with this list, but which emphasize the importance of stressing positive coping strategies and defence mechanisms. Such strategies are, perhaps, the key to the whole nursing role in helping the patient adapt to a new body image.

This chapter is based on an earlier version by L. May, published in the first edition of the book.

**References**

Andreason, N.J.C. and Norris, A.S. (1972) Long-term adjustment and adaptation mechanisms in severely burned adults. *Journal of Nervous Mental Disorder* **154**, 352–362.

Belfer, M., Harrison, M., Pillemer, F. and Murray, J. (1982) Appearance and the influence of reconstructive surgery on body image. *Clinics in Plastic Surgery* **9**(3), 307–315.

Bernstein, N.R. (ed.) (1976) *Emotional Care of the Facially-burned and Disfigured*. Boston, Little, Brown.

Berschied, E. and Gangestad, A. (1982) The social psychological implications of facial physical attractiveness. *Clinics in Plastic Surgery* **9**(3), 289–295.

Blakeney, P. (1995) School reintegration. *Journal of Burn Care and Rehabilitation* **16**(2), 180–187.

Bowden, M. (1980) Self-esteem of severely burned patients. *Archives of Physiological Medical Rehabilitation* **61**, 448–452.

Bradbury, E. (1991) Healing the scars within. *The Independent* November 12, 15.

Burns, B., McCauley, R., Murphy, F. and Robson, M. (1993) Reconstructive management of patients with greater than 80 per cent TBSA burns. *Burns,* **19**(5), 429–433.

Cason, J. (1981) *Treatment of Burns.* London, Chapman and Hall.

Chang, F.C. and Herzog, B. (1974) Burn morbidity: a follow up study of physical and psychological disability. *Annals of Surgery* **183**, 34.

Collyer, H. (1984) *Facial Disfigurement, Successful Rehabilitation.* London, Macmillan.

Cope, O. (1976) In: Bernstein, N.R. (eds) *Emotional Care of the Facially-burned and Disfigured.* Boston, Little, Brown.

Di Maria, R. (1989) Post-trauma responses: potential for nursing. *Journal of Advanced Medical-Surgical Nursing* **2**, 41–48.

Department of Health (1995) *Hospital Statistics, vol. 1.* London, Department of Health.

Eggleston, J., Bentrem, D., Bromberg, W., London, S., Biesecker, J. and Edich, R. (1994) Adaptive clothing for persons with mobility disorders after burn injury. *Journal of Burn Care and Rehabilitation* **15**, 269–274.

Gaukroger, P., Chapman, M. and Davey, R. (1991) Pain control in paediatric burns – the use of patient-controlled analgesia. *Burns* **17**(5), 396–399.

Gilboa, D., Friedman, M. and Tsur, H. (1994) *Journal of Burn Care and Rehabilitation.* **15**, 86–94.

Goffman, I. (1963) *Stigma: Notes on Management of a Spoiled Identity.* Harmondsworth, Penguin Books.

Helm, P. and Walker, S. (1992) Return to work after burn injury. *Journal of Burn Care and Rehabilitation* **13**(1), 53–57.

Iafrati, N. (1986) Pain on the burn unit: patient vs nurse perceptions. *Journal of Burn Care and Rehabilitation* **7**(5), 413–416.

Johnson, J., Greenspan, B., Gorga, D., Nagler, W. and Goodwin, C. (1994) Compliance with pressure garment use in burn rehabilitation. *Journal of Burn Care and Rehabilitation* **15**, 181–188.

Kinsella, J. and Booth, M. (1991) Pain relief in burns: James Lang Memorial Essay 1990. *Burns* **17**(5), 391–395.

Kinsella, J., Glavin, R. and Reid, W. (1988) Patient-controlled analgesia for burn patients: a preliminary report. *Burns* **14**, 500–503.

Kolman, P.B.R. (1983) The incidence of psychopathology in burned adult patients: a critical view. *Journal of Burn Care and Rehabilitation* **4**, 430–436.

Konigova, R. (1992) The psychological problems of burned patients. The Rudy Hermans Lecture 1991. *Burns* **18**(3), 189–199.

Kubler-Ross, E. (1969) *On Death and Dying*. New York, Macmillan.

McBride, M. (1979) *The Fire That Will Not Die*. ETC Publications.

McCaffrey, M. and Beebe, A. (1989) *Pain*. St Louis: C.V. Mosby.

McGregor, F.C. (1953) *Facial Deformities and Plastic Surgery: A Psychosocial Study*. Springfield, IL, C.C. Thomas.

McNee, J. (1990) The use of silicone gel in the control of hypertrophic scarring. *Physiotherapy* **76**(4), 194–197.

Morse, J. and O'Brien, B. (1995) *Journal of Advanced Nursing* **21**, 886–896.

Muir, I. (1990) On the nature of keloid and hypertrophic scars. *British Journal of Plastic Surgery* **43**, 61–69.

Muir, I.F.R. and Barclay, T.L. (1974) *Burns and their Treatment*. London, Lloyd-Luke.

Partrige, J. (1993) The psychological effects of facial disfigurement. *Journal of Wound Care* **2**(3), 168–171.

Piff, C. (1985) *Let's Face It*. London, Gollancz.

Price, B. (1990) *Body Image: Nursing Concepts and Care*. New York, Prentice Hall.

Quinn, K., Evans, J., Courtney, J. and Gaylor, J. (1985) Non-pressure treatment of hypertrophic scars. *Burns* **12**, 102–108.

Richardson, S. (1962) *Social and Psychological Consequence of Handicapping*. Unpublished paper presented at 1962 American Sociological Association Convention, Washington, DC.

White, A.C. (1982) Psychiatric study of patients with severe burn injuries. *British Medical Journal* **284**(13 February), 265–467.

Wilson-Barnett, J. (1985) Principles of patient teaching. *Nursing Times* **81**, 28–29.

CHAPTER 14

# A neurological perspective

*Margot Lindsay*

**Introduction**

It is among neurologists that one finds some of the earliest thinking about body image. They were forcefully confronted with the concept in terms of the unusual and bizarre attitudes which patients with brain damage often adopt towards their bodies. Patients with various brain lesions manifest a whole gamut of distorted body ideas. They may, for example, be unable to distinguish the left side of the body from the right, deny the existence of various body parts, be unable to acknowledge the incapacitation of paralysed body parts; they may falsely attribute new or supernumerary body parts to themselves or experience undue heaviness of one half of the body. These experiences indicate that the individual is no longer thinking about his or her body in the same way as prior to the illness (Fisher and Cleveland, 1968; Walsh, 1978).

The two parietal regions are those most closely connected with the zones which analyse kinesthetic and visual perception. The superior parietal areas are closely connected to the lobes in which the lower limbs and trunk are represented, which is important for the integration of movements of the whole body. The close proximity of the occipital lobe, which is responsible for visual reception of images from the eyes, means that this is an important area for the formation of the body image. The brain tissue in the temporal, occipital and parietal lobes is intermediate between the auditory and visual zones of the cortex, and, therefore, is involved in analysing the most complex forms of auditory and visual reception, in particular relating to the semantics of spoken and written language.

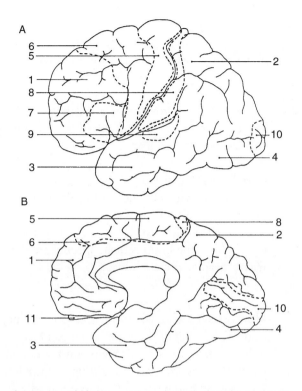

***Figure 14.1***   Areas of the brain. (A) Supero-lateral surface of left hemisphere. (B) lateral section through brain: 1, column frontal lobe; 2, parietal lobe; 3, temporal lobe; 4, occipital lobe; 5, motor area (pre-central) gyrus; 6, pre-motor area; 7, motor-speech area; 8, sensory area (post-central gyrus); 9, auditory area; 10, visual area; 11, olfactory bulb. From *The Human Body on File*, reproduced by kind permission of Diagram Visual Information Ltd.

**Disturbed body image caused by brain damage**

A lesion of the parietal lobe in the non-dominant hemisphere may lead to an inability to attend to subtle variations in form, to the extent that the patient may confuse their water jug and another jug of the same shape. Lesions at the occipitoparietal lobe of the non-dominant hemisphere may cause difficulties in understanding and remembering relationships of places to one another, so that patients are unable to find their way in familiar surroundings. They may even fail to recognize the buildings and furnishings among which they have lived and worked (topographical disorientation).

Whereas lesions situated in the occipital or parietal cortex cause disturbances of complex forms of visual or tactile perception, the agnosias, lesions of zones situated in the parietotemporo-occipital regions, are the 'overlapping zones' of the visual, auditory and tactile analysers, which may lead to far more complex disorders. Lesions of these zones of the cerebral cortex may cause appreciable disturbances of orientation in space.

## What can happen to the brain to disturb body image experiences?

A *stroke* (a cerebrovascular accident) which causes a clogged or burst blood vessel to block the blood supply to the brain means that brain tissue in a specific area degenerates and can no longer function.

A *tumour* (an abnormal accumulation of cells) expands and disrupts the activities of the surrounding brain tissue because of the pressure or infiltration of cells.

*Trauma* (a blow to the head, either accidentally or surgically) can damage the brain cells in specific areas, so leaving the patient with a permanent disability.

## Understanding patients' experiences

How does it feel if, whenever you look at a page of a book you see only the left half of the page; when you focus on the first word, you only see its left half, and when you try to concentrate on the first letter of the word, only the left half of the letter is there? What if you were able to write, but could not read your own writing? How does it feel to find yourself outside your own home and yet be unable to go for a short walk because you might get lost? These are a few of the problems that patients with body image disorders experience when they have disturbance of the parieto-occipital region of the brain.

## Apraxia

Apraxia is the inability to carry out purposive or skilled acts owing to brain damage when there is no weakness, paralysis or sensory loss (Walsh, 1978). It results from cerebral lesions of either or both hemispheres in the parietal lobe areas, and may take several forms, including motor and dressing apraxia. Two or more apraxias usually occur together – only rarely is one type found in isolation (Siev and Freishtat, 1976).

*Dressing apraxia* is the most common. Patients have difficulty in dressing to the extent that they may not be able to relate the articles of clothing to their body and/or may not be able to relate the parts of the clothes to each other. Patients make mistakes of orientation in putting clothes on backwards, upside down or inside out. The true constructional apraxic defect in dressing shows itself in a total disarray, whereby garments are put on in the wrong order, or at the wrong end (trousers over head; shirt over legs). Often patients with right-sided lesions will neglect to dress the left side of their body or put both legs in the same trouser leg (Critchley, 1953; Siev and Freishtat, 1976).

*Motor apraxia* is believed to be a loss of kinesthetic memory patterns which results in the patient's inability to perform a purposeful motor task on command, although it is apparent that the patient understands the concept and purpose of the task. The patient may be able to carry out simple motor tasks automatically, but cannot complete a complicated sequence.

*Constructional apraxia* means the patient may have difficulty in breaking down and building up again an object in either two or three dimensions. Although constructional apraxia is rarely specifically complained of by the patient, there are occasions when indications of this phenomenon can be detected in the history. The patient may have little or no insight into this difficulty, and the story emerges from the independent account given by relatives or friends. Certain domestic activities become difficult, if not impossible, for a patient with constructional apraxia. The patient may be at a loss to lay the table for a meal, and may have trouble in making the bed, or in packing and tying a parcel. He or she will encounter great difficulty with such recreations as jigsaw puzzles or any sort of assembly work, as well as in writing and arithmetic (Critchley, 1953).

*Disorders of spatial thought – topographical disorientation*

A sense of disorientation in space, spatial aptitude or topographical sense consists of an inability to find one's way about without getting lost. In patients with parietal disease, the symptom of losing oneself often constitutes a conspicuous feature in the case history. In such an event, the patient finds it difficult to conjure up a mental picture of a familiar environment – their home, office, the streets in their neighbourhood. This impairment may occur independently of other visual images and may alert the relatives to the fact of illness, although, oddly enough, it rarely distresses or interests the patient.

Critchley (1953) and Luria (1973) have provided many vivid examples of the dramatic effects of damage to the parieto-occipital region of the brain. Most of the people whose experiences were described had received penetrating head injuries so that the precise area of damage was readily identified.

*Topographical disorientation*

1. A soldier with a left parieto-occipital lesion no longer had any sense of space. He could not judge relationships between things, and perceived the world as broken into thousands of separate parts. As he put it 'space made no sense'; he feared it, for it lacked stability (Luria, 1973).
2. A man who had lived in the same place for 10 years was quite unable to describe the area, but he could give a satisfactory description of his wife's appearance. 'It's so weird – I simply can't orientate myself to a place, just have no sense of space' (Luria, 1973).
3. 'She enjoys a walk but suddenly she may lose all sense of direction. Streets which are normally well-known to her now appear as if belonging to a foreign city. Often she has wandered for hours vainly trying to find a certain bus stop, or the house of a friend, or her own home and the houses appear very strange, being larger and floating' (Critchley, 1968).

*Anatomical consideration for patients with visual perceptual difficulties*

A disturbance of the anterior sections of the occipital area can mean that the person continues to see objects as clearly as before, but their vision is dramatically changed. This is because small cells that synthesize individual characteristics of objects perceived into complete wholes have stopped functioning. They still distinguish individual parts of objects but can no longer synthesize them into complete images; they can then only guess the total from these separate parts. The disturbances of visual perception arising in lesions of the right hemisphere can be understood as lack of control over the patient's searches when assessing an object, such as being unable to recognize people's faces (Luria, 1973).

If someone whose brain has been damaged in this way is asked to look at a picture of a pair of spectacles, they see one circle, then another, then a crossbar, and finally, two cane-like attachments. They guess it may be a bicycle. They cannot perceive objects, even though they can distinguish their individual features. They experience 'optical agnosia' – inability to recognize the meaning of visual stimuli (Luria, 1973).

*Visual perception difficulties*

A patient who had a lesion in the parietal lobe of the non-dominant hemisphere said: 'I don't recognize anybody till I have seen them a long time'. He knew that he had seen someone before, but he was unable to make the connection between a person's name and face. The man was able to recognize his own face in the mirror, he was unable to identify prominent political figures, but he could easily recognize pictures of animals. He said that he could visualize his wife's face clearly but not other people's. He could only imagine certain traits, such as a moustache, or a bald head, but not the overall features.

| | |
|---|---|
| *Autopagnosia* | Described by Pick (1922), autopagnosia is the loss of the ability to localize and name body parts. It may be associated with visual defects, apraxia or aphasia. People with this defect have difficulty in finding, describing or naming body parts even when they can see or touch the parts on themselves or on the examiner. Placed before a mirror, the subjects still cannot point or otherwise identify body parts. Some patients seem to be fully aware of their defect while others are not. |

Inability to point out various parts of the body may be interpreted as a disorder of personal space. At a later stage still, it may seem as though the frontiers between personal and extra-personal space become less sharp. Patients confuse their own limbs with those of the examiner. This is likely to happen, in particular, when the examiner holds one of the patient's limbs; the patient may then imagine that the examiner's hand is their own or that their own leg is part of the examiner. When a pin is stuck into their arm, the patient, whose eyelids are shut at the time, may point to a similar region upon the examiner's limb as being the spot stimulated. Those who are unaware of their defect may suggest that the body part that they cannot designate has been lost. The patient described by Pick (1922) looked for his own hands at the table or in the bed, believing he had lost them. One of Hecan's patients accused the doctor of having taken away her hand (Critchley, 1953; Hecan and Albert, 1978).

Finger agnosia is a fragment of autopagnosia entailing an inability to recognize, name or point out on request, various parts of the subject's own body. It may also apply to the anatomy of other persons; this is practically the only instance of an isolated or localized autopagnosia. Patients may point out correctly and unhesitatingly each part of the body until they reach their fingers. It is interesting to observe the patient identifying without trouble each toe on the two feet, but failing where the hands are concerned (Critchley, 1953).

*Asomatognosia*

At times, a patient may suffer from an acute and painful impression that one side of their body has disappeared and despite evidence to the contrary, be uncertain of the integrity of their body. When this happens the person fails to recognize a portion of their body as being their own and may attribute that body part to another person. If the examiner were to pick up this patient's paralysed left arm, the patient would declare that the arm in question belonged to the examiner.

Asomatognosia may manifest itself to the patient, not so much as a continued phenomenon, but as a recurring episode. The arm and leg of the affected side may seem to disappear, or to fall out of corporeal awareness. When this happens, there may also be an involuntary deviation of the head and eyes towards the other side, and a feeling of great anxiety may temporarily supervene. The patient may grope with their good hand so as to palpate the paralysed limbs and thus assure himself or herself of their existence (Critchley, 1953).

When a hypnotic suggestion was made to four amnesic patients – 'You will forget everything about your body when you awaken' – they not only lost their ability to name their body parts but also manifested markedly decreased capability for doing various other things. One patient found it difficult to name objects and to draw geometric figures. Another lost the ability to recognize articles of clothing, and made many gross errors in evaluating the length, thickness and parallelism of lines. But overall, the hypnotic suggestion to forget everything about the body resulted mainly in errors of differentiation of the right and left sides of the body, difficulty with arithmetical calculations, breakdown of the ability to draw figures, and faulty recognition of objects. The most important result of the study is that it shows a relatively intact body image to be a foundation necessary for the performance of certain judgements and skills (Fisher and Cleveland, 1968).

*Unilateral neglect*

The inability to integrate and use perceptions from the left side of the body or the left side of the environment is known as unilateral neglect, which may occur independently of visual deficits or be compounded by left hemianopsia. There may be no trace of motor weakness, but an expanding lesion produces other clinical troubles. The patient may become generally confused, which elaborates the unilateral neglect in a striking and often bizarre fashion. To passive disregard is added active neglect. Patients may cease to pay heed to one half of their anatomy, to attend to its hygiene and cleanliness, and they may be observed to be getting untidy, and even dirty, in appearance. For example, a man may only comb the hair on one half of his head, while a woman may apply cosmetics to one side only of her face and lips, and leave her hair unkempt on one side, while the other is neat. In the bath, the patient may soap only one side of their face and body, and a moment later, proceed to dry one half only. He or she may step out of the bath with just one leg and leave the other foot in the water: then, on attempting to cross the bathroom floor may fall heavily (Critchley, 1953). Unilateral neglect may cause the patient to neglect the food on the left side of the plate or to read starting in the middle of the line. They may bump into things on their left or constantly be turning to the right.

*Anosognosia*

Body agnosia is often associated with lack of awareness of disease or disability, known as anosgnosia, where patients either fail to perceive or deny that a part of their body, such as an arm and leg, is paralysed. When patients deny and are indifferent to their hemiplegia, there is a failure to integrate one side of the body into consciousness of the whole body, a one-sided reduction of the body image.

Anosognosia for hemiplegia usually occurs when the right side of the brain is damaged, as in vascular disease, but also happens with a tumour in that part of the brain. It may occur immediately after an acute vascular lesion of the right hemisphere and, after persisting for some days, then disappears. As the initial state of confusion slowly recedes, so patients begin to realize their disability. Anosognosia is, as a rule, a transitory phenomenon.

Anosognostic patients will frequently be unaware that they have other gross disabilities at the same time as their paralysis. Thus they may also show an apparent ignorance of, or imperception for, such states as blindness or deafness (Critchley, 1953).

The reaction of patients when forcibly confronted with the hard facts of their paralysis does not necessarily conform to a pattern. Anosognosic patients who are compelled to face their disability may react in one of the following ways:

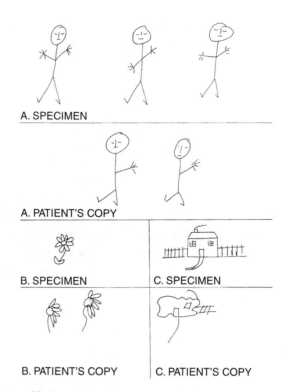

**Figure 14.2** Unilateral neglect in a patient with a lesion in the right parietal occipital region.

1. Register a puzzled admission of this disease.
2. Admit the fact with reluctance.
3. React with unexpected light-heartedness.
4. Concede that they are paralysed but show little or no distress on that account.
5. Obstinately reject the obvious facts of the handicaps. The patients may describe their paralysed arm as having a 'will and purpose of its own' or 'it is tired' or that 'it always was a lazy arm' (Sacks, 1985), and may accuse the doctor of exaggeration or error.
6. Admit the disability but attribute it to some local lesions or claim that the limb has always been 'a bit odd'.
7. Realize the trouble and develop a reactive depression on that account.

In the course of a single interview the patient may run through the gamut of these psychological reactions with complete inconsistency.

*Case study*

A 62-year-old woman had a right cerebral thrombosis in the front pari-etal region. When in her kitchen on 23 December, she was seen to sway on her feet. She complained of pins and needles in the left arm, and then the left leg felt weak. By the following morning there was profound weakness of the left face, arm and leg, with loss of feeling. There was no loss of consciousness, and no confusion was noted by her relatives, but lit-tle movement of the left arm or leg was seen over the next few days and she was admitted to hospital where examination revealed that she had experienced a cerebral thrombosis. When the patient was asked about her illness, she described the incident in the kitchen correctly, but whereas she was aware she had lost power in the left leg, she insisted that the left arm had not been affected and that it was normal.

On 2 January she still maintained that the left arm and leg were 'all right' and moved the right instead. On the next day she said that the left hand was 'all right', but on being asked to show it, showed the right instead. When shown the left hand she recognized it, and after trying to move it said, 'will not lift' and that it was 'very naughty'. She described the left leg as 'all right' but moved the right instead. On 4 January the patient again denied her hemiplegia. On being told to move the left hand, she merely wagged it with the right hand and appeared satisfied with the result. The next day her attitude to her hemiplegia was chang-ing, she tended to make light of her disability. When she could not move her left hand and was asked why, she said it was 'dopey' and described the left leg as 'much better'. 'Is it dopey?' 'No I am moving it all the time' (she was only moving the right leg). By 16 January the disability of the left arm was no longer ignored but was treated in an objective fashion – the patient described it as 'poor little withered hand'. There was still some neglect of the left leg both in bed and when sitting out in the ward. By 18 March the patient's attitude to her left side was not obviously abnormal, and there was no neglect or denial of disability (Gilliatt and Pratt, 1952).

*Gerstmann's syndrome*

In 1924, Josef Gerstmann described a woman of 52 years of age with a dominant hemisphere lesion, located in the parietal lobe, in or near the angular gyrus. She had a striking inability to recognize her own fingers, or to name them, or to point out an individual digit when asked. This same inability applied not only to her own fingers, but also to those of other people. The patient had not been aware of this difficulty until it was revealed by the doctor's exami-nation. Although there was no weakness in her fingers, she was unable to move some of her fingers when asked to do so.

Gerstmann regarded this particular symptom as a disorder of the body image and termed it 'finger agnosia'. There was also a right–left disorientation, particularly for parts of her own body and for the bodies of others. Furthermore, she showed difficulty in carrying out arithmetical calculations and in writing spontaneously.

The striking thing about this syndrome is that it includes four kinds of dysfunction which may appear to have nothing in common. Finger agnosia is unique in that rarely does one find an agnosia for any isolated part of the individual's body. Although there are four cardinal manifestations of Gerstmann's syndrome – finger agnosia, right-to-left disorientation, acalculia and agraphia – sometimes these are not all present at the same time, although usually all are present. The emphasis may be uneven, so that one or two of the features are more prominent than the others (Critchley, 1953). An analysis of 456 patients with cerebral disease found that 111 had one or more Gerstmann symptoms: 33 with one symptom, 32 with two, 23 with three and 23 had all four symptoms (Heimburger *et al.*, 1964).

*Finger agnosia* is a disturbance of the body image which declares itself in the patients' inability to name and localize parts of their own body. One of the most commonly described disorders in this category is finger agnosia where patients cannot point to or show the examiner the various fingers of each hand. Even with their eyes open, patients may be unable to respond with a correct finger movement when a finger is touched, although there is no evidence of weakness in the fingers. Errors are generally more marked with the three middle fingers than with the thumb or little finger. Subjects tend to be unaware of or to deny their disability and make no effort to correct errors. Such patients may be able to thread a needle or play a piano.

*Right–left disorientation* is present when the patient, when asked to indicate the right or left hand (ear, eye, shoulder or foot), displays confusion and makes many mistakes in sidedness. The patient will also make mistakes when asked to perform this test on the person of the examiner or looking in a mirror. Right–left confusion will also be displayed when the patient is asked to indicate one or other side in a two-dimensional picture or representation of a human body. This disorientation may possibly apply to inanimate objects, such as a doll or a statue, and to articles of dress, such as a shoe or glove. In early cases of progressive parietal disease, patients may show no right–left confusion as far as their own anatomy is concerned, but only when the examiner uses tests with a mirror, or their own person, or pictures, puppets or clothing.

Unlike finger agnosia, the disorientation affects all parts of the anatomy, but it may not extend into outer space so as to involve inanimate objects. It is common, however, for the disorientation to include the anatomy of other individuals (Critchley, 1953).

*Acalculia*

In doing calculations on paper, patients with a parieto-occipital lesion cannot point to a figure in a multifigure number representing the tens, hundreds or units column. They will confuse the spatial position of the figures and often refuse to tackle such a comparatively simple problem. In severe cases they cannot even manipulate numbers in a tens column, and can calculate only by counting one by one with the aid of their fingers (Luria, 1966b).

People who have investigated the significance of the hand in body-image disorders draw attention to the primitive use of the fingers in counting, a practice which was so fundamental as to mirror itself in the Latin word *digitus*, meaning both 'numeral' and 'finger'. In some communities, both in remote times and today, complicated systems of counting and bargaining are mediated by way of the fingers. The arithmetic dysfunction might, therefore, be the breakdown of the person's body image which involves the hand and fingers because of the basic importance of the fingers in counting and other arithmetical calculations.

*Agraphia*

Agraphia is a disorder of writing caused by a lesion of the dominant cerebral hemisphere. Patients can copy from a pattern offered, they can read and understand the content of what they read, but they may have difficulty in writing spontaneously without something from which to copy. A lesion in the parietal lobe may cause agraphia, with patients still able to read, but if the lesion is deeper into the area of the brain where analysers of body image and spatial orientation merge, other difficulties may also occur (Espir and Rose, 1983).

*Patient's experience – acalculia and agraphia*

Lesions in either the right occipital region or the left parietal region caused visual disturbance for a short time after the injury, but gradually receded. One man reported that he could see objects well, but he had difficulty in deciding what they were. He could not distinguish between symmetrically arranged figures, or distinguish letters placed the right way round from mirror images: he thought that the letters K and Я were identical. He showed considerable writing defects, being unable to orientate the individual elements of letters accurately in space.

Another patient said that he could no longer read and write because he had 'forgotten' the shape of the letters and could not draw the strokes in the proper direction. He could perceive only one object at a time. When shown a six-pointed star, inside which was drawn a cross and a circle, he saw one of the points of the star first, and was completely unaware of the other elements inside it. He was unable to write individual letters properly, but introduced mirror-image elements. Difficulties of a similar nature sometimes appeared when he was asked to read the numbers he had written (Luria, 1966b).

Another man said: 'I was always confusing numbers and couldn't get the answers when I tried to add or subtract in my head. . . . Often I'm not sure whether five 5s are 25, 35, or 45, and I've completely forgotten some of the less obvious examples, like 6 × 7'. He explains that he does not try to work out money when he goes shopping, he just tells the cashier what he wants and puts the money down (Luria, 1973).

*Phantom limb sensations and body image*

When an individual continues to experience the sensation of a body part which has been amputated, this is the result of the persistence of a body image which has not yet adjusted to the body loss and which distorts the meaning of stimuli in order to deny the loss. The phantom limb shows how resistant the body image is to the effects of mutilation (Fisher and Cleveland, 1968).

The phenomenon is found following amputation of limbs or other body parts in 90–100% of cases, and is also seen after surgery on any part of the body (e.g. breast, eye), tooth extraction, mutilating diseases of the limbs, limb agenesis, and lesions of various parts of the nervous system. A phantom may follow an injury to the brachial plexus. Transverse spinal disease may cause a paraplegia with phantom legs. Following amputation, the illusion appears almost immediately and persists for relatively long periods of time (months or years) (Critchley, 1950).

In some instances, this phantom limb may seem very real to individuals and be the apparent source of great pain to them.

(Some people have reported sensations, such as pain, paresthesia, heat, cold and cramps, related to the phantom limb.) They may have the feeling that they can move it and at times will unthinkingly begin a sequence of action whose completion assumes the reality of the phantom. In the process of recovery, the phantom limb may progressively become smaller and less well defined – telescoping.

One patient described how he must 'wake-up' his phantom in the mornings. Firstly, he flexes the thigh-stump towards him, and then he slaps it sharply – like a baby's bottom – several times. On the fifth or sixth slap the phantom suddenly shoots forth, rekindled, fulgurated, by the peripheral stimulus. Only then can he put on his prosthesis and walk (Sacks, 1985).

Although phantom limbs occur in the vast majority of patients with limb amputation (Melzak, 1990), the persisting belief in the existence of an additional limb after a stroke has been regarded as very unusual (Cutting, 1989). However, a recent case study (Halligan *et al.*, 1993) concluded that: 'The apparent rarity of supernumerary phantoms after cerebral lesions may be misleading; such phenomena could be more common were investigators to specifically look for them'. The case study reported that: 'Unlike patients with other anosognosic phenomena which are usually observed in the acute stages of stroke, this patient was unusual in that he continued to hold a strong and persisting belief in the existence of a third arm for several months'. He was interviewed by doctors many times and he was always unwilling to volunteer additional information unless specifically asked. He later asked that doctors would not ask about this aspect of his illness as the subject clearly disturbed him. Extracts from an interview follow:

*Examiner:*  How is the middle one attached to your body?
*Patient:*  It is not . . . I don't know. I really don't know. I'm in a muddle about this.
*Examiner:*  Does it get cold?
*Patient:*  Yes, it does get cold.
*Examiner:*  Can you feel it?
*Patient:*  Yes, I do!
*Examiner:*  What do you think of a person having three hands?
*Patient:*  It's an odd situation! . . . I'm a bit vague about it I must say.
*Examiner:*  Can you raise your middle hand?
*Patient:*  No, I can't . . . it's dead . . . it's not connected to me anymore.

| | |
|---|---|
| *Examiner:* | Whereabouts is it? |
| *Patient:* | It's tucked away down here! (points to left side) |
| *Examiner:* | Can you touch it? |
| *Patient:* | Yes, I can. I can find bits of it in the bed . . . it's in three pieces . . . I think. This arm is an awful nuisance, it keeps getting in the way. It's an unusual number . . . unusual . . . I don't know. I'm in a muddle about it, I really don't know what to call it . . . There seems to be quite a lot of heat in it. It's quite warm . . . warmer than the other hand. |

The authors of this case study emphasized that: 'The main point to stress in any discussion of the patient's behaviour is that he appeared completely rational on all topics broached other than those concerning the "third arm". The patient was well aware of the irrationality of what he claimed to be experiencing. He was obviously unhappy about holding his belief in the "third arm", he was annoyed and dismayed by it and did not have any psychological gain from the belief, in other words, when we do not understand a condition, we must not assume that the patient is crazy'.

*Vertigo and body image distortions*

Many influences contribute to normal balance and momentary disturbance of any one of these may cause giddiness. Balance is maintained by the interaction and co-ordination in the brain of nerve impulses from the inner ear, the eyes, the neck, muscles and joints in the limbs. The vestibular system lies in the brainstem and receives information from the inner ears; the eyes and proprioceptive impulses which all help to maintain a person's posture. Generally speaking, vision, balance organs (the vestibular system) and proprioception determine our position in space. Normally, all of these work together. If one fails, the others can compensate, or substitute – to a degree (Sacks, 1985). 'The vestibular system is of paramount importance in maintaining perfect balance, but proprioception and vision are also important' (Luxon, 1986a).

Vertigo constitutes one of the best examples of distortion of the body image. The patients may seem unusually light, they may appear to float through the air, or to sink through the bed, they may seem to be rotated or jerked abruptly in one direction or another (Critchley, 1950).

Bonnier (1893) described a patient with attacks of labyrinthine vertigo during which he would seem to be divided into two persons, one looking at the other from outside. One of Lhermitte's patients with vertigo felt the left side of the body 'heavy, doughy, as if clamped in steel'. The whole left side seemed filled with some foreign matter (Critchley, 1950). Patients suffering from vertigo caused by a neurological or otological disease often say that they feel outside themselves, watching their own body; patients may often describe a sensation that their brain is swimming around their head and when they turn round they feel the brain is lagging behind their head (Luxon, 1986b).

**General principles for care of the patient with perceptual disturbance**

We develop a knowledge of body image by being able to move, touch and feel objects in close proximity to us, and by being able to touch different parts of ourselves. In general:

1. Simplify the environment. Reduce the number of objects, noises, choices and people – a more subdued environment permits the patient to concentrate on the task at hand with minimal distractions.

2. Good lighting is essential in helping to overcome these perceptual deficits. It eliminates shadows and distortions, which only complicate the problem. Bright colours on certain items may help the patient to pick out objects against a background.

3. It is important not to place the patient's bed at the far end of the ward with their 'good' side facing a blank wall. They probably have significant sensory deprivation without compounding it by thoughtless positioning of the bed.

4. Personification of the affected limb by staff or relatives who may give the useless limb a name and, therefore, a separate identity is to be avoided. For successful rehabilitation, the patient as a whole must be considered and anything else which distances the patient from his or her paralysed limbs must be prevented.

5. Video equipment can be very helpful for some patients who can see their own difficulties more clearly when they view a video film of themselves in action. However, care must be taken before exposing patients to their own image in this way, as some may find the experience unduly disturbing. Mirrors are cheaper and more commonly used, but the mirror image can be confusing and is not suitable for all patients. Those with visual perception problems or with severe disorientation may not find them helpful, and elderly and confused patients

may be totally disturbed and not relate the mirror image to themselves at all (Atkinson, 1986).

*Practical tips*

1.  Patients who no longer understand the concepts of up and down, left and right, may need special help in self-care. Point to the left arm and have the patient practise putting that arm in the sleeve first. The patient who has difficulty finding the left sleeve or the top of the shirt may need to learn helpful hints such as that labels are always on the top, and perhaps to look for a special mark on the left sleeve.
2.  Patients may be positioned so that they can see the affected part and have their attention drawn to it frequently.
3.  Constant handling of the area and helping the patient to simulate normal activities with the affected limb may be of value.
4.  If the patient accepts an abnormal position as being normal, this must be pointed out and explained in an understandable way.
5.  If the patient has, for example, a visual agnosia, he or she will be unable to see or to perceive things on the affected side; placing the bedside locker to the affected side will encourage him or her to cross over to that side to reach the locker.
6.  If a patient cannot carry out a task because of apraxia, try another approach. By breaking instructions down into small steps, using plenty of repetition and practice, and giving positive reinforcement for small attempts and successes, much can be achieved.
7.  The patient's spectacles should be brought into hospital, used and kept clean.
8.  It may be necessary to provide mnemonic aids, either by pictures or lists, so that the correct sequence for dressing is always undertaken.

Thus, much can be done to help neurologically impaired patients to adjust to their change in body image.

**References**

Atkinson, H. (1986) Principles of treatment. In: Downie, P.A. (ed.) *Cash's Textbook of Neurology for Physiotherapists*, 4th edn. London, Faber and Faber.

Bonnier, P. (1893) Cited in Critchley, M. (1950).

Critchley, M. (1950) The body-image in neurology. *Lancet* **i** (February 25), 335–340.

Critchley, M. (1953) *The Parietal Lobes.* London, Edward Arnold.

Critchley, M. (1968) A personal account of a complicated case of parietal disease. *Medical Society of New York, Supplement* **26**, 73–82.

Cutting, J. (1989) Body image disturbances in neuropsychiatry. In: Reynolds, E. and Trimble, M. (eds) *The Bridge between Neurology and Psychiatry.* Edinburgh, Churchill Livingstone.

Espir, M.L.E. and Rose, F.C. (1983) *The Basic Neurology of Speech and Language.* Oxford: Blackwell Scientific Publications.

Fisher, S. and Cleveland, S.E. (1968) *Body Image and Personality.* New York: Dover Publications.

Gilliatt, R.W. and Pratt, R.T.C. (1952) Disorders of perception and performance in a case of right-sided cerebral thrombosis. *Journal of Neurology, Neurosurgery and Psychiatry* **15**, 264–271.

Halligan, P.W., Marshall, J.C. and Wade, D.T. (1993) Three arms: a case study of supernumerary phantom limb after right hemisphere stroke. *Journal of Neurology, Neurosurgery and Psychiatry* **56**, 159–166.

Hecan, H. and Albert, M.C. (1978) *Human Neuropsychology.* New York: John Wiley and Sons.

Heimberger, R.F., Demeyer, W.F. and Reiton, R.M. (1964) Implications of Gerstmann's syndrome. *Journal of Neurology, Neurosurgery and Psychiatry* **27**, 52–57.

Luria, A.R. (1966a) *Higher Cortical Function in Man.* New York: Basic Books.

Luria, A.R. (1966b) *Human Brain and Psychological Processes.* New York: Harper and Row.

Luria, A.R. (1973) *The Man with a Shattered World: History of a Brain Wound.* London: Jonathan Cape.

Luxon, L.M. (1986a) Physiology of balance. In: Downey, L.J. (ed.) *Current Approaches – Vertigo.* Southampton: Duphar Medical Publications, pp. 1–8.

Luxon, L.M. (1986b) Personal communication.

Melzak, R. (1990) Phantom limbs and the concept of a neuromatrix. *Trends in Neuroscience* **13**, 88–92.

Pick, A. (1922) Störung der Orientierung om eigen Korper. *Psychologische Forschung,* **1**, 313–318.

Sacks, O. (1985) *The Man Who Mistook His Wife for a Hat.* London: Duckworth.

Siev, E. and Freishtat, B. (1976). *Perceptual Dysfunction in the Adult Stroke Patient.* New York: Charles B. Slack.

Walsh, K.W. (1978) *Neurological Psychology.* Edinburgh: Churchill Livingstone.

**Further reading**

Carleton, V. (1995) Sexuality after a stroke. *Kai Tiaki: Nursing New Zealand* **1**(5), 13–15.

Jacono, J. and Keehn, B. (1990) Psycho-social adjustment to adult onset epilepsy: a theoretical framework. *Canadian Journal of Psychiatric Nursing* **31**(4), 12–15, 17.

McGregor, I. and Bell, J. (1993) Voyage of discovery . . . people with dementia retain their basic personalities. *Nursing Times* **89**(36), 29–31.

Nijhof, G. (1995) Parkinson's disease as a problem of shame in public appearance. *Sociology of Health and Illness* **17**(2), 193–205.

Piotrowski, M.M. (1982) Body image after a stroke. *Rehabilitation Nursing* **7**, 11–13.

Rubio, K.B. and Van Deusen, J. (1995) Relation of perceptual and body image dysfunction to activities of daily living of persons after stroke. *American Journal of Occupational Therapy* **49**(6), 551–559.

Samonds, R.J. and Cammermeyer, M. (1989) Perceptions of body image in subjects with multiple sclerosis: a pilot study. *Journal of Neuroscience Nursing* **21**(3), 190–194.

Schwalb, D. and Zahr, L. (1985) Nursing care of patients with an altered body image due to multiple sclerosis. *Nursing Forum* **22**(2), 72–76.

Weir, A.M., Pentland, B. and Cosswaite, A. (1995) Bell's palsy: the effect on self-image, mood state and social activity. *Clinical Rehabilitation* **9**(2), 121–125.

CHAPTER 15

# Spinal cord injury and changes to body image

*Peter S. Davis*

**Impaired physical mobility**

The focus of this chapter is predominantly the changes to body image encountered by the spinal cord-injured person. However, many of the principles of nursing care apply generally to individuals with impaired physical mobility, that is, orthopaedic patients. These patients have noticeable body changes owing to a variety of causes and origins (Table 15.1).

For example, Crowther (1982) uses the framework of identifying three types of amputee: the hero, the dependent and the depressive. Each type is readily identified in amputees, but more fundamentally ensures they are stigmatized and labelled as disabled. These types are also identifiable in many other individuals who encounter changes to body image as a result of impaired physical mobility. This includes those with injuries to the spinal cord.

The ordinariness of amputation was also explored by Crowther (1982) and described as a major characteristic. Children, for example, react undramatically to amputation and are initially perplexed by the postamputation presents and attention that they

*Table 15.1* Body changes related to cause and origin. Reproduced with permission from Davis (1994).

| Aetiology | Example of body change |
| --- | --- |
| Congenital | Muscular dystrophy, spina bifida |
| Hereditary | Osteogenesis imperfecta (brittle bones) |
| Medical/disease | Arthritis |
| Trauma | Spinal injury |
| Surgery | Amputation |

receive. The profile of Bill, later in this chapter, illustrates the ordinariness in terms of the spinal cord injury leading to a big adventure for the first 18 months.

**Spinal cord injury**

Spinal cord injury (SCI) is more than a loss of sensation and the inability to move. Functions such as micturition, defecation, control of vasomotor tone and sexuality are also affected. In addition, the spinal cord-injured individual has to adjust to the psychological and social ramifications.

Until the 1940s the victims of severe SCI in the United Kingdom were doomed to a relatively slow and uncomfortable death from infection, pressure sores and mental anguish. Today, modern health care systems perceive the spinal cord-injured individual as physically disabled but as a healthy person, able to make a significant contribution to society. It is the skills of the interdisciplinary team and the motivation of the individual that determines how successfully the transition from a recently injured dependent patient to a fulfilled, productive member of the community is made. This chapter explores the nurse's role, as a member of the interdisciplinary team, in facilitating the individual's transition through to acceptance, or otherwise, of the changes to body image that SCI inflicts.

**Causes of spinal cord injury**

Grundy and Swain (1993) provide statistics (see Figure 15.1) for their spinal injury unit that may be considered as typical for the UK and are similar to those in the USA, except that acts of violence account for three times as many SCIs in the USA. Further

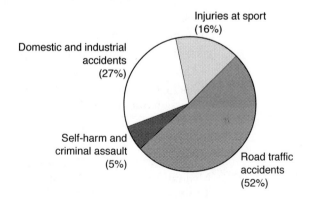

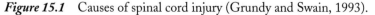

*Figure 15.1*   Causes of spinal cord injury (Grundy and Swain, 1993).

analysis shows that, of the road traffic accidents, 27% were due to cars, vans or lorries, and 21% due to motorcycles. Almost half of the sport injuries were due to diving into shallow water.

SCI primarily affects young people (Zejdlik, 1992) (see Figure 15.2). With early onset of physical disability and advances in health sciences that offer almost full life expectancy, a tension is set up between human disability and care and social economics. Estimated costs of lifetime care are predicted at in excess of £500 000. The young age of the person at the time of injury means most are single. The average age is 29.7 years and the most frequently occurring age at injury is 19 years (Stover and Fine, 1986). Males tend to be more susceptible than females; 82% of all SCIs occur in the male population (Porth, 1986).

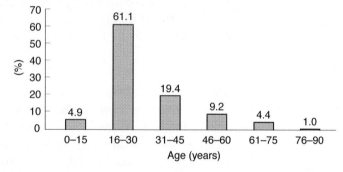

*Figure 15.2*   Age at injury.

**Terminology**

Paraplegia refers to paralysis of the lower part of the body, which includes the legs and possibly the trunk. It occurs with injury to the second thoracic segment ($T_2$) or below. Because upper body strength is preserved, the paraplegic person has the potential physical ability to become independent in all aspects of activities of living.

Quadriplegia, or tetraplegia, refers to paralysis of the lower and upper parts of the body including part or complete involvement of the arms and hands. It occurs with injury to the first thoracic segment ($T_1$) or above. Rehabilitation is more complex with the level of injury affecting abilities and the independence potential of activities of living and wheelchair mobility. Also the autonomic nervous system does not function normally and there may be a threat of respiratory insufficiency.

**Spinal cord**

The central nervous system consists of the brain and the spinal cord. The spinal cord extends from the medulla oblongata at the base of the skull to the level of the first or second lumbar vertebra. The cord is divided into cervical, thoracic, lumbar and sacral segments. The cord enlarges in the cervical and lumbar areas to receive additional nerves from the upper and lower limbs. As the cervical and lumbar areas of the spine are most mobile, these areas of the cord are particularly vulnerable to injury. The cord ends in a tapered comb called the conus medullaris which contains major reflexes for bowel, bladder and sexual functions (Zejdlik, 1992).

The functions of the spinal cord are (Davis, 1994):

- To carry nerve impulses via sensory nerve fibres through ascending tracts to the brain.
- To carry nerve impulses from the brain via motor nerve fibres down the descending tracts to muscle or glands.
- To act as a centre for reflex actions.

**Autonomic nervous system**

The autonomic nervous system causes involuntary responses to control visceral functions within the body. It exerts an influence on arterial blood pressure, sweating and body temperature, gastric and intestine mobility, and secretion and urinary bladder emptying. It is controlled by groups of nerve cells in the brainstem, hypothalamus and spinal cord. It subdivides into the parasympathetic and sympathetic system.

Generally, the higher the level of the SCI, the greater the effects on the autonomic nervous system become and particularly for those with injury at the level of $T_6$ or above. Symptoms are bradycardia, hypotension, postural hypotension and a tendency to assume the temperature of the environment.

**Changes in body image**

The introductory and subsequent chapters have discussed and defined altered body image extensively. Of particular relevance in SCI is the adolescent and young adult population who are at greatest risk as they also constitute the age group most concerned with appearance and at a critical period in body-image development and maintenance. Young adults are seeking their place in society and independence from their family. Yet, SCI often necessitates dependence on various mechanical devices and a multitude of people for survival. In addition, the spinal cord-injured person may experience losses of privacy, environmental control, communication, security, trust, resources, finances, friends, support systems, independence, and physical and emotional health (French and Phillips, 1991).

Morse and O'Brien (1995) describe how the priority of trauma care on the maintenance of life has a physical emphasis and that the psychosocial experience of the trauma victim has been relatively ignored in the literature. It is important to recognize that the experiences of the spinal cord-injured person are dynamic and that the psychosocial aspects of their injury may bear little importance to them in the immediate postinjury period, but take on an increasing priority as their rehabilitation progresses. The interdisciplinary team must also change their emphasis from physical to psychosocial care.

A change in body image is an important psychosocial factor in response to SCI as the patient experiences interactional changes within their family and the community. How the spinal cord-injured person attempts to deal with these changes is crucial.

**Case study: 'I felt it was a big adventure'**

*Bill was injured 13 years ago at the age of 19 years. His SCI was at level $T_4$. Since the injury he has striven to make a full and rewarding life for himself and his family. He met Alice ten years ago and they were married a year later. Bill is a keen skier and sportsman and has taken part in the Paraolympics. About four years ago, Alice and Bill decided to try for a family and Richard was born 9 months ago. As health care professionals, we must never assume or try to dictate how the spinal cord-injured person will respond to changes in body image, the best we can do is to try to understand fully the meaning of the change to the individual, and offer support and guidance on their journey. The following is Bill's description of what some aspects of the SCI has meant to him. Names have been changed but Bill, Alice and Richard are a real family, and I thank them for their important contribution to this chapter.*

'I didn't know what it meant at time of injury but it helped that all those in the ward with me were a similar age, late teens to early twenties, and with similar injuries. I wasn't frightened, and accepted what had happened. The injury was my own fault to a certain extent. I never really got depressed at all. It was a big adventure as it was my first time away from home and I met a lot of new people. In the first year, disability was not a problem. I got into a social life about 2 months after the injury. In the first 18 months I had a lot of new and positive experiences. The implications of the injury hadn't sunk in and a lot of things I saw as challenges. After 18 months the reality sunk in: I returned to my family in an environment where disability was not fully understood and found I often had to cope for my family as well. Initially, I felt pressurized to have children and was not really excited when Alice became pregnant. It struck home when the birth was almost imminent, just a few weeks before Richard was born. Richard's birth was quite an event. I am concerned, that as he gets older, he might be taunted at school about his father being a cripple. Children can be very hard. Before Richard was born I tended to avoid children and was very apprehensive around them.'

**Change theory and adjustment to SCI**

There can be little doubt that SCI is a major change in any individual's life. It is sudden and devastating in its effects. A broad understanding of change and its meaning to individuals from a sociological perspective forms the foundation of much of what is contained in the literature on SCI.

Davis (1991) suggests that three themes concerning change and the individual are of importance for all concerned, and may be utilized to aid adjustment. These are the need for the spinal cord-injured individual to be:

- self-empowering, helping, caring or motivating;
- resilient to change and reflective in approach;
- able to perceive the change as a learning experience.

The literature on altered body image and SCI overwhelmingly describes a transitional period from the time of injury where the individual moves through a number of related stages or phases in order to adapt (Hohmann, 1975; Thompson and Lott, 1980; Trieschmann, 1980; Vash, 1981; Flannery, 1990; French and Phillips, 1991; Partridge, 1994; Morse and O'Brien, 1995).

The concept of linear progression through stages is a useful description as it enables the carer and spinal cord-injured person to recognize what they are experiencing, and that they are not the only individuals who have had these feelings or responses. Also the stages provide a series of targets for assessment and goal planning. However, the stages or phases must not be adopted in a rigid, inflexible manner or to 'label' individuals. The spinal cord-injured person may not reach the end stage of acceptance or adjustment. They certainly will not progress in a linear or predictable manner through the stages. Often they may become stuck for a long period in one stage or skip a stage altogether. Patients and carers must use the stages flexibly to help them understand the meaning of their experience, and not as a 'labelling' process on which they may become hooked or blinkered in their progress. In reality, progress is often a series of blocks, false starts, backward slides, calm periods and leaps forward.

Broome (1989) describes how psychoanalytic views of adjustment liken disability to loss. Again, this provides a useful concept to aid understanding of the SCI and body image experience, but should not be used too enthusiastically. Not every spinal cord-injured person needs to 'work through' every stage of the grieving process, and not every person will necessarily go through episodes of significant despair and depression.

The general concepts of change theory provide a more lateral approach to the understanding of the meaning of the experience to the spinal cord-injured person. A useful model that describes the process of change for the individual is that proposed by Woodward and Buchholz (1987). The model describes the reaction to change in three phases: Endings → Transitions → Beginnings.

It is proposed that change occurs when some things end. These endings are often painful or confusing, and before the person can progress, they must come to terms with the changes and resolve them. If they are unable to let go of the past, excess emotional baggage will be carried by them into the future. Transitions are the periods between the old and the new, when the individual becomes conscious of what is ending and what is beginning. At this time, support for the individual is of great importance. Once the new is accepted, the challenge of beginning starts, when the individual must identify a purpose and vision.

Perspectives of change and their effects on individuals shows us that, as individuals or social groups, we have a desire or need to maintain stability (equilibrium and balance are also used to describe this concept). Schön (1971) refers to this as the stable state and proposes that it reflects an individual's belief in the unchangeability and constancy of central aspects of our lives. This belief in the stable state is essential because it protects against the threat of uncertainty that change often elicits. The paradox is that the erosion of the stable state that a SCI engenders means that the individual lacks security and stability when they need it most. Schön refers to the individual's attempts to maintain the stable state as 'dynamic conservatism', that is, a tendency to fight to remain the same. In this light, the spinal cord-injured person's initial responses of denial, bargaining, questioning, etc. are wholly understandable, and may be considered as essential mechanisms for them to survive and adjust. It may be that they can only come to grips with aspects of their own experience, such as changed body image, if they hold other areas of their experience in a stable state, either temporarily or permanently.

The inevitable and massive changes the spinal cord-injured person has to make to adjust to and cope with an altered body image leads to stress. In general, Toffler (1970) refers to this human response to change as 'future shock' and describes it as producing symptoms ranging from anxiety and hostility to helpful authority and seemingly senseless violence to physical illness, depression and apathy. When this concept is applied more specifically to health and social readjustment, the possible detrimental effects of change may be clearly identified. Holmes and Rahe's (1967) social adjustment scale suggests that, if an individual scores more than 150 units due to stress in the past 24 months, then they have a 30% chance of a serious change in their general health in the next year. Suggested scores for some events are:

| | |
|---|---|
| Personal injury | 53 |
| Sex difficulties | 39 |
| Change in financial state | 38 |
| Change to different line of work | 36 |
| Change in living condition | 25 |

It would seem that SCI predisposes an individual to an inevitable change in general health after the injury. Selye (1956) proposed that individuals adapt to stress in a series of stages. Following the initial 'alarm reaction' and the stage of 'resistance', adaptation is achieved. However, during the adaptation period the individual's ability to respond to further stress is greatly reduced.

Conversely, the stress and conflict caused by changes in body image may be an ingredient for growth (see the case study earlier in this chapter). Further, too little stress can have an adverse effect on the equilibrium of the individual. Each individual's ability to respond and adapt to change is different, and will also vary in the individual depending on the context, timing and substance of the change.

The stage theories discussed so far portray a personality-based adjustment process by the individual to spinal cord injury and use a psychoanalytic perspective. A typical example of the stages are Krueger's (1984):

- Shock
- Retreat, denial or disbelief
- Grief/mourning and depression
- Hostility and anger
- Adjustment

These theories have been criticized. For example, Trieschmann (1980) suggests that depression is not a necessary phase in adjustment. Although grief is common, it is by no means a universal reaction to disability and should not always be anticipated.

From a sociological perspective, adjustment has been related to the strength of social networks and control over resources. This more pragmatic view claims that economic considerations are paramount and may be of greater importance than professional help in determining an individual's response to changes in body image and disability. Wright (1983) considered many aspects of the potentially hostile and restrictive environment which disabled people encounter, and vehemently challenged the assumption that disabled people must be suffering emotionally. The general population, including caring professionals, assume that the spinal cord-injured person must be emotionally disturbed, and adopt a patronizing and pitying attitude towards them. Weinberg and Williams (1978) propose that disability may bring positive effects, such as an increased sensitivity to others and the provision of a challenge.

**Self-empowerment**

Self-empowerment is a means by which an individual can draw on their inner strengths and resources. Everyone can become more self-empowered: care professionals, spinal cord-injured persons and families. The more self-empowered an individual becomes, the more they will be able to help bring out this process in others. Self-empowerment may be considered as 'a process of becoming increasingly more in control of oneself and one's life, and thus increasingly more independent' (Fenton, 1989).

Rotter (1966) described individuals who believe they have a lot of personal control over events as having an internal locus of control. Alternatively, those who believe that they have little control over events and situations, who believe instead in luck or fate, are defined as having an external locus of control. Frank and Elliott (1989) found that spinal cord-injured persons who believe that they are primarily responsible for their health show less depression and greater adaptive behaviour than those who have more externalized beliefs. Powerlessness is described by Richmond *et al.* (1992) in SCI in terms of lack of this personal control and they are therefore describing the same concept.

Increasing the self-empowerment capacity of the spinal cord-injured person enables them to take control of situations so that they move more effectively along the road to adaptation to changed body image. Self-awareness and liking oneself are essential for adjusting to the changed body image of SCI. To promote adjustment, the spinal cord-injured person and carers must believe that:

- Each individual is unique, valuable and worthy of respect.
- Once people have learned to respect, love and value themselves, they will be able to respect, love and value others.
- It is helpful to differentiate between the behaviours which encourage the developing parts of a person, and those which serve to anchor them in states of depressing hostility, fear and/or insecurity.
- People with disabilities are sexual beings who can choose their sexual orientation from a number of equally valid options (from Fenton, 1989).

The relationship between concepts such as change theory, disability and empowerment and the specific nursing diagnosis of 'body-image disturbance' may not always be apparent [see Ackley and Ladwig (1993) for a descriptor of the term body-image disturbance as a nursing diagnosis]. However, changes in body image are the result of a multitude of complex, individualized, dynamic, interrelated occurrences and perceptions involving the spinal cord-injured person, their environment, other individuals and the society in which they exist. Therefore, a broad spectrum of understanding and skills are needed so that the nurse is able to assess, diagnose, plan, implement and evaluate appropriate care. More importantly, to make significant choices and take appropriate action, then empowerment must be achieved for the spinal cord-injured person, the health care team and carers.

## Nursing and body-image disturbance

*Nursing diagnosis*

People tend to take being able to move for granted. It is not until they temporarily or permanently suffer restrictions to their mobility that they realize what the effects of changes, such as impaired physical mobility, mean to them as individuals. Broadly speaking, physical disability and impaired physical mobility are the same in their effects (Davis, 1994). However, categories of physical disability have been derived from medical diagnoses and are perceived as disabling conditions, for example, stroke or paraplegia. While a medical diagnosis is useful when caring for the spinal cord-injured person, it is not always essential to nursing care. A medical diagnosis indicates what condition an individual has in order to plan medical care, while a model of nursing, used to formulate a nursing diagnosis, provides a comprehensive picture of the individual's problems in order to plan nursing care. Using nursing diagnosis as a stage of the nursing process enables nursing practice to be problem-solving and, more importantly, to be problem-finding (Kirk, 1986).

Body-image disturbance, as a nursing diagnosis, is related to four main areas of change (Ackley and Ladwig, 1993):

- Biophysical
- Cognitive/perceptual
- Psychosocial
- Cultural or spiritual

These areas have already been discussed but require a model of nursing to enable comprehensive care to be provided for the spinal cord-injured person with body-image disturbance.

*Model of nursing*

Davis (1994) proposes that, by blending activities of a living model with an ethos of empowerment, it is also possible to glean the essence of self-care and adaptation models. The addition of patient problem identification, as a nursing diagnosis, to Roper *et al.*'s (1990) activities of living, systematic approach to individualizing nursing, will also be of benefit.

The modified activities of the living model (Figure 15.3) (described by Davis, 1994) will be used in the remainder of this chapter as the framework for nursing care. The model's nature is that it centralizes mobilizing as a key element in the care of orthopaedic and spinal-injured patients.

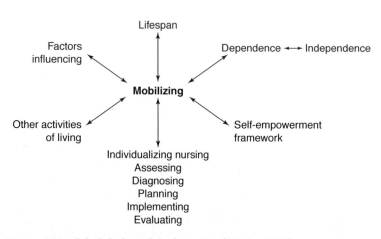

***Figure 15.3*** Modified model of nursing (Davis, 1994).

*Assessment*

Understanding the patient's and the family's background provides a basis on which to offer psychosocial support for potential body-image disturbance. Assessment must be a continual, ongoing process and must consider that, to the patient, there may not be a problem even though the circumstances may appear negative to the health care professional making the assessment. Also the problem of body-image disturbance may arise or disappear rapidly and without logical explanation. Humans are rarely rational and particularly so in the situation of SCI.

Price (1990) has developed a model of body image care that uses, amongst others, components of body reality, body ideal and body presentation to aid assessment:

*Body reality*:   the body as it really exists, constrained by the effects of human genetics, and the wear and tear of life in the external environment.

*Body ideal*:   the picture in our heads of how we should like the body to look and to perform. It is profoundly influenced by society and cultural norms, by advertising and by changing attitudes towards fitness and health.

*Body presentation*:   is the balance between body reality and our body ideal standards, and is how the body is presented to the outside through the way we dress, groom, talk, move and use props such as wheelchairs.

Examples are: the need to insert urinary catheters intermittently for the rest of one's life (body reality); the desire for a return to normal continence (body ideal); the wearing of sporting/jogging bottoms to disguise the need for frequent and easy access for catheterization (body presentation). One of the major effects on body image and self-esteem for the spinal cord-injured person is the fear of an 'accident', either faecal or urinary. The nurse needs to assess the reality and extent of these types of fears as they may have profound effects and lead to body-image disturbance. Good listening when assessing is also good intervention as empathy and attention are therapeutic.

Influencing factors that need assessing, as they aid adjustment, are: youth, emotional maturity, good self-esteem, intact family supports, higher levels of education, and financial and job security. The spinal cord-injured person whose work and leisure activities are more physical might find the onset of SCI more disruptive than those less physically inclined (Trieschmann, 1980).

*Nursing diagnosis and goal setting*

A nursing diagnosis, or patient problem, derived from an assessment is an important bridge in determining patient-centred goal statements in care planning. These goals should be measurable and indicate criteria for achievement. Price (1990) affirms that, because body-image care often deals with emotions, then goals should be stated in terms of what the spinal cord-injured person expresses about their feelings, mood or confidence.

The nursing diagnosis of 'body-image disturbance' should be considered along with that of 'fear' related to powerlessness over loss of body function. To identify these fears and implement ways of reducing or eliminating them through appropriate action can do much to help the spinal cord-injured person with body-image disturbance. The fear of faecal incontinence, for example, when at work or out of the home can undermine confidence, self-esteem and a positive body image. For example, realistic goals set to allow monitoring of faecal incontinence after the instigation of a bowel programme can boost confidence as the spinal cord injured person sees directly that they can remain continent when out. Thompson and Lott (1980) describe how success at physical and physiological tasks also achieve social success: 'a night out with others – with a consistent control of bodily functions – can lead to the kind of self-certainty which fosters greater interactions in the future'.

It is important that the model of nursing used to make nursing diagnoses and set goals is patient centred. All health care professionals have their own definitions of health, but it is essential for the spinal cord-injured person to be treated and cared for in an environment that is consistent in its approach and ideology. The injury causes an altered health state for which Parse's (1981) definition of health provides a useful foundation for the spinal cord-injured person and the health care professional to set goals from: '... a state of physical and mental reality which enables the individual to participate in the achievement of his/her own identified goals. It is more than a wellness of body and mind, in that it incorporates into his/her cultural reality a realistic movement towards his/her dreams of living'.

With this perspective of health, nurses can help the spinal cord-injured person to discuss their future expectations and perceptions of reality, which may be different from those of the health care team. The aim must be to help the individual to address the problems of the injury and balance them with the reality of the need to make changes in their attitudes and lifestyle. Success at achieving this while simultaneously encouraging the individual's motivation to fulfil personal aspirations is the yardstick against which nursing care is judged. It forms the cornerstone in minimizing or preventing body-image disturbance. We all have aspirations for our lives, many of which we may never achieve, so we must not deny the spinal cord-injured person the same opportunity to strive to achieve their dreams. For many it is the struggle to achieve them that produces an acceptable body image and self-esteem.

As the majority of spinal cord-injured persons are young, there has been a profound impact on their ability to plan for their future. Because of their stage of development, they may have difficulty in controlling impulsive, verbally aggressive outbursts, and require more guidance and assistance in setting limits on a day-to-day basis. However, younger individuals tend to have a greater capacity to adjust and adapt to new situations than older individuals. An understanding of these aspects of SCI enables nursing care to be sensitive, directive and supportive in enabling goals to be set by the individual.

It is not uncommon for the spinal cord-injured person to inflict injury on the non-functioning part, directly or indirectly, at some time. For example, the individual may be potentially capable of carrying out a correct intermittent catheterization procedure, but repeatedly forgets to do it at the appropriate time and puts themselves at risk of injury or infection by poor technique. The individual may be described as having a body-image disturbance related to non-acceptance of the change in their ability to maintain normal urinary continence. Helping the individual to identify and accept this as a problem will be a major step forward and is the first goal. A second goal, with measurable criteria, stating that the individual will be able to carry out appropriate and safe intermittent catheterization by a specified time period, such as within 3 weeks, is also necessary. The second goal is measurable and provides evidence of success in achieving the first goal.

*Implementation*

Nursing care of the spinal cord-injured person and their family must respond to their choices and stage in their rehabilitation. Communication must be open, honest and provide hope. The nurse should recognize their own needs in the nurse–client relationship, as often the nurse will feel depressed and helpless in the SCI scenario, or may also feel elated at times of success.

Selecting the appropriate time and occasion for a quiet and serious manner is important, but so too is the time for a lighter more humorous approach. Fry (1995) argues that humour is a contributor and manifestation of our mental health which helps release the hold that emotions, such as fear, anger, depression and disappointment, have on nurses and patients. The manner in which care is provided is as important as what is done and does much to alleviate or exacerbate body-image disturbance. Humour can be a useful coping strategy for the spinal cord-injured person but must not be used too extensively so as to mask their denial and non-acceptance.

Zejdlik (1992) advises applying sensitivity to the patient's needs for social acceptance especially in regard to sexuality. The mix of a predominantly young male client population with a predominantly young female nursing population often produces difficulties for both sides. Emotional attachments may cause confusion about the role of caregiver as opposed to romantic partner. Maintaining an appropriate professional relationship in these circumstances is almost impossible. However, this does not imply that the nurse should adopt a cold, unfeeling approach to care.

An important part in any individual's self-image is concerned with sexual attractiveness to the opposite sex. It is necessary for the nurse–client relationship to recognize and acknowledge this. For either partner in the relationship to compliment the other on how they look or behave can do much for maintaining a positive body image. The nurse may help the spinal cord-injured person to address their sexuality and support them in developing a loving relationship with a significant other in their life. A skilled, disciplined and perceptive approach from the nurse is needed so that appropriate relationships may be established.

Nurses may feel obligated to patients and uneasy about a refusal to meet patients' requests as this may lead to a lowering of their self-esteem. Nurses need to be confident and clear in their role in order to avert complicated emotional situations developing during rehabilitation.

By empowering the patient through strategies such as health education the nurse is providing a means for the spinal cord-injured person to control and ensure their care needs are implemented. To provide health education or promote a 'healthy' lifestyle, the nurse must have a fundamental understanding of his or her own and the spinal cord-injured person's beliefs about health. For example, does the spinal cord-injured person perceive themselves as 'unhealthy', with little control over outcomes, because of their injury.

McBean (1991) describes the model of health (eudaemonistic model), which contains themes of independence, interdependence (family, friends and community) and control. The research identified categories in which individuals used phrases to describe their beliefs about health. Of importance to body image were ideal weight, to look good and have good feelings about your body. To be self-fulfilled the individual needs to be able to achieve goals, reach their optimum, and be productive and self-aware.

The nurse educator should continuously provide knowledge and teach the spinal cord-injured person about their care so that they understand and have control over it. Equally important is developing the individual's beliefs and attitudes about their health as, without this, the spinal cord-injured person will not take control and become dependent, seeing responsibility for their health and progress as solely the responsibility of the health care professionals.

Many interdisciplinary teams provide a nurse educator to take responsibility for the spinal cord-injured person's education in its widest sense. Empowering the spinal cord-injured person and the family in this way takes time, and a skilled and knowledgeable nurse. The benefits of success are, however, enormous, particularly for promoting a positive body image and high self-esteem. Caution is required when applying this approach to teenagers as they may not be sufficiently developed to be self-directing or ready to accept that certain behaviour may have adverse consequences. They may not be prepared to make decisions about and implement their own care.

Unreasonable, unsocial behaviour is not unusual in the spinal cord-injured person, particularly as the rehabilitation programme progresses. The use of alcohol and drugs may be a result of peer pressure, or to alleviate boredom and the difficulties of dealing with the reality of disability; they provide an escape. Zejdlik (1992) recommends management of recreational and leisure time, particularly in the evenings and at weekends. Mind-altering substances may help individuals to forget their problem of body-image disturbance in the short term, but ultimately they must accept the reality of their situation and strive to come to terms with it. Alcohol and drugs can often put the spinal cord-injured person into a downward spiral of depression and despair.

*Evaluation*

Evaluation of body-image care needs to scrutinize the short- and long-term outcomes of nursing interventions. Many interventions extend over long periods of time and may not come to fruition until much later in the rehabilitation. Body image is continually changing, owing to progress, setbacks, and the fluid nature of the support environment and networks. Short-term goals are necessary as are longer term goals. The former are more responsive and provide rapid feedback, the latter are necessary to gauge the fundamental underpinnings of progress. Success or failure should take account of the spinal cord-injured person's views as well as those of the nurse. What the nurse may perceive as success in body-image care may not be seen as such by the injured person. Contentment, a joy for life and the ability to take a worthwhile role in society are indicators of long-term success, but remember that any spinal cord-injured person can have their 'off' times and require support to boost their body image.

**Conclusion**

With today's advances in medicine, survivors of SCI can anticipate a normal life expectancy. It is important for health care professionals to recognize the need to make these lives worthwhile and fulfilling. Attention to body image and the effects of body-image disturbance is essential and a key aspect of nursing care. The future is one in which the spinal cord-injured person can expect and will receive expert physical care, but they must also have a right to the best possible psychosocial care and all the benefits that this engenders.

**References**

Ackley, B.J. and Ladwig, G.B. (1993) *Nursing Diagnosis Handbook; A Guide to Planning Care*. St Louis, C.V. Mosby.

Broome, A. (1989) *Health Psychology*. London, Chapman & Hall.

Crowther, H. (1982) New perspectives on lower limb amputees. *Journal of Advanced Nursing* **7**, 453–460.

Davis, P.S. (1991) The meaning of change to the individual within a college of nurse education. *Journal of Advanced Nursing* **16**(1), 108–115.

Davis, P.S. (1994) *Nursing the Orthopaedic Patient*. Edinburgh, Churchill Livingstone.

Fenton, M. (1989) *Passivity to Empowerment*. London, Royal Association for Disability and Rehabilitation.

Flannery, J. (1990) Guilt: A crisis within a crisis. *Journal of Neuroscience Nursing* **22**(2), 92–99.

Frank, R.G. and Elliott, T.R. (1989) Spinal cord injury and health locus of control beliefs. *Paraplegia* **27**, 250–256.

French, J.K. and Phillips, J.A. (1991) Shattered images: Recovery for the SCI client. *Rehabilitation Nursing* **16**(3), 134–136.

Fry, W. (1995) Cited in Naish, J. Taking fun seriously. *Nursing Standard* **9**(29), 18–21.

Grundy, D. and Swain, A. (1993) *ABC of Spinal Cord Injury* London, BMJ.

Hohmann, G.W. (1975) Psychological aspects of treatment and rehabilitation of the spinal cord injured person. *Clinical Orthopaedics and Related Research* **112**, 81–88.

Holmes, T.H. and Rahe, R.H. (1967) *Journal of Psychosomatic Research* **11**, 212–218.

Kirk, L.W. (1986) Framework. In: Hurley, M.E. (ed.) *Classification of Nursing Diagnosis*. St Louis, C.V. Mosby.

Krueger, D.W. (1984) *Rehabilitation Psychology*. Rockville, M.A. Aspen Publishers.

McBean, S. (1991) Health and health promotion. In: Perry, A. and Jolley, M. (eds) *Nursing: A Knowledge for Practice*. London, Edward Arnold.

Morse, J.M. and O'Brien, B. (1995) Preserving self: from victim, to patient, to disabled person. *Journal of Advanced Nursing* **21**, 886–896.

Parse, R.R. (1981) *Man – Living – Health: A Theory of Nursing*. New York, John Wiley & Sons.

Partridge, C. (1994) Spinal cord injuries: aspects of psychological care. *British Journal of Nursing* **3**(1), 12–15.

Porth, C.M. (1986) *Pathophysiology: Concepts of Altered Health States*, 2nd edn. Philadelphia, J.B. Lippincott Company.

Price, R. (1990) A model of body image care. *Journal of Advanced Nursing* **15**, 585–593.

Richmond, T.S., Metcalf, J., Daly, M. and Kish, J.R. (1992) Powerlessness in acute spinal cord injury patients: a descriptive study. *Journal of Neuroscience Nursing* **24**(3), 146–152.

Roper, N. Logan, W.W. and Tierney, A.J. (1990) *The Elements of Nursing*. Edinburgh, Churchill Livingstone.

Rotter, J.B. (1966) Generalised expectancies for internal versus external locus of control of reinforcement. *Psychology Monograph* **80**, 1–28.

Schön, D.A. (1971) *Beyond the Stable State*. London, Pelican.

Selye, H. (1956) *The Stress of Life*. New York, McGraw-Hill.

Stover, S.L. and Fine, P. (1986) *Spinal Cord Injury: the Facts and Figures*. University of Alabama, National Spinal Cord Injury Research Data Center.

Thompson, D.D. and Lott, J.D. (1980) Psychological redevelopment of the spinal cord injured person. *Spinal Cord Injury Digest* **2**, 6–9.

Toffler, A. (1970) *Future Shock*. London, Bodley Head.

Trieschmann, R. (1980) *Spinal Cord Injuries, Psychological, Social and Vocational Adjustment*. New York, Demos Publications.

Vash, C. (1981) Disability as a transcendental experience: a personal perspective on learning to live with a disability. In: Eisberg, M. and Falconer, J. (eds) *Treatment of Spinal Cord Injured – An Interdisciplinary Perspective*. Springfield, Charles C. Thomas Publisher.

Weinberg, N. and Williams, J. (1978) How the physically disabled perceive their disabilities. *Journal of Rehabilitation* **44**(3), 31–33.

Woodward, H. and Buchholz, S. (1987) *Aftershock*. Chichester, John Wiley & Sons Ltd.

Wright, B. (1983) *Psychosocial Aspects of Physical Disability*. London, Harper Row.

Zejdlik, C.P. (1992) *Management of Spinal Cord Injury*, 2nd edn. Boston, Jones and Bartlett.

## CHAPTER 16

# Eating disorders and body image

*Louise Woodhead, Linda Davis, Mary Levens and Bridget Dolan*

**Introduction**

This chapter will concentrate on the altered body image that occurs in people who suffer from eating disorders. It is hoped to increase the nurse's understanding of the more common ones, bulimia, obesity and, particularly, anorexia nervosa, on which the most research has been done in relation to altered body image. However, it should not be forgotten that weight gain or loss is not just psychological in origin. For example, weight gain can be caused by steroid treatment and weight reduction by malignant disease. The aim will be to help the nurse to become more aware of the sometimes profound psychological nature of these illnesses, for, if any real progress is to be made, patients will need help if they are to understand why their eating disorder has developed. Some of the research carried out and its findings will be discussed alongside, for example, how altered body image affects the treatment of anorexia and the other eating disorders, and the nurse's role within the broad treatment plan, with particular reference to art therapy and group psychotherapy, as these are two important avenues for treatment on the writers' unit.

It is important to realize that not only do as many as 2% of adult women suffer with a clinical eating disorder (Cooper *et al.*, 1987) but more than half the female population between the ages of 15 and 50 years suffer from some form of eating problem (Orbach, 1983). Not only is the magnitude of the problem seen from this statement but one must question why women feel the need to alter the shape of their bodies (Dolan and Gitzinger, 1994). As nursing is a female-dominated profession, there will be those among the profession who suffer, often secretly, from some degree of eating disorder. However, it must be stated that anorexia nervosa and bulimia are not solely female-orientated problems: there is a small, but increasing, incidence of both in males. Finally, the discussion will centre on the nurse's own attitudes and responses when he or she is nursing patients who have eating disorders.

**Anorexia nervosa**  Anorexia nervosa usually develops in young adolescent girls, either during or a few years after puberty. It is characterized by a substantial loss of weight which is self-induced, amenorrhoea (usually secondary), an intense fear of normal body weight and of becoming fat (Russell *et al.*, 1975). They will also have a disturbance of their body image, which some researchers claim can become almost delusional (Phillips *et al.*, 1995). The illness is often precipitated by remarks made about a girl's developing shape: sometimes family members may joke affectionately that she has become 'a little tubby'. In themselves, these comments do not cause anorexia, but they occur at a time when the girl feels vulnerable and often ill at ease with her newly developing body. She also may have experienced her first sexual encounter, for which she may have felt ill-prepared and, sometimes, extremely guilty about. Gradually, she may reach the conclusion that to re-establish a form of control and order in her life, she must lose weight, thus reducing the comments about her shape and reducing the possibility of further sexual advances, no matter how innocent.

Anorexia nervosa seems to be an illness of denial (Bemporad *et al.*, 1988). The anorexic girl attempts to deny her own needs, psychological and physiological, denying in the face of all the evidence the body's inevitable development towards womanhood. She may gain a sense of pride and self-esteem by denying her fundamental needs and begin to feel special and rather superior towards those who openly acknowledge their needs, particularly in relation to food. This sense of specialness and superiority is often a new experience for these young girls, who have, in the past, often lacked confidence and had a low self-esteem (Vitousek and Manke, 1994).

She will adamantly deny that there is anything wrong and finds it difficult to comprehend why others are so concerned about her weight. 'Can't they see I'm huge', she exclaims, even when she is obviously very thin. She may glory in other people noticing her emaciated figure and commenting on her willpower in the face of so much temptation. One anorexic girl was said only to feel happy 'when my ribs are sticking out'.

This denial of thinness in the face of objective reality illustrates the disturbed body image. Before any change can be facilitated, this altered image has to be acknowledged by nursing staff and not dealt with by reassuring comments such as 'Of course you are not fat', which mean little to the anorexic individual.

To lose weight or maintain an abnormally low weight, the anorexic girl will avoid food, in particular carbohydrates such as cakes, potatoes and bread, only eating low-calorie foods such as salads, fruit and vegetables, often in very small quantities. Foods seem to be divided into 'good' and 'bad', carbohydrates being the bad foods particularly feared as they seem to represent the individual's vulnerability and lack of control. She may also abuse laxatives, purging herself of any residual food, often describing how cleansed she feels afterwards. A cycle of bingeing and vomiting may develop. Vomiting may take place after ordinary meals or after a massive binge, where a vast amount of carbohydrate food is ingested, then immediately vomited, thus avoiding any weight gain. Although weak and tired, she will often plan a strenuous routine of daily exercise, running miles a day, swimming and cycling. The suppression of her basic bodily needs for rest and nourishment seems to bolster her fragile self-esteem.

Those suffering from anorexia nervosa also suffer from a marked sleep disturbance, waking early in the morning between 3 and 5 a.m. and unable to get back to sleep. Dreams often mirror the poor nutritional state and food is their dominant topic. Sometimes the patient may wake in an agitated state, as during a dream in which she has allowed herself to enjoy a meal. Sleep is often the only time a relaxation of the strict control over her desire for food occurs. As the nutritional state of the patient improves the sleep disturbance readjusts itself.

Sadly, as the condition continues, the anorexic girl becomes more and more isolated from friends and family. Losing interest in previous hobbies and activities, she lives a rather secretive existence where food, avoidance of food and preoccupation with weight are of paramount importance. Eventually, the increased self-esteem, sense of power and control obtained from the above behaviour is replaced by a sense of desperation, emptiness (physiological and psychological). This may be the time when the person begins to want to change, but because she is alone it is difficult to allow herself to acknowledge needs without feeling a sense of intense guilt.

Although the anorexic girl denies herself food, she enjoys and takes great pleasure in seeing others consume it. This is no selfless enjoyment for the gratification of others but another way of enabling her to feel superior in her resolve not to eat. In the past, the anorexic girl has found it difficult to express individuality and this behaviour can be seen as a maladaptive way of telling others, for instance, her family, that she is unlike them, and also as a means of expressing her independence. However, it is obvious that this behaviour is ultimately a self-destructive way of establishing her individuality. One of the major aims of treatment is to help her to express her personality in a more constructive and fulfilling manner.

Many anorexic girls think that if they develop normally, gaining weight, their family will not express their love for them, that they will become ignored members within the family, losing their 'specialness' and the attention gained from being emaciated. They feel that their only positive quality is their resolve not to eat, and the control and determination this entails. Weight and shape are associated with adulthood; anorexic girls feel that adults are rejected if they express their need for love and security. This misperception reinforces their dependent, childlike stance. They see adulthood as a state of total self-reliance for which they rightly feel they are ill-prepared, finding it difficult to conceive that adults have feelings of insecurity and self-doubt. Enabling the anorexic to see her needs as worth some acknowledgement, and to enable her to accept them without shame or fear of rejection, is an extremely important area of treatment.

**Bulimia nervosa**

Women suffering from bulimia nervosa often describe a period during their adolescence that meets the diagnostic criteria for anorexia. The women who ask for help with this disorder differ from anorexics in that they are often older, ranging between their early and late twenties. They tend to be of normal or slightly above normal weight, although often extremely unhappy with their weight. There is a tendency, like anorexics, to overestimate their body size, particularly bust, waist and hip sizes. They often experience a sense of self-disgust concerning their bodies, which causes a great deal of distress.

Bulimic women experience a powerful urge to overeat, especially carbohydrate foods, from which they would normally abstain. They avoid the fattening effects of these foods by inducing vomiting, or abuse of laxatives, often using both methods. They describe a morbid fear of becoming fat. Again, as with anorexia, the eating disorder is a symbolic way in which psychological distress is enacted and represented; it is only when the disturbed eating disorder is controlled by treatment, which relies on the motivation of the individual to change, that the emotional disturbances can be addressed.

These young women are often well-educated and capable individuals, giving the impression that their lives are well-ordered and controlled. This is often very different from the way in which they experience their lives. The emotional chaos experienced is reflected in their chaotic eating habits, often abstaining throughout the day, planning a binge for that evening. The binge is an extremely secretive occasion: the individual often feels ashamed of her behaviour but is unable to control it. She buys vast amounts of carbohydrate foods, such as biscuits, cakes and bread (the calorific value of this food can reach 20 000 daily) and then binges on it, only to vomit the food.

Just after the binge, which is described as a frantic experience, the woman may panic about the amount she has eaten and the amount of weight that would be gained if she allowed her body to absorb the food consumed. She has an intense feeling of disgust and guilt after bingeing and vomiting, but also a feeling of relief that she has been able to 'have her cake and eat it' without gaining the weight. After a period of overeating, the women will often abstain, cutting back on all foods, but particularly avoiding carbohydrates. This behaviour has an addictive quality as there is often a sense of relaxation and calm afterwards. The frantic intake and regurgitation of food seems to promote a release of energy which enables the individual to relax and gain some sort of peace of mind. This is reported by many who have performed this ritualistic behaviour.

As with anorexia, bulimia must be seen as symbolic of profound emotional distress. Women who suffer from bulimia often describe themselves as 'empty', having 'no identity' or sense of individuality. They have developed an image of themselves which is extremely negative. This self-hatred seems to be focused on the individual's body. These women often describe feeling overwhelmed by their own emotional needs for love, security and a sense of identity, which they fear will never be satisfied. The binge metaphorically, if only temporarily, fills their empty inner space (psychologically and physically). The response to stress or lack of confidence is to turn to food and the comfort this gives. However, there is an extremely ambivalent relationship with this food. The desires and needs that these women use food to meet are not satisfied as they are not needs of a physical nature.

They experience their bodies in a similar way to their emotions, seeing them as extreme and too needy. They are guilty about their size, although often within the normal range, and attempt to reduce it by abstaining from food between binges. Many women describe vomiting after a binge as getting rid of the 'evil' inside them. It is also an expression of intense anger towards themselves or, unconsciously, someone they are close to. Women also describe vomiting as a punishment for the amount of satisfaction they gained during the binge. They often believe they are unworthy of pleasure and must pay the price if they achieve some form of comfort. They may include the use of diuretics or laxatives in their scanty diet. These also have the effect of making them feel clear and purified after bingeing. Gradually, the bulimic's life will become much more focused on her chaotic eating habits. All areas of life are affected; she will become lonely and isolated, sometimes actively seeking isolation to enable her to concentrate on her ritualized behaviour.

## Disturbed body image in obesity

One might expect that all obese people have derogatory feelings about their condition and that these are the major feature. However, this does not seem to be the case. Some obese individuals manage to escape without any severe disturbance, and in those that do suffer from some form of disturbance, three main factors seem to have a great influence.

Firstly, the age of onset. Major body-image disturbance usually occurs in those who have developed obesity during childhood or adolescence. The latter seems to be the time in which the disorder is most likely to develop. Secondly, people who develop a disturbance of body image and also experience other emotional problems seem to focus their attention on their physical size, seeing this to be central to any emotional problem that they may experience. Thirdly, an obese person is also more likely to have a negative attitude towards his or her shape if significant others, i.e. parents, spouse, children, and so on, respond negatively to their size. They may develop feelings of self-loathing and disgust, which does little for their motivation to change. If, however, a child is brought up in a family where being large is valued and looked upon as a sign of strength and health, they seem to escape a disturbance of body image. Although there are short-term fluctuations in the intensity of feelings about body image, depending on the way life is experienced, the body-image disturbance persists with little change for long periods.

As with anorexia, alteration of weight seems to have little effect on the perceptions of the body. Neither the extent of weight reduction nor its duration seems to have a significant effect on the disturbance of body image. As in the other eating disorders, the underlying psychological problems need to be expressed before any lasting change can occur. Stunkardo and Mendelson (1967) state: 'In each of five persons suffering from the disturbance, who were significantly benefited by long-term psychotherapy, there was a concomitant improvement in body-image disturbance which has persisted for as long as six years'.

Again, as with other eating disorders, there is a preoccupation with shape, weight and food, and the person seems to experience himself or herself in terms of weight. Stunkardo and Mendelson continue: 'It may make no difference whether the person be talented, wealthy or intelligent; his weight is his overriding concern and he sees the world in terms of body weight'. Because of low self-esteem and self-consciousness, the obese person often has a problem in relating to others, particularly those of the opposite sex. They may feel that this is directly due to the obesity but it may be more to do with a disturbed body image and the negative views they have about themselves.

Obesity may sometimes be experienced as a shield that protects and defends the individual against stressful situations. It may also be a reason for not putting himself or herself in difficult situations such as 'I didn't go to the party because I'm too fat and people would laugh at me', rather than saying 'I didn't go to the party because I find talking to people very difficult, especially those of the opposite sex'. Obesity is seen as the main problem, and the difficulties in communicating or being assertive are seen as a direct result of size. Although obesity may, in a maladaptive way, serve to provide a form of refuge, it may also lead to feelings of isolation and loneliness which do nothing to improve self-esteem and confidence. It is vital that nurses who are involved in the care of obese patients should be aware of their own stereotyped and preconceived ideas about obesity. They should be able to look beyond size and shape.

**Disturbed body image and creative therapies**

In this section it is intended to look at the way in which these therapies can be of value to people with disturbed body image related to the eating disorders anorexia and bulimia. To understand this further a much wider meaning is attached to the concept of disturbed body image to emphasize the emotional as well as the perceptual aspects which cause the distortions.

The term 'creative therapy' refers to the use of any medium, but particularly art, drama and music, to enable patients to express their feelings and explore their difficulties in ways other than the purely verbal. They may be used with all psychiatric disorders; however, certain aspects will be of importance for specific problems. Patients with eating disorders will frequently symbolize their difficulties through their feelings about their bodies. Common problems with assertion, or becoming independent may be *unknowingly* fought out with their own bodies, rather than with significant others. The psychological body image depends upon a number of things, but particularly on individuals' life events and the symbolic meaning that they (or their families) have attached to their bodies or, perhaps, parts of them. If sexual development carries with it feelings of shame or disgust, it is less likely that individuals will easily be able to accept all parts of themselves.

Body image also depends upon developing a sense of identity, one of the early stages of which is the development of the concept of having a body boundary. Most people experience this with no thought at all, but those who have disturbed feelings about their body may be less confident about it; some may feel that, even after eating very little, their whole shape may grossly enlarge. Many patients also have great difficulty in recognizing what they feel about something. Some are so enmeshed with their families that it seems as if they hardly know where they end and their parents begin! It is for this reason that the creative therapies may be of particular value, for they require patients to take an active role in their own treatment.

Anorexic people are often perfectionists. Creative therapies are never to do with 'getting something right', i.e. a correct painting or a beautiful dance; they are to do with being able to express oneself. For this reason they can be a valuable tool for those who find their own complicated feelings intolerable and certainly imperfect. These patients are frequently physically inhibited and emotionally restricted. This is demonstrated by the type of movements they make in dance therapy, where encouragement may be needed to try out more expressive movements. Using a wider definition of disturbed body image, one also sees how 'out of touch' with their own bodies, and feelings originating from within, patients with eating disorders can be. They do not recognize accurately their feelings of hunger, sadness or anger, and the body is often experienced as something rather alien and separate from the real self and, frequently, monstrously large.

In order to be 'in touch' with one's feelings, one has to be able to bear having them, whether they be bodily or emotional. Some patients cannot bear many feelings, and hope to gain total control over themselves. It is an important aspect of their therapy that some of this control should be relinquished. In drama therapy, trust exercises may be used to encourage patients to hand over some control to others, which is only possible if they are able to trust them. For instance, by permitting others to support them physically, they can allow themselves to feel physically dependent in a safe way.

The anorexics have a great fear of becoming too close to people or dependent upon them – they struggle for independence. Movement and drama allow patients to try out different ways of behaving, or responding to difficult situations. Through role play, fear of being overwhelmed (or of overwhelming) can be acted out and worked out. Assertion techniques encourage practice in standing up for oneself, whether it be to a dominating family or when making a complaint in a shop.

This wider perspective of the concept of distorted body image includes disturbed feelings about one's sense of identity. The difficulties of recognizing and then accepting feelings can be worked on through various means of self-expression. The use of art as a form of therapy enables certain issues such as the use of 'space' and 'territory' to be focused on. Both of these are symbolized by the use of the paper and materials. The bulimic patient will frequently cover many large sheets of paper, using a great deal of paint and leaving very little empty space in her paintings. A number of patients have described this as feeling like a binge. However, this is potentially a far more useful binge than the type that leaves them feeling disgusted, guilty and ashamed. Painting gives patients the chance to explore the feelings behind the need to binge which may emerge during the actual painting, such as the anxiety felt when faced with large empty spaces. Some patients have related this to their frantic use of food to deal with feelings of emptiness. The frequent guilt about needing so much, whether it be food or art materials, may sometimes contribute to the size a person feels. One patient said 'When I feel like I need so much from people . . . I feel absolutely enormous with this great empty hole inside'.

Art therapy can be done individually or in groups (Doktor, 1995). Certain areas come to light when an anorexic and a bulimic patient paint together. The bulimic may be frightened by her own powerful feelings and less able to keep them in control. She may end up taking the lead on paper, with the anorexic compliantly and carefully adding to the bulimic's work as if the latter did not have the right to exist. Issues of assertion, passivity and fears to do with relating to people, such as literally how much space should one take up in relation to another, are brought to life through this activity.

With specific reference to body image, certain art therapy techniques focus on, for example, drawing around the outline of the person's body. It may be that this 'mirror image' will be disbelieved or reacted to with horror by the skeletal anorexic in a false perception of it seeming to be immense. Of course, severe malnutrition does produce perceptual distortions but a significant psychological effect occurs even when the individual is not malnourished. Dealing with the reality of one's size may be very difficult: for the anorexic asked to fill in the body outline, she is in some way defining herself.

Self-portraits of desperately thin anorexics may be of large, obese figures, or idealized, childlike figures standing in a bed of roses. Often in the first stages of treatment, the patients deny that anything is wrong. However, their pictures reveal how they actually feel about themselves. Disturbed body image is, therefore, very much to do with how one feels about one's body. It is understandable how patients who feel large, clumsy and actually 'in the way' at home can hope that by being very small, they will take up less space and be more wanted. One patient who felt this painted herself in very large, clumsy ways. The image which patients with eating disorders paint of themselves is often distorted, whether boy-like or doll-like, but art therapy will often reveal aspects of people's feelings of which they are unaware. Sad or angry faces, or backs turned on people, allow patients to begin to recognize these feelings in relation to their own lives.

Suggested themes which patients can explore through the medium of art include a number of concepts related to body perception, such as 'myself when I have reached target weight' or 'myself before and after a meal'. These may reveal the horrific fears that the anorexic has of how she will look if she gains weight. For the anorexic, mind and body are often split in two: the former is superior, and the latter base and in need of total control. She is, therefore, unable to accept parts of herself, both emotionally and literally. Thus, the role of creative therapies must include encouraging the patient to become aware of the areas she cannot tolerate in herself, and to develop ways of being able to accept both her emotions and her body.

Problems of a sense of identity separate from their parents is common. These patients will frequently have experienced the world (or their family's) as having imposed things upon them, and in effect, having defined their identities for them. As with every adolescent, they need to define themselves, but for these patients this has not been possible for them as they feel powerless except in one area – that being control over their own bodies. This can be seen as a final resort in striving for some act of independence.

In art therapy, the patient has to decide how to use a blank sheet of paper. In drama or music therapy, she has to find her own means of self-expression, with no one else defining it for her. When she describes what her art means to her, she is, in fact, learning to define herself. The passive compliance shown by many anorexics has to be challenged in an activity which demands active participation. Art therapy allows for self-direction as well as the testing of previously forbidden feelings. Patients with eating disorders often pay great attention in their art to painting the boundary around their body. It is as if their difficulties about being a separate individual are expressed by emphasizing (often by painting over and over again) the outer line. This gives the onlooker a clear understanding of how unsafe it can feel to accept the actual boundaries of their bodies. To conclude this section, it should be emphasized that the concept of disturbed body image should be far wider than just the misjudgement of size. The confused sense of identity, the extreme sense of powerlessness and the feeling that one has no capacity to influence things around one, are not only to do with distorted perceptions of physical size, but are almost a denial of having any existence at all! (Levens, 1995).

**The nurse's contribution to care**

Women are easily persuaded that by changing their shape they will gain a sense of achievement and belonging. They seem willing to sacrifice physical health in exchange for society's approval and acceptance. It is necessary for nurses to be conscious of these processes within themselves and their patients, so as to be able to empathize. To be of any other than the conventional shape, the accepted norm, is often to feel inadequate, worthless and often lonely. Having accepted these influences, one must not have a simplistic view of why eating disorders develop. They are complex disorders, which demand more subtle explanations. 'Anorexia nervosa is a much more complex disorder than dieting out of hand. These youngsters seriously misinterpret their biological functioning and social role, and they attempt to correct this by changing their body size, they interpret fashions, demand to be thin in an exaggerated concrete way. They truly believe that they can achieve respect and very special recognition through excessive thinness' (Bruch, 1973).

In bulimia nervosa there is little outward sign of the inner emotional chaos. As mentioned earlier, bulimic women are often successful in their jobs and seem socially skilled, appearing confident and self-assured. However, to maintain this outward show, they feel they need to suppress their own psychological needs. This in turn leads to a lack of a sense of self and identity. They may often feel isolated, unfulfilled and experience themselves as empty or a void. They strive to mould themselves to an image which is acceptable to their family and society. A binge after a period of self-imposed starvation may temporarily fill the sense of personal emptiness, but the disgust and guilt which goes hand in hand with such behaviour results in vomiting.

The nurse must try to understand the symbolic nature of this activity, and its connection to the mental state of the patient, so as to help the patient gain insight and understanding. There is also an educational role, as often both bulimic and anorexic patients have little practical knowledge of what they need nutritionally to maintain and control their weight.

Obesity, like anorexia nervosa, is obvious to all. It is an outward expression of the inner self. Also, as in anorexia, obese patients describe their outward appearance as some form of shield or protection from various pressures, whether these be sexual or more broadly social. In both conditions, if the nurse were to ask how they saw themselves as individuals, often the reply would be focused on the size and shape of their body. In all three conditions, the body is used to express psychological distress in a non-verbal way. The nurses' role is to develop a trusting relationship with their patients and to facilitate insight into these problems by discussing openly, and in a non-judgemental manner, issues the patients consider relevant. Often the ventilation of these issues releases the focus on weight and size.

As one of the key workers in the multidisciplinary team, the nurse is deeply involved in the care and treatment of those suffering from some form of eating disorder. Nurses have much to contribute when planning the total treatment regimen, as they have a great deal of contact with the patients throughout their stay in hospital. They take part in many different aspects of care, some of which are not normally associated with 'nursing duties', including family therapy and supervised individual therapy. It is fruitless to attempt to alter the disturbed body image in isolation. The approach must be holistic, treating the whole being of the patients, allowing them to take an active part in their own treatment.

*Nursing care of patients in hospital*

Although the care given by the nurse during a patient's stay in hospital will be discussed here, it should be remembered that the roles of members of the multidisciplinary team are often blurred – experience is shared between the various disciplines (Conrad *et al.*, 1992). As treatment progresses, patients' fears about gaining and maintaining weight become less dominant and are replaced by issues of sexuality, interpersonal relationships, feelings of worthlessness and depression. Nurses need to use their skill and experience to suggest a link between these feelings and the way in which the patients perceive their bodies (Love and Seaton, 1991). The following treatment programme was devised by Professor A.H. Crisp, an international specialist in the treatment of anorexic patients (Crisp, 1980; Crisp and McLelland, 1994; Crisp *et al.*, 1994).

*Treatment programme for anorexia nervosa*

The treatment programme can be divided into three main areas: refeeding, psychotherapy (small group, large group and individual therapy) and education. Nurses may be active participants in all three areas. They must develop a therapeutic relationship, which will be maintained throughout the patients' admission. This relationship will, in itself, pass through many stages. Initially, nurses may find that patients are extremely dependent, continually asking for reassurance and assessing the genuineness of the nurses. As treatment progresses, patients respond to the sense of safety they find within the treatment framework. This enables them to express their own views and personality without fear of punishment. They tests limits, often challenging the authority of staff and the established rules. This new-found sense of rebellion must be acknowledged and seen as healthy. It mirrors the adolescent stage within a family, where the young girl feels that others are 'together' enough to cope with her questioning. Staff must try not to appear too defensive at this stage and should treat enquiries, etc. with respect. If patients, who are still extremely vulnerable, perceive staff as disapproving, they may withdraw again.

The patient's stay in hospital is divided into two phases: pre-target weight and post-target weight. The length of the former is obviously affected by the weight on admission, but that of the latter is usually between six and eight weeks. The programme is structured to meet the particular needs of the patients at the various stages of their admission. Initially, the staff want to foster dependence and compliance with the programme, but as treatment develops, there is a gradual removal of support to allow the patients to take more responsibility for their own care.

## Refeeding

Patients are each admitted to their own cubicle, where they will remain until they have reached their target weight. Meals are served to them by the nursing staff, and they are expected to eat all food prescribed. The daily calorie intake will be high, approximately 3000, to ensure weight gain: it will be reduced once the target weight is reached.

The target weight is calculated by measuring the patient's height, estimating the age of onset, and sex. If the age of onset is very young the patient's present age or an intermediary age will be chosen. Anorexia nervosa tends to stunt psychological growth so a weight that reflects the psychological age of the patient is felt to be more acceptable to the patient. However, in reality, all weight gain is viewed with fear and apprehension. It is important that, once set, the target weight should not be changed. Staff, and particularly nurses, because they have the most contact with the patient, will be tempted to agree to minor changes in the target weight, but it is necessary to stand firm when any reduction is requested because to respond would be colluding with the patient's anorectic stance. Patients would also lose trust and confidence in the staff's judgement if they felt they could undermine the decision.

Successful treatment relies upon the patients' level of motivation to change their self-destructive behaviour and discover the underlying conflicts. Both staff and the patients need to be aware that gaining weight alone will not produce health. If psychological issues have not been addressed by the time of discharge, patients will merely revert to their original anorexic situation. Birtchnell *et al.* (1985) state: 'We hope to create a forum for examining the underlying difficulties with the subsequent lessening of the displacement of conflicts into dissatisfaction with weight'. Nurses should accept that they can only encourage change, not create the motivation necessary for it. This may leave them feeling sad and frustrated when patients fail to respond to treatment, even though they are gaining weight.

### Psychotherapy

As treatment progresses and their stay in hospital comes to an end, patients often spend much time reflecting on their experience. They may need staff to help them recall the stages they went through, putting them in some sort of understandable framework. The aims of treatment can be seen as short, medium and long term. There is often a necessary bias towards physiological care initially. Anorexia can be a fatal disorder and at an extremely low body weight, the priority is obviously to save life and establish a refeeding programme. Any attempt to explore psychological issues at this stage would be fruitless.

As the patients gain weight, there will be a gradual reawakening of their personalities. It is a frightening time; all emotions are experienced as chaotic, contradictory and, maybe more importantly, out of *their* control. In response to these feelings, the perception of their body changes: instead of seeing their emaciated form they perceive themselves as disgustingly gross. Intense emotional experiences tend to have a direct effect on their body image. These areas of concern can be shared with staff and other patients, particularly in a small group setting. To compound their problems, it is at this time that they start to develop sexually; below approximately 45 kilograms gonadotrophins (sex hormones) are inactive, but as weight increases, they again start to influence body shape. Breasts enlarge and there is a rounding of the thighs and abdomen. They will feel conspicuous and extremely self-conscious, gross and unacceptable to others. The clothes they choose to wear will be baggy, covering their developing form. Moods become erratic, sadness often being the predominant emotion. The patient is often unaware of the origins of these feelings. The fear of continued weight gain is immense at this time as weight is seen to be the cause of these confusing and unwanted feelings. Long gone are the days when they were blissfully shielded from uncertainty and self-doubt.

The nurse must attempt to examine with the patients the connection between their emotions and the way in which they perceive their body. If patients feel secure within the relationship with the nurse, they will be able to discuss their very ambivalent feelings regarding weight gain. They will hanker after the controlled and predictable world of anorexia. This will often affect their involvement and commitment to treatment. They may start to leave apparently insignificant amounts of food, particularly carbohydrates. This proves to themselves that they have retained some control at a time which seems chaotic. The nurse must not miss the opportunity to highlight this behaviour and discuss its implications and meaning by means of advising or sensitive listening. Initially, patients may be defensive but, in time, will often feel relieved that the nurse has noticed their difficulties.

The treatment offers many avenues for the patients to express their feelings and compare their experiences with others. One important form of therapy is the small group. This is where patients (up to ten) formally gather together for one hour at regular periods during the week. The therapists facilitate involvement and interpret silences, splits, scapegoating and so on, that occur within the group meeting. The anorectic patients are encouraged to attend these groups once they have reached a weight previously mentioned (45 kilograms approximately). Before this point they are often unable to focus their attention on to their psychological problems and are still very preoccupied with food issues alone. The role that the anorexic patients may adopt within the group sometimes mirrors that which they adopted within the family. The feedback and information they receive during the group sessions, particularly from their peers, often has a profound effect on their attitudes. Throughout the treatment programme, they will continue to attend these groups. Once reaching target weight, and moving out into the main ward, they often become a more active member of the group.

Family therapy is also an extremely important form of treatment. Often, the patient lived at home prior to admission and had a profound effect on the household. Therapy is useful in helping each member of the family to communicate their feelings openly. This is often difficult prior to treatment and it is crucial that they have the opportunity to discuss the effect of having an anorectic member within their midst and how their attitude may unconsciously be maintaining the anorectic stance.

### Education

As mentioned earlier, there is a strong educational element within the latter part of the treatment programme. The nurse is an important model which patients use to assess their own progress. The nurse will help patients to learn how to maintain their weight and cope with the anxieties associated with target weight. Patients are strongly encouraged to take part in activities that they would normally avoid, such as shopping for clothes, cooking the occasional meal for themselves and eating with others. They take back the responsibility for choosing their own meals, so that they can gradually get to know their own requirements. Often, they have not eaten normally for many years, and prior to that their mothers were in charge of the amount they ate.

As treatment progresses, the programme will become more flexible and patients will have much more free time. They will often find these unstructured times difficult to handle, as they lack the ability to assess what they would enjoy doing. Their time in the past has been spent meeting and adapting to others' needs but now they are encouraged to meet their own. This may initially seem quite alien to them as they experience themselves as undeserving. They may describe themselves as being unaware of their own likes, dislikes and opinions; therefore, it is easier to fit in with the plans of others. It is a crucial stage in treatment for the patient to develop a sense of self-identity. The greater their self esteem, the less likely are they to focus on shape and size as a means of coping with psychological problems.

The anorexic patient feels unworthy of a separate identity, but to change needs to gain self-awareness and autonomy. Therapy must be directed towards evoking awareness of impulses, feelings and needs that originate within themselves. Patients are, therefore, embarking on a road of discovery which will, it is to be hoped, lead to an independent existence. However, it is important to remember that skilled psychiatric help will have formed part of their inpatient treatment and may have to be continued in the future.

**The nurse's contribution to the care of bulimia**

As in the care of anorexia nervosa, the nurse has a particularly important role in the treatment and care of patients with bulimia nervosa. Bulimic patients may have had a past history of anorexia nervosa. Although within a normal range of weight when they first seek help, they are preoccupied with body shape and they are extremely fearful of becoming obese. Unlike anorexic patients, they are not unduly frightened by normal body weight. Although maintaining weight, they do this by eating irregularly, developing a chaotic, ritualized eating pattern. This behaviour eventually encroaches on all aspects of their lives: work, relationships and health are all seriously affected.

Like anorexia, the eating disorder can be seen to symbolize psychological distress. During treatment, when the behaviour stops, patients will experience depressive, sad and angry feelings. It is inappropriate to try to get rid of these feelings by prescribing medication, as it is much more helpful for the nurse to explore why such feelings exist. They may arise from the shame felt when acknowledging past behaviour, but more often seem to be connected with past experiences and deep feelings of self-disgust. Many bulimic patients seem to have experienced some form of sexual abuse, either rape or incest. They have rarely come to terms with such experiences and seem to turn the anger and disgust they feel on to themselves. Vomiting is often described by these patients as getting rid of the unwanted and frightening emotions which they seem to experience as 'bad' or 'evil'.

The nurse needs to encourage patients to talk about their emotions, so that they feel some release. Once again, the nurse has an important educational role, teaching patients that eating three meals a day will not only reduce the possibility of bingeing, but will maintain weight. Bulimic patients will often have starved themselves between binges, severely restricting carbohydrate foods, leading to an intense preoccupation with food, in particular, those foods which are restricted.

When admitted to hospital, patients may be able to eat regular meals surprisingly quickly without vomiting, because they see the food as being prescribed by others. This seems to reduce the guilt when they allow themselves to eat normally. The fear of becoming obese is severe and, owing to their lack of experience, they perceive eating normally and not vomiting as leading inevitably to obesity. The bulimic's world revolves around food, the avoidance of it between bingeing, and the planning and preparation for the next binge. When this behaviour stops, patients experience a sensation of emptiness and lack of substance. Time is seen as endless and something to be filled, rather than enjoyed for its own sake. They have little knowledge of themselves and their own needs.

The nurses' role is to help their patients discover themselves, not to impose their own view of how the patients should think or behave. Bulimic patients are often extremely emotionally needy and will demand much support. They will benefit from a firm, structured contract, which they must agree to before treatment begins. Nurses and other members of the multidisciplinary team must be clear about their expectations and make sure that the patients understand.

For success in patient care, patients must be asked not to binge and vomit during treatment, to maintain their weight and eat three meals a day. Patients will often find this difficult but should be supported by staff who give them plenty of opportunity to discuss their feelings. An emphasis on the psychological is important, as often their patients have denied this area of their lives. Various avenues can be used to help them gain insight and try out new ways of coping: small groups are useful in encouraging patients to share feelings, thus reducing their isolation. Also, the sense of belonging that is gained from attending a group increases their self-esteem, which in turn helps them to communicate. Community meetings that are attended by all inpatients initially cause the individual patients great anxiety but will eventually help them to become aware of others and their difficulties, which are often similar to their own. The realization that they are not alone tends to have a very beneficial effect upon their self-image. Individual therapy concentrates in greater detail on their inner emotional life, exploring the reasons why their focus of attention has been directed towards their bodies.

In all the above areas of therapy, nurses have a great contribution to make. They will not only gain immense experience of those suffering from an eating disorder, but often begin to understand their own personalities and development in more depth.

**Nurses' attitudes and the need for self-awareness**

The first step when nursing patients with eating disorders is to establish a warm, trusting relationship. This relationship forms the foundation for many learning experiences and is a very vital part of treatment. Three phases of the relationship can be described: getting to know the patient, allowing and encouraging dependency, and encouraging independence and initiating motivation to maintain the new coping methods that have been learnt. Encouraging and facilitating the expression of feelings is a necessary nursing skill in building relationships.

Anorexic and bulimic patients will be in hospital for at least 3 months and very often for as long as 6 months. This gives nurses the opportunity of getting to know and help patients in a variety of ways. It can be as therapist in group situations or individual work, but also participating in as well as encouraging patients in involvement with the rest of the ward and its community environment. (It is necessary to state that the following assumes that both nurse and patient are female; aspects concerning male patients and male nurses are looked at later.)

The nurse–patient relationship becomes very meaningful because the patient will use it to try out new ways of relating to others. The nurse, therefore, has to learn to accept feelings of hostility, anxiety, anger, sadness, guilt and inadequacy, and also to enjoy success and achievement with the patient (Cahill, 1994). It is necessary for the nurse to understand the defence mechanisms used by the patient and the displaced anger that often occurs. Manipulation may be an unconscious process through which the patient attempts to deal with a conflict. At the beginning of treatment, the biggest conflict of all is whether or not to eat. Emphasis is not, in fact, placed upon observing whether the patient eats or not, as the ultimate weight gain will be reflected in the weight chart. This alleviates the problem of the patient eating to please the nurse and also confirms that the nurse–patient relationship is based upon trust and respect for the individual. Motivation for change has to come from the patient and this can be difficult for the nurse to accept. Real commitment to treatment can take some time to cultivate, thus causing feelings of frustration.

Seeing individuals in an emaciated state can sometimes provoke maternal feelings and it can be tempting to deal with patients as though they were children. When the individual does gradually put on weight, the nurse may think that progress is being made when, in fact, many major psychological changes still have to occur. A therapeutic tool that is valuable in measuring psychological change is a log-book or personal diary kept by the patient which can be used as a basis for discussing feelings. It provides structure for time spent alone, and the nurse's role is to clarify the feelings that the patient has recorded.

Because the overestimation of body size is such a common phenomenon, and is not confined to eating disorders, it is reasonable to assume that nurses themselves may not be entirely happy with their shape or size. Nurses are often weight-conscious and have difficulty eating regularly because of unsocial hours. A patient may well ask 'Do you count calories?' and the response should emphasize healthy eating rather than calories. The important thing to convey to the patient is a sense of each individual being happy with her own body and its functions. Fear of sexuality and menstruation are major issues for the anorexic patient and the nurse will find herself discussing these. Patients use the nurse as a model and she can be an example of someone who is happy with her relationship to her body. In order to do this, it is necessary for the nurse to recognize that she herself may be envious of the thinness of the anorexic patient who is just reaching target weight.

It can be especially difficult to understand the mentality of a person starving herself when food is plentiful. The nurse needs to realize that the starving equates to control and that the only control that the anorexic patient feels she has is over her own body size, and that her feelings of powerlessness both in the family and in society have resulted in the anorexic behaviour. The nurse should understand fully the treatment regimen described, realize how the boundaries and limit-settings make the patient feel secure, and why all control is taken from the patient and then gradually given back to her. This is in no way a punitive treatment approach but is based upon the fact that the patient needs to eat alone in her cubicle because, psychologically, she cannot cope with eating with others. The nurse should understand the utter fear and panic that gaining a few pounds can bring, and be sensitive and realize that, if she says to the patient 'Oh, you're looking well', this may be interpreted as 'I must be looking fat'.

The anorexic patient often feels that eating food is a great self-indulgence, as is taking a bath or buying clothes, and this feeling can also extend to the nurse–patient relationship with the patient thinking that she does not deserve the nurse's attention. These feelings can be counteracted if the nurse is seen to be giving freely of her time and by encouraging and listening to their expression. Non-verbal communication such as touch is vital and goes a long way towards telling the patient that she cares. It is important that the nurse should be able to accept assertiveness in others, especially other women, and recognize and encourage it from the patient and not feel threatened by it. Consequently, the nurse will feel pleased when the patient begins to recognize her own needs.

It is a common misconception that all anorexic patients are manipulative. Of course, some are extremely devious and will go to great lengths to convince staff they are eating their food when, in fact, they are disposing of it, but whenever the nurse feels that she is being manipulated, she should remember that how this makes her feel will often be how the patient is feeling or may have felt in the past. There can be unconscious manipulation in which the patient tries to split or win-over staff. It is, therefore, extremely important to communicate with all colleagues who are involved in the patient's treatment. A staff support group that provides a forum for nurses to ventilate their difficulties and frustrations is a necessity because these feelings must be expressed or they will eventually be made known unconsciously to the patient.

It is also vital to bear in mind the prognostic aspects of treatment – whether or not it is the patient's first admission and her treatment has been planned to 'cure' her, or it is intended to maintain her at below normal body weight because this is seen to be a realistic objective. Female nurses may find themselves relating to patients with eating disorders because of problems they themselves have about food and may well wonder why strong feelings about food occur. Our three basic needs – for food, security and love – are all combined and felt as one when a baby. When anorexic people hunger for food they are, in fact, hungering for acceptance and security. Hunger for food is felt to be unacceptable so they control it, fooling themselves that they are controlling their hunger for acceptance. Coupled with this is a tremendous fear of their feelings and a dread that they can never be satisfied. Their need to control the emotions is expressed in their control of food. The nurse, therefore, has to recognize her own desires and feelings and be aware of how she responds both to the patient and to her own needs.

For anorexic and bulimic women to become well they have to examine the issues of sexuality, femininity and body image. Body image is not something that is external but comes from an inner sense of self and femaleness. It also comes from what others think and what is generally accepted by society. The nurse has to decide what makes her feminine; is she trying to keep her waist at size twelve, and is she eating low-fat yoghurt at break times; what is she trying to suppress – is she frightened that her urges and emotions will get out of control? Being feminine, assertive and powerful while also being warm, taking responsibility and accepting one's own feelings, all come into this very special nurse–patient relationship.

It will be noted that, although it has been assumed that both nurse and patient are female, there are increasing numbers of male nurses and male anorexics. It can be disconcerting for the nurse, whether male or female, to see a man express his emotional difficulties through dieting. Male nurses often see that the bulimic patient is out of control of her eating and they may find this attractive in a sexual way. They may also find the vulnerability and helplessness of the anorexic patient appealing. These feelings are in no way bad or guilty, but if male or female nurses find themselves spending more time than usual with a patient, it may be due to underlying sexual attraction. It is important also to recognize other underlying motivations, some of which may not be so obvious and may operate on an unconscious level. Any strong feelings should be discussed either in the staff support group or on a one-to-one basis with a colleague.

Anorexic patients usually have great difficulty in relating to men so the male nurse can provide a non-threatening environment in which to experiment with their feelings. Male patients with anorexia also need to talk about their sexual feelings and it can be easier for them to share these with a male nurse (Köpp, 1994; Stockwell and Dolan, 1994).

It is both stimulating and demanding working with anorexic and bulimic patients, and imagination and skill are needed to create a safe relationship in which these patients can explore hidden aspects of themselves. Although this very special nurse–patient relationship presents many difficulties, it does provide the opportunity to share someone else's initial experience or renewal of a sense of self and of pleasure in life.

**References**

Askevold, F. (1975) Measuring body image. *Psychotherapy and Psychosomatics* **26**, 71–77.

Bemporad, J.R., Ratey, J.J., O'Driscoll, G. and Daehler, M.L. (1988) Hysteria, anorexia and the culture of self-denial. *Psychiatry* **51**(1), 96–103.

Birtchnell, S.A., Lacey, J.H. and Harte, A. (1985) Body image distortion in bulimia nervosa. *British Journal of Psychiatry* **147**, 408–412.

Bruch, H. (1973) *Eating Disorders, Obesity, Anorexia Nervosa and the Person Within*. New York, Basic Books.

Cahill, C. (1994) Implementing an in-patient eating disorders program. *Perspectives in Psychiatric Care* **30**(3), 26–29.

Casper, R.C., Halmi, K.A., Goldberg, S.C., Eckert, E.D. and Davis, J.M. in (1979) Disturbances of body image estimations related to other characteristics and outcome in anorexia nervosa. *British Journal of Psychiatry* **134**, 60–66.

Cooper, P., Charnock, D. and Taylor, M. (1987) The prevalence of bulimia nervosa: a replication study. *British Journal of Psychiatry* **128**, 549–554.

Conrad, N., Sloan, S. and Jedwabny, J. (1992) Resolving the control struggle on an eating disorders unit. *Perspectives in Psychiatric Care* **28**(3), 13–18.

Crisp, A.H. (1980) *Anorexia Nervosa: Let Me Be.* Hove, Lawrence Erlbaum Associates.

Crisp, A.H. and McLelland, L. (1994) *Anorexia Nervosa: The 'St. George's Approach.* Hove, Lawrence Erlbaum Associates.

Crisp, A.H., Joughin, N., Halek, C. and Bowyer, C. (1994) *Anorexia Nervosa and the Wish to Change.* Hove, Lawrence Erlbaum Associates.

Doktor, D. (1995) *Art Therapies and Clients with Eating Disorders: The Fragile Board.* London, Jessica Kingsley.

Dolan, B. (1994) Introduction. In: Dolan, B. and Gitzinger, I. (eds). *Why Women? Gender Issues in Eating Disorders.* London, Athlone Press, pp. 1–11.

Dolan, B. and Gitzinger, I. (eds) (1994) *Why Women? Gender Issues in Eating Disorders,* 2nd edn. London, Athlone Press.

Garner, D.M. and Garfinkel, P.E. (1982) *Anorexia Nervosa; A Multidimensional Perspective.* New York: Bruner/Mazel.

Glucksman, M.L. and Hirsch, J. (1969) The response of the obese patient to weight reduction. *Psychosomatic Medicine,* **31**, 1–7.

Huon, G.F. and Brown, L.B. (1986) Body images in anorexia nervosa and bulimia nervosa. *International Journal of Eating Disorders* **5**(3), 421–439.

Köpp, W. (1994) Can women with eating disorders benefit from a male therapist? In: Dolan, B. and Gitzinger, I. (eds) *Why Women? Gender Issues in Eating Disorders,* 2nd edn. London, Athlone Press, pp. 65–71.

Levens, M. (1995) *Eating Disorders and Magical Control of the Body.* London, Routledge.

Love, C.C. and Seaton, H. (1991) Eating disorders: highlights of nursing assessment and therapeutics (review). *Nursing Clinics of North America* **26**(3), 677–697.

Orbach, S. (1983) *Food, Fatness and Femininity*. Institute of New York: The Women's Therapy Centre.

Phillips, K.A., Kim, J.M. and Hudson J.I. (1995) Body image disturbance in body dysmorphic disorder and eating disorders: obsessions or delusions? *Psychiatric Clinics of North America* **18**(2), 317–334.

Russell, G.F.M., Campbell, P.G. and Slade, P.D. (1975) Experimental studies on the nature of the psychological disorder in anorexia nervosa. *Psychoneuroendocrinology* **1**, 45–56.

Schilder, P. (1935) *Image and Appearance of the Human Body*. London, Kegan Paul, Trench & Trubner.

Stockwell, R. and Dolan, B. (1994) Women therapists for women patients? In: Dolan, B. and Gitzinger, I. (eds) *Why Women? Gender Issues in Eating Disorders*, 2nd edn. London, Athlone Press, pp. 57–64.

Strober, M., Goldenberg, I., Green, J. and Saxon, J. (1979) Body image disturbance in anorexia nervosa during the acute and recuperative phase. *Psychological Medicine* **9**, 695–701.

Stunkardo, A. and Mendelson, M. (1967) Obesity and the body image. *American Journal of Psychology* **123**(10), 1296–1300.

Touyz, S.W., Beaumont, P.J.V., Collins, J.K. and Cowie, I. (1985) Body shape perception in bulimia and anorexia nervosa. *International Journal of Eating Disorders* **4**(3), 259–265.

Vitousek, K. and Manke, F. (1994) Personality variables and disorders in anorexia and bulimia nervosa. *Journal of Abnormal Psychology* **103**(1), 137–147.

Willmuth, M.E., Leitenberg, H. Rosen, J.C., Fandacaro, B.A. and Gross, J. (1985) Body size distortion in bulimia nervosa. *International Journal of Eating Disorders* **4**(1), 71–78.

Wingate, B.A. and Christie, M.J. (1978) Ego strength and body image in anorexia nervosa. *Journal of Psychosomatic Research*, **22**, 201–204.

# Some useful addresses

**Arthritis Care**
18 Stephenson Way, London NW1 2HD

**Association to Aid the Sexual and Personal Relationships of the Disabled (SPOD)**
286 Camden Road, London N7 OBJ

**Association for Spina Bifida and Hydrocephalus (ASBAH)**
Asbah House, 42 Park Road, Peterborough PE1 2UQ

**Breast Cancer Care**
Kiln House, 210 New Kings Road, London SW6 4NZ
The Nationwide Freeline Tel: 0500 245 345
Helpline Tel: 0171 384 2344

**British Association of Cancer United Patients (BACUP)**
3 Bath Place, Rivington Street, London EC2 3JR

**British Association for Counselling**
1 Regent Place, Rugby, Warwicks CV21 2PJ

**British Colostomy Association**
15 Station Road, Reading, Berks RG1 1LG

**British Epilepsy Association**
Anstey House, 40 Hanover Square, Leeds LS3 1BE

**British Heart Foundation**
14 Fitzhardinge Street, London W1H 4DH

**British Lung Foundation**
8 Peterborough Mews, London SW6 3BL

**The British Red Cross Society, Cosmetic Camouflage Service**
9 Grosvenor Crescent, London SW1X 7EJ

**British Sports Association for the Disabled (BSAD)**
The Mary Glen Haig Suite, Solecast House, 13–27 Brunswick Place, London N1 6DX

**Cancerlink**
17 Britannia Road, London WC1X 9JN

**Changing Faces**
1–2 Junction Mews, London W2 1PN

**Cleftlip and Palate Association**
134 Buckingham Palace Road, London SW1W 9SA

**Cystic Fibrosis Research Trust**
5 Blyth Road, Bromley, Kent BR1 3RS

**Disabled Living Foundation**
380–384 Harrow Road, London, W9 2HU

**The Disfigurement Guidance Centre and Laserfair-Childfriend**
PO Box 7, Cupar, Fife KY15 4PF

**Eating Disorders Association**
Sackville Place, 44 Magdalen Street, Norwich NR3 1JU

**Haemophilia Society**
123 Westminster Bridge Road, London SE1 7HR

**Ileostomy and Internal Pouch Support Group**
Amblehurst House, PO Box 23, Mansfield, Notts NG18 4PF

**John Groom's Association for Disabled People**
50 Scrutton Street, London EC2A 4PH

**Motor Neurone Disease Association**
PO Box 246, Northampton NN1 2PR

**Multiple Sclerosis Society**
23 Effie Road, Fulham, London SW6 1EE

**National Aids Helpline**
Tel: 0800 567 123

**National Aids Trust**
New City Cloisters, 188–196 Old Street, London EC1 V9FR
Tel: 0171 814 6767

**National Association for Colitis and Crohn's Disease**
4 Beaumont House, Sutton Road, St Albans, Herts AL1 5HH

**National Association of Laryngectomy Clubs**
Ground Floor, 6 Rickett Street, Fulham, London SW6 1RU

**National Asthma Campaign**
Providence House, Providence Place, London N1 0NT

**National Eczema Society**
163 Eversholt Street, London NW1 1BU

**Royal National Institute for Deaf People**
19–23 Featherstone Street, London WC14 8SL

**Scoliosis Association UK**
2 Ivebury Court, 325 Latimer Road, London W10 6RA

**Scope** (formerly the Spastics Society)
12 Park Crescent, London W1N 4EQ

**Spinal Injuries Association**
76 St James's Lane, London N10 3DF

**The Stroke Association**
CHSA House, Whitecross Street, London EC1 8JJ

**The Terence Higgins Trust Ltd**
52–54 Grays Inn Road, London WC1X 8JU
Tel: 0171 831 0330

**Urostomy Association**
Central Office, Buckland, Beaumont Park, Danbury, Essex
CM3 4DE

# Index